Born in the Desert

BORN
IN THE
DESERT

*The Education of a
Saudi Nomad and
the Rise of Modern
Saudi Arabia*

ॐ

DR. FAISAL AL-BASHIR
AL-MERSHED

Westphalia Press
An Imprint of the Policy Studies Organization
Washington, DC

Westphalia Press
An imprint of Policy Studies Organization
1367 Connecticut Avenue NW
Washington, D.C. 20036
info@ipsonet.org

ISBN: 978-1-63723-544-7

Cover and interior design by Jeffrey Barnes
jbarnesbook.design

Daniel Gutierrez-Sandoval, Executive Director
PSO and Westphalia Press

Updated material and comments on this edition
can be found at the Westphalia Press website:
www.westphaliapress.org

To my country, the Kingdom of Saudi Arabia,
who was so generous in educating its people.

TABLE OF CONTENTS

(Cont'd.)

Acknowledgements

My oldest son Sami has a lot to do with this book. As a matter of fact, without his help, the book might not have been published. He was the liaison between me (the author) and the publisher. He structured the book to make it more readable and chose some titles. To my Sami, I am grateful for his help which was tremendous despite the fact he is not a Bedouin.

PREFACE

I began to write this story in the summer of 1968, at the urging of many friends.

Then, I lost interest, until 1991, when I picked it up again.

Then, again somehow, I lost the desire to continue, mostly because I did not want to remind myself of certain sad incidents in my life.

In the later part of 2020, I gathered the courage to finish it.

I tell you this so that what is described here can be understood in the context of the time frame in which it was written.

This book is a personal as well as a tribal autobiography. It is my story, it is the story of the tribe I come from, and, in addition, it tells the story of the development of Saudi Arabia, starting in the 1960s. Primarily, it is written to record the events that transformed a single man from an illiterate, nomadic person, wandering in the desert, to an urban, educated person, and a public figure who played a role in his country's government. In a way, it is written to familiarize the world with the sociopolitical and economic set-up of tribal society, especially the Bedouins in Arab countries of the Middle East, and to recount the transformation of a country called the Kingdom of Saudi Arabia.

This book is presented in three parts, to reflect how it was written at three distinct moments in my life, and to focus on three primary stages in my development. First, I was a Bedouin in the desert, who went to school and was urbanized; then I was a college student in the United States; and ultimately, I came home to Saudi Arabia.

I don't claim absolute objectivity, nor do I guarantee the total absence of emotion from the story I tell. But I assure you, my dear reader, that truth was the light that I followed all the way through the book. I beg your forgiveness if you notice emotional outbursts here and there, because it is my life and I am telling you about it, with all of its beauty and ugliness, sadness and happiness.

While writing, I cried sometimes, not because of pity and regret, but rather due to my feeling that I did not meet the expectations of those who loved me so much and protected me until I left them. By their standards, I was one of the greatest failures in this world, especially at the time. On the other hand, if I judge my achievements by the standards of urban people, I am something like a hero.

Due to the application to myself of these two conflicting standards, you sometimes find me the most miserable human being around. At any time, I might be thinking that neither a doctorate degree, nor a high government post mean much, as long as my tribe thinks that I have failed them. At other times, you find me happy, because those who know me, especially from my tribe, are beginning to feel that the road I followed was the right one.

Throughout this book, I move back and forth between those poles, between judging myself a failure, and regarding my life as a relative success. Such is the perspective of someone who has changed over the years as I have, who has the heart of a tribesman and the mind of an educated city-dweller. And such is the split perspective that informs this book, which tells the story, not only of my life, but that of the great country I call home.

PART ONE

1

—

CHILD OF THE DESERT

I was born in the desert between Syria and Iraq, in the summer of 1940, or so I was told by some of the elders of my tribe, Al-Sba'a. I was called by this name, Faisal, on the insistence of my grandmother from my father's side, who came from Al-Hajj, from Makkah, in Saudi Arabia. Thanks, Grandma—you saved me from living with an ugly name. Tribal tradition was to name a person, most of the time, after the place he was born.

And so Faisal ibn (son of) Sfouq Bashir Al-Mershed was welcomed by the Al-Sba'a Tribe. In shortened form, my name is Faisal Al-Mershed. Al-Sba'a, is one part of the Great Aneza Tribe. Al-Sba'a is headed by the Al-Mershed family, and my uncle was Rakan, chief of the tribe. My father, Sfouq, was the right hand of his brother Rakan, his senior by about 13 years. The setup between the two brothers was like Rakan was the Chairman of the Board, and Sfouq the CEO. The younger brother moved with the tribe in search of better grazing areas for the herd, mostly camels at that time, all over areas roamed by Arab Tribes of the Middle East, primarily Northern Saudi Arabia, Iraq, Jordan, and Syria.

When he reached the age of 20, my Uncle Rakan left his father Bashir's tent, aspiring to do his best to create his own position in the tribe, so as to claim leadership someday. Rakan was a hard competitor to beat. Although the rivalry between him and his cousins for the leadership of the tribe was fierce, the contest played out within the established family and tribal rules. Every male child of the Al-Mershed family was urged to do his best, so he might someday become a leader of Al-Sba'a. In reality, that kind of competition among the Al-Mershed children was very healthy for the tribe and led to the choice of the best one from many. Later, Rakan proved to be the best, and was for many years the Chief of Al-Sba'a Tribe.

When Bashir Al-Mershed, my grandfather, died, my father became the rightful heir to his wealth, estimated at about 120 camels. In 1967, a full-grown camel was worth about $300, making his animals worth about $36,000.00 at that time. My Uncle Rakan realized that my father was too young to take care of his inheritance, and so the two brothers joined together to live as one family. That relationship generated much animosity between the brothers when they decided to divide the lot around 1951.

My father proved to be a loyal and hardworking brother, leaving aside all personal gains and working for the welfare of the whole family. He lived most of the time in one tent. Due to an increase in our number, it eventually became necessary to live in two separate tents.

My uncle's tent was seven sections, my father's tent was five sections, and each section measured about four square meters. Later yet, my father's tent was obliged to move with the tribe, while my uncle's tent (the largest) was usually left behind near wells.

In some ways, Bedouin tents are like any habitation. They are like houses, in that no two houses are quite the same, and based on the wealth and status of the owner, they can vary dramatically in size. I grew up in a large tent, relatively speaking, as my family was prominent. My father's tent, with its five sections, was about 90 feet across, with two sections set aside for women, and three sections for the men who lived in it.

Bedouin tents are rectangular, and open in front, some also in back. In my youth, they were mostly made of goat hair and were thus black in color. In later years, the tents of the well-to-do were made of cotton during the summer, a much cooler material.

As far as furniture, we had rugs, sometimes quite ornate, and pillows for sitting. I remember one woman from Iraq who was never married, but who considered my uncle and my father her brothers. She stayed with us for several years, and while she was with us, she made a divider for our tent, to keep the line between the men's and women's sections demarcated. It was beautiful and sewn by hand.

The tent belonging to the head of the tribe is like a hotel. It is open 24 hours a day to whomever might need it. When I was growing up, when a guest would arrive, it didn't matter what time they appeared and announced themselves. Even in the middle of the night, we would wake up and welcome them. It was up to the men to slaughter a lamb—more than one, if the guest was important—and the women would prepare a meal. And remember, at night in the desert it gets extremely cold.

Readers who have not been to Saudi Arabia might picture it as it has been portrayed in films, as a place of endless, rolling sand dunes pocked with wells and oases. While we have our share of desert in Saudi Arabia, we have our more verdant regions, too, and much of our wandering was done so as to seek what were the most fertile areas at any one time.

Al-Sba'a Tribe is the subtribe of Greater Aneza, which came from Najd, the central part of Saudi Arabia. Loyalty was and continues to be to the government of Saudi Arabia, regardless of where the tribe was camping or even owned property.

This relationship with Saudi Arabia was enforced by the claim of King Abdulaziz, its founder; that Aneza Tribe was part of Saudi Arabia. He allocated something like a salary per year for the heads of the subtribes of Aneza.

Living with the tribe was tough, but it gave me rich examples of a human being's ability to adjust to nature's fluctuations. Nomadic life is the life most conditioned by what nature gives. It is a lovely life when rain is abundant, and a very hard and intolerable life when there is no rain.

This kind of life gave me a sense of pride, by maintaining the honor of the tribe and the family to which I belong. Every male child was

Dr. Faisal Al-Bashir Al-Mershed

looked at as the property of the tribe as a whole, and he had to be raised according to its laws.

ψ ψ ψ

Tribal law had been in place for many, many years by the time I was born into it.

Since the dawn of history, human beings have striven to better their lives by whatever means they had, physical or non-physical. This was what tribes in the Arabian Peninsula did, especially in the late nineteenth century. The Peninsula was poor and had no established governments to protect its inhabitants and secure their livelihood—no matter how meager it was. Tribes were in constant warfare, raiding each other to survive and dominate. Usually, the strongest at the end was the victor for a while, until they weren't.

And so, life continued back and forth without many changes. Traditions perpetuated, and the way of nomadism was inherited from one generation to another.

At that time, most of the Arab lands in the Middle East were part of the Ottoman Empire, and there were no borders as such to restrict tribal movement. I say *movement*, not *migration* or *immigration*, because tribes were not moving across established borders. They were powerful enough not to need permission from anyone.

Two tribes in particular are of concern to me. Greater Aneza was supposedly the largest Arab tribe in the Middle East with many subtribes, including Al-Sba'a, which I belong to from my father's side. The second tribe is Shammar, the one I belong to from my mother's side, considered to be foreign, and an adversary to Al-Sba'a and the Greater Aneza Tribe.

Both major tribes, and most of their branches, began to move north and northeast in the late nineteenth century, to what we now call Syria and Iraq, in search of better grazing areas to sustain their herds of camels. Shammar Tribe moved as far as the Al-Jazirah

4

region in Syria and Iraq, by crossing the Euphrates River, where the Turkish border lies today. The Greater Aneza Tribe, with its branches, ended in areas in Syria and Iraq, south and southeast of the Euphrates River, almost as far as the Al-Nofud Desert in what is now Saudi Arabia.

Both major tribes found those areas in Syria and Iraq to be more prosperous and suitable to their herds than areas they came from, mostly the central part of Saudi Arabia (Najd). In the late nineteenth century, both tribes remained nomadic, roaming the desert from Diyarbakir in what is now Turkey, to Al-Nofud in present-day Saudi Arabia. With the passage of time, some began to live semi-settled lives, especially those from the Shammar Tribe. Both major tribes began to call on relatives who had stayed back in Najd to join them in areas they found so rich that some even fed bread to their camels, which was rare in Najd at that time.[1]

While most areas of Al-Jazirah across the river were known to be Shammar Tribe areas, Aneza subtribes, with passing years, reached some unwritten understanding about imaginary demarcation lines between them. Al-Sba'a, for example, ended in the desert areas east of Hama and Homes city to connect with their kin called Alomarat, in and around the Iraqi borders. Other subtribes of Aneza, like Alfedaan, were east of Aleppo City, in Al-Rowalah, east of Damascus, and so on.

Mind you, what I mention here about areas of interest to this tribe or another is not exact. Maps drawn by the Royal British Geographical Society may be more accurate. The important point I wish to make is that tribes remained nomadic at this time, roaming all over deserts from the Turkish borders to Al-Nofud, in what are now the Saudi and Iraqi deserts.

At the beginning of the twentieth century, and especially after the defeat of the Ottoman Empire after the First World War, most Arab countries of the Middle East were directly or indirectly controlled

---

1   There is, in the nomadic folklore of Aneza, a poem to that effect.

by foreign rule—except some of the Arabian Peninsula, like Yemen, and parts of what became Saudi Arabia.

Saudi Arabia was established in 1932. At that time, Iraq, Transjordan (now the Hashemite Kingdom of Jordan), and Palestine were under British rule, while Lebanon and Syria were ruled by France. All this division happened after the two superpowers of that time, Great Britain and France, reneged on their promises of independence made to the Arabs, both the tribes and the urban people, who fought with them to defeat the Ottomans.

The famous movie *Lawrence of Arabia*, although not an accurate historical record, gives a quick summary of what happened. Tribes throughout those countries were almost happy, because their traditions as well as nomadic way of life were respected and not disturbed. Borders, which were not really exact and recognized, were left open, leaving tribes free to roam the desert like before.

The term "Displaced Arab Tribes" came into being to refer mainly to Aneza and Shammar, to distinguish them from the indigenous tribes of those areas, and to directly relate them to where they were displaced from, which was and still is, mainly Najd.

That term created a lot of headaches for the occupying powers when they were negotiating border demarcations, mainly in Iraq, with the founder of Saudi Arabia, King Abdulaziz Ibn Saud. When asked, "Where are your borders?" King Abdulaziz said that they were where tribes who came from Najd camped, which really meant big areas of Syria and, especially, Iraq. It was a clever answer.

One might ask, what about the nationality of those so-called "Displaced Arab Tribes?" During that time, and up until the 1950's, I think, nationality in the region was not so important, nor precise. Borders, relatively speaking, remained easy to cross for nomadic tribes. And most, Aneza in particular, knew from where they came—Najd—so nationality was not on anyone's mind. Nomadic tribes were notorious for being secretive about their family members and the number of sheep and camels in their herds, mostly from fear of military service or taxation. And so, when a nomadic tribe camped for a few months in a country, that country usually tried to take its census, which turned out to be inaccurate and misleading, as far as the names recorded, as well as the number of people. As far as subtribes of Aneza, including my Al-Sba'a Tribe, I would not be surprised to find us registered as nationals of most Arab states of the Middle East, except Saudi Arabia, at that time, (because there was no need to do so).

Few members of the Aneza Tribe knew what the future held for them. Tribal members never doubted their origin, and felt no need for a piece of paper to say where they came from and where they belonged. They were very powerful, and under the shadow of that power they were able to go anywhere, without papers or permission from any government. Furthermore, if nationality meant loyalty and belonging to a place, they never doubted where they belonged.

At the same time, host countries, and especially members of their own mostly settled or semi-settled indigenous tribes, never let Aneza and Shammar forget that they were displaced Arabs who came mainly from Najd, and should go back. Unfortunately, some subtribes of Aneza neglected to have the necessary papers specifying their nationality when times began to change. It's sad to say, but that negligence or delay in realizing the importance of nationality papers, created many problems for members of those subtribes of Aneza.

I say sadly, but in reality it hurts when some—and, I repeat, *some* —cousins, who remained in Najd when Aneza and Shammar conquered the north, and lived in relative prosperity, never forgot those cousins who denied helping them when they dropped by looking for jobs in Syria or Iraq. And so, the so-called Displaced Arab Tribes expected their cousins to receive them with open arms when they moved south, mainly to Saudi Arabia and Kuwait.

To be fair, from experience, the leadership of Saudi Arabia never to my knowledge denied what most subtribes of Aneza claimed; that they were Saudi nationals. But bureaucracy has its own wisdom and pseudo-wisdom, sometimes with many shapes and colors. With this brief background about tribes - back to my personal side of this story.

ψ ψ ψ

In a way, as a member of Al-Sba'a Tribe, I lived in one of the largest families in the world. My immediate family was Al-Mershed, but in reality, my most important family was the whole tribe. These relationships caused me to believe in the need to work hard to increase the welfare of my small and larger family at the same time. This belief dominated nearly every tribesman during those days.

Some people may think that it would be very difficult to reconcile these dual family interests. But this was easy in a tribal society, such as the one in which I was born and raised. As a person who was furthering the well-being of his immediate family, I had no doubt that I was also furthering the well-being of the tribe as a whole. As a matter of fact, we were like sailors who took care of a ship. All of them work to keep the ship going, and all tribes work hard to defend the honor and retain the good name of each, through financial as well as political power.

Cooperation was and remains the basis for tribal existence. Certainly, exceptions came up, for some reason or another, and that usually led to less cooperation, which ultimately diminished the power of the tribe. Conflict arises in any community of people, and this is the case even among those whose lives are so tightly interwoven with one another.

Nomadic life is a routinized life, in that it offers very little variation and change. However, at times it is so erratic in its character, and its events proceed with so much speed, that only the most tolerant men can live with it.

At this stage, it is appropriate to briefly discuss the socio-economic and political setup of Al-Sba'a Tribe. What is stated about my tribe can be generalized to many others throughout the Arab countries of the Middle East.

During the 1940s, and up to 1951, the wealth of Al-Sba'a Tribe was mostly camels. Sheep ownership did exist, but with less emphasis. After 1951, an almost complete reversal took place. By 1970 (the year I wrote this), only about 100 camels were left in the tribe, as far as I know. Those camels remained only because the elderly people in certain tents objected to the total disappearance of camels while they were alive.

The nomadic life of each tribe has two major yearly cycles. The first includes the last part of the fall season, winter and spring. This is when the Bedouins' movement from one place to another is predominant. The second cycle is the summer season and most of the fall, when tribes usually camp around the water wells.

The existence of these two cycles depends mainly on rainfall. Rain usually falls only in the first cycle. And so, by the last part of the fall season, as clouds begin to appear in the sky, the Bedouins always become restless. The whole tribe will often start preparation to leave the summer place the moment some clouds appear.

Travelers are frequently the best carriers of rain and pasture news. But each tribe will also send out a few of its horsemen, who will spend from a week to a month in search of rain and pasture. If a Bedouin traveler arrives to a tribe from the direction where the last cloud went, a thorough questioning period will inevitably take place, traditionally in the tent of the tribe's chief. After establishing the identity of his tribe, meaning his tribal association, its location, and his name, the chief of the tribe will continue:

> The chief: From where did you come?
>
> The traveler: From the East.
>
> The chief: How far?

The traveler: About three days riding.

The chief: Did you pass any Bedouins?

The traveler: Yes (or, no).

The chief: How was the land you passed?

The traveler: Not bad (and he proceeds to describe the vegetation of the area).

The chief: (trying to be more specific) Valley x and y in that area have places that usually hold water. Did you pass them?

The traveler: I passed that vicinity, but it seems from your description that my way was below the mentioned valleys.

The chief: (here is the crucial question after all the above maneuvering) About ten days ago, we saw many clouds heading in that direction. We believe that any rainfall from them would have had to have hit the area you passed, and the valleys we know. Did you see any trace of rain?

The traveler: (at this point, every Bedouin in the chief's tent is anxious for an answer) From what I have seen, it appears that the area was hit by rains not long ago. But I cannot tell how much rain fell.

With that response, the questioning will usually end. And at night, the chief of the tribe, after a secret consultation with some of his tribesmen, will send horse or camel riders to inspect that area. This kind of mission is done with the utmost secrecy, so as to avoid spreading the news and attracting neighboring tribes.

The mission will serve as a double-check for the good news brought by the traveler. I say it is good news, despite the unenthusiastic statements of the traveler. Usually, when a Bedouin describes an area as "not bad," he means it is a good one. This is due to the Bedouins' modesty and tendency to refrain from exaggeration, especially in describing rain and pasture. If the traveler were not telling the truth, because he was the scout from another tribe, he would resort to all kinds of arguments to convince those questioning that the area was not worth consideration. Thus, the mission of the chief and his tribe is to reach the decision to move or not to move to that specific area.

Most often, the tribe will not move until the scouts have returned. If their news is good, then Al-Raheel (the movement from one place to another) will begin. The night before Al-Raheel, the chief will order a man to ride a horse or a camel and to begin shouting, "Al-Arab Raheel Bakr (tomorrow the tribe is moving)."

This announcement will be followed by two steps:

1. Informing all the men in the chief's tent of the decision that the chief took with the consent of other tribesmen and,
2. Sending all sheep and most camels ahead by one or two days in advance.

Preparation for the day of Al-Raheel is tedious. To have a good early start at the first sign of dawn, camels are separated into two groups—one for loading, and the other for any other arising needs. At dawn, the lady of the tent will prepare breakfast, and some loaves of bread and dates to feed the children during the movement of Al-Raheel. Lunch is unthinkable for adults during that day. Next, the lady, with the help of other members of the family, will begin packing the light belongings of the tent. After the lady has done her job, it is the responsibility of the men to carry the heavy goods and all packed items, to be loaded onto camels. Then, only the empty tent remains. It is usually the last thing to be loaded.

During the process of loading, in preparation for the movement of Al- Raheel, there is a lovely but sad musical symphony all over the Bedouins' camp. It has neither regular players nor a conductor. Not even a rehearsal period. Moreover, it has no quiet audience and no established stage. It is composed of the camels' sounds, Bedouins shouting, horses neighing, and dogs barking. The natural setting is the stillness of the desert, as large and empty as only the desert can be. Here and there you hear a Bedouin shouting, while chasing a stubborn camel who has refused to accept his load peacefully. You hear the sad bark of a dog, seeming to realize that it will be left behind, or perhaps Bedouins are singing, as encouragement to carry a heavy load.

To a Bedouin, that symphony is the most beautiful one possible. It is one of the things most deeply rooted in nomadic traditions, and it is generally a sign of good news. What could a Bedouin want more than to move to a good grazing area?

I will not forget the gradual disappearance of that symphony as long as I live. It will not stop suddenly, and there remains here and there, the sound of young camels who happen to be receiving the first load of their lives. And the sound of dogs, still persistent in following Al-Raheel, despite their owners' decision to leave them behind to fight for survival alone. That symphony to me represents the true nomadic life. That life is cruel, sad, honest, fast, hospitable, and suspicious to an outsider—the strangest life he may be able to imagine. It represented in a concrete way the survival of the fittest, long before the appearance of Darwin's sophisticated theory.

Al-Raheel will not start moving until the chief's tent is loaded. It is almost always the last tent to be folded. This delay in folding the chief's tent is intentional and traditional, as it serves as a flag to rally the tribe in case of a sudden attack, anytime during the preparation to move. Many tribal raids failed because the attack took place while the chief's tent was still pitched. To a Bedouin, his chief's tent and camels must be defended like a country's flag. It represents the honor of the tribe, not the chief's personal possession.

During Al-Raheel, ladies and children will be left with the loaded camels. The men move ahead on their horses and camels in a group called Aslaf. However, Aslaf will stay close enough to the loaded camels (Al-Madhaheer) to serve as protector in case of a raid. I never saw a raid firsthand, but I knew what was to be done if ever one took place.

Conversation among the men of Aslaf varies. It ranges from reminiscences of a drought year to the best year anyone can remember. It covers the day the tribe defended its camels, and the time when the men of the tribe attacked another tribe and lost. During those conversations, some individuals will be pursuing their hobbies of hunting with prized falcons and salukis—a graceful dog, somewhat like a greyhound.

Al-Raheel continues moving all day long. About one hour before sunset, unloading starts with the tents first. Dinner has to be prepared, despite the wet wood that sometimes comes along with an area of recent rains. I have a strong impression of us having to leave the tent because it was full of smoke from wet wood. No matter what the condition of the wood, the ladies in the tribe must prepare a hearty dinner. No excuses were accepted.

Neither rain, wind, nor cold stops the Bedouins from Al-Raheel the next day. Al-Raheel continues day after day, sometimes for months, until a grazing area is found.

I remember one year we started from the northern desert of Saudi Arabia, and spent the summer in Al-Jazirah, in the northern part of Syria, bordering Turkey. When we saw clouds going to the south, we started Al-Raheel again, continuously moving through the desert of Iraq, down to an area near the combined borders of Jordan, Saudi Arabia, and Iraq, and where the grazing was best.

This description of the Bedouins' movement, starting at the end of the fall season, is a typical process followed by all tribes of the area, whether they own sheep or camels. Al-Raheel is an agonizing process of movement, but it is the core of nomadic life. It is the dividing line between a settled person and a nomadic one.

Every member of a nomadic family must perform some duties, especially during Al-Raheel. Even children of the age of five or so are assigned tasks to perform. Thus, the existence of each nomadic family will depend first on its members' cooperation. Secondly, it depends on the tribe's power of self-protection. This is why it is sometimes disturbing to me, to live isolated and to think about my immediate family far away. No member can sit around while others are performing their duties. He will be repugnant, and his reputation will be damaged, not only within his immediate family but all through his larger family (the tribe). Girls will come to loathe his name, and children as well as adults will make his life miserable.

Competition and the fulfillment of duty within the established rules of the tribe are respected and encouraged. This side of the Bedouins' character has been ignored by many sociologists, economists, anthropologists, and especially popular writers, who describe the Bedouin as a lazy person who has no ambition to upgrade his position and look ahead for a better life. Those urban-educated people too often judge the Bedouin by their standards, and not by standards suited to nomadic life. They fail to understand nomadic life and refuse to admit this is so.

Frankly, some lack the intellectual integrity to be as objective as possible. You cannot judge a Bedouin by using the mores and morals of an urban society. To understand the nomadic person very well, one has to study him within his small as well as his larger family, the tribe he belongs to, and whom he could hardly live without.

2

—

BEDOUIN JUSTICE

I have not personally seen any kind of society, aside from the tribe where I grew up, where individual achievements are the property of the community as a whole, regardless of whether that individual happens to be the chief's son or an insignificant (in some peoples' eyes) shepherd. In this kind of a society, laziness cannot be tolerated, and competition is encouraged.

It is not a concern that a nomadic person does not aspire to the "better life," defined by intellectuals as the urban way of life. The nomad feels he is living the most honorable life of all, despite the intellectuals' disrespect for it. He is consciously fighting to preserve that way of living, because it was his father's and forefathers' way, and he respects them so much.

In reality, a nomadic person has not only an aim, but a very honorable one: to defend, protect, and perpetuate his history, and that of every tribe and every nomadic person. To sociologists, economists, anthropologists, and other well-educated writers who misunderstand nomadic life, I say, please leave your fancy offices long enough to try understanding and judging nomadic culture through its own environment, rather than through the fairytales of Hollywood movies.

Everyone who has lived a nomadic life is aware that some specific, strong personality traits do exist in the Bedouin. He is sharp, definite, and precise. Those qualities of a nomadic person's personality result from his illiteracy, and the need, in a nomadic life, to make quick decisions. He is faithful when one establishes trust in him. But cheat him even once, and he becomes the most suspicious human being. The past will not be forgotten, and, accordingly, tribes always consider their past as a strong influence on their current lives.

ψ ψ ψ

The family is the smallest unit in the tribe. To a Bedouin, this does not mean parents and children only, but rather it implies the extended family, including all blood relatives. After the family, Al-Fekhth (the smallest branch of a tribe) is the next segment of the tribe, followed by the subtribe, and then by the tribe proper.

For example, my family is connected to the Al-Sba'a Tribe as follows:

Al-Mershed (Immediate family)
Al-Ameerah (Fekhth)
Al-Gmosah (five or six Fekhth)
Al-Sba'a Botainat (sub-tribe)
Al-Sba'a (the tribe as a whole)
Aneza (the group of tribes of which Al-Sba'a is a part)

The chief of a tribe is its absolute leader. In a way, he is the political leader as well as a commander-in-chief of the military power of the tribe. This kind of centralized and absolute leadership is required in nomadic life. Consequently, a weak leader will usually not stay in power long, as his weakness reflects on the tribe's name and honor.

The word "absolute" should not be interpreted literally. It has its limitations, based on well-established tribal laws. For example, a chief of a tribe cannot kill one of the tribe members without being subject to revenge by the family or Al-Fekhth of the killed person. Accordingly, the chief should be flexible, and should use his power sparingly within his tribe only after peaceful means have failed. Likewise, possessions of any Bedouin of the tribe cannot be touched by the chief without the consent of the owner.

In a way, a crude democracy does exist in tribal society. Each member is entitled to defend his home, property, and relatives, even against the powerful chief. The Bedouin society is one in which the least significant member will get the support of the tribe in defending himself against the powerful chief, if that leader is not just.

It is worth stating some well-established laws in my tribe (most of which are followed by other tribes too), in order to enlighten outsiders about ways a tribe settles its disputes.

If a man from my tribe, Al-Sba'a, kills one of his tribesmen, the relatives of the murdered person will attempt to kill him on the spot. But if he escapes, and enters the nearest tent, he is safe. No one can touch him because the owner of the tent will protect him to the last. This process is called Al-Wajh. It means that the accused is under the protection and honor of the tent owner and his relatives, extending most of the time up to Al-Fekhth.

But protection has its limit, especially when the killing is intentional. The Al-Wajh system is not a means to encourage murders within the tribe, rather, it is an immediate protective device, respected by every tribesman, to save the tribe from fighting within itself.

Eventually, the murderer almost always pays dearly for his action. Al-Wajh provides protection for three days only. After that time, the relatives of the victim have the right of revenge.

If the killing is not intentional, then compensation in the way of a "blood payment" is the only solution. Usually, the killer has to pay about thirty camels, plus his horse and rifle—except in the case where the victim's relatives are poor, in which case the blood payment is often waived. The Bedouins reason that God has decided that such a thing should happen; thus, for the sake of tribal unity, the payment should not be made. However, if the victim's relatives insist on having the compensation, then they are entitled to get it without any impediment.

Once, when Al-Sba'a Tribe was camping, in spring of 1950, in the Syrian desert, an unintentional killing took place. I heard this story being told over and over again by members of the tribe.

Two young men were playing with a pistol. The poorest one happened to kill the only son of a very respected, well-to-do old man. The killer immediately went to that old man and told him, "Ana fi wajhak (I am in your protection)." The old man, without asking what for, announced that the young killer was under his protection. To the old man's agony, he was protecting the killer of his only son. He refused to accept compensation, reasoning that he had lost a son, but God also gave him a son.

I heard that as late as 1967, the innocent killer was still supported by that old man's wealth, for the sake of all the ladies who were left without a guardian because of his unintentional killing of their brother. The killer, in actuality, became a member of the victim's family. This is the kind of unity and cooperation the tribal law tries to establish. It has succeeded in many cases but has also failed in others.

Al-Wajh has another aspect, besides being a temporary preventative measure to stop fighting from starting within the tribe. It also has what is called a lasting and permanent clause for the future. If a case of murder is solved by blood payment, upon paying, the guilty party will pick a member of the tribe to provide him with Al-Wajh. This is done to discourage the still-young relatives of the victim from trying to seek revenge for their lost relative when they grow up. This is why I call it a lasting and permanent clause, as opposed to the temporary one, which normally lasts only three days.

Only once, as far as I know, was the lasting and permanent clause of Al-Wajh violated in Al-Sba'a Tribe. It happened in 1949, the year when my nearest subtribe of Al-Sba'a called Al-Botainat almost went to war with the other sub-tribe of Al-Sba'a, called Al-Ebedah. That episode was a classic in tribal cases, featuring diplomacy and determination beyond one's imagination. Almost every member of the Greater Aneza Tribe, scattered throughout the Arab countries of the Middle East, were aware of the case and awaited the outcome.

Exactly twenty years before the event, in 1929, a member of Al-Ebedah killed one of his relatives. He took refuge with Shammar Tribe in Iraq for twenty years. After that, when the son of the murdered person had become an adult, the case was solved by blood payment. The murderer paid and picked my family, Al-Mershed, to be his protector for future days (the lasting and permanent clause of Al-Wajh). Usually, a family such as mine should not accept the murderer's choice, because as head of the tribe we should avoid being part of any internal conflict. But the case was so crucial that my Uncle Rakan accepted it for the sake of tribal unity.

After that, the accused moved back from his refuge with Shammar Tribe to the area of our tribe. When he encountered the son of his murder victim, the son instantly attacked, wounding him in the arm. Although the wound was not serious, this did not make much difference in the consequence. Whether he was killed, wounded, or merely slapped, it meant one thing: that my family Wajh was violated.

When my uncle heard the news, he was furious and immediately rode, accompanied by my father and other men, with the intention to kill any immediate relative of that young man. It took our men a few days to find the man in our Wajh, but they found no one to attack in order to defend our Wajh. After the attack, the son (young man) and his immediate relatives left the tribe at once and took refuge, ironically enough, far away with the Shammar Tribe.

Why Shammar? Because it was foreign, as far as our tribe, Al-Sba'a, was concerned. And tribal law stipulates that the place of refuge should be with a foreign tribe and as far as possible from the killer's tribe.

All our men could do was to bring the wounded man in our Wajh back to our place. I remember him very well. He was about 45 years old, with features as sharp as a falcon. He was as much of a humorist as one can imagine, but privately most members of the tribe hated him, because he came to symbolize the tribe's disunity.

For two years, emissaries went back and forth, between the attacker's family and my family, to solve the case. My uncle insisted that the law was clear and must be applied to the last word. They must bring the attacker to my family to do what was appropriate (in this case, Al-Mershed family was entitled to kill him on the spot) or he and his relatives were subject to attack, no matter where they lived. The law was also clear about what would happen if the relatives of the attacker decided to come back to the tribe, leaving the attacker with the Shammar Tribe. In that instance, they would have to pay eighty camels, most of them being theirs and those of their nearest Fekhth in Al-Ebedah. This still left the attacker liable to be killed in future days.

Al-Ebedah refused to abide by the law, on the grounds that the law was applicable only in non-cousin cases. In Al-Sba'a Tribe, everyone is a cousin, therefore, the law is void. My uncle tried to convince them otherwise, but they refused his arguments. Within six months, if the case was still unsolved, any member of Al-Ebedah would be liable to our attack. This did not mean from Al-Mershed only, but rather from an attack by any one from Al-Botainat.

The case had reached the highest point of danger and sensitivity, because the two subtribes of Al-Sba'a were bound to fight in the very near future. Al-Ebedah was worried, and Al-Botainat was also. In fact, every tribe that belonged to the Greater Aneza Tribe was worried.

Finally, Al-Ebedah sent its dignitaries to the judge of blood cases for all Aneza subtribes. He was the chief of Al-Fedaan subtribe in Syria. They asked him his opinion of the law, and whether my uncle's interpretation was the right one. Ibn Mhaid told them that what Rakan Ibn Mershed (my uncle) said was the truth, and that they'd better execute the law.

Two or three months later, Al-Ebedah came to ask for a waiver. When we refused, they agreed to pay the 80 camels for the return of the attacker's immediate relatives only.

The day of payment was the most agonizing test for all concerned.

Al-Ebedah was angry because this payment (even if it was legally right) was going to damage the tribe's unity for a long time to come. My subtribe was frustrated for the same reason. Some of my sub-tribesmen argued with my uncle and father that the law was very harsh, especially since the attacker had not killed the man in our Wajh. But my family refused to reverse their stand, and insisted we must show Al-Ebedah that we meant business.

Our tents were filled with women and children of Al-Ebedah, asking for mercy. But they had no success. I remember Al-Ebedah paying the camels on a sunny day. At about 4:00 p.m., when my uncle asked one of his men to check the marks on the camels, to establish whether or not they came from the attacker's family and Fekhth, the examiner found that there were only 79 camels. When my uncle then insisted that the last camel must be paid, we all felt that he was too harsh and inflexible. But Rakan was aiming at much more than a mere camel. He was aiming to establish his authority and to reunite the tribe of Al-Sba'a.

The final camel was paid in the same afternoon, paid while all the dignified men of Al-Ebedah were present, and paid by those loyal and respected men of Al-Ebedah. Oh! Uncle, it was too much to disgrace those men of Al-Ebedah. Uncle, they were too respectable to be humiliated to that extent. But, despite all that you did, you proved to be the firm leader who would come out on top in the end.

For about one month, my family, Al-Mershed, owned the 80 camels. Owned them while our tents were still full of children and ladies from Al-Ebedah. Then, my uncle called the dignitaries of Al-Botainat to discuss the matter. My father insisted, and my uncle agreed, that we had proven to everyone that our Wajh was not a game with which to play. Now, for the sake of the tribe's unity, all 80 camels should be sent back to our cousins Al-Ebedah of Al-Sba'a Tribe. Our cousins (Al-Ebedah) appreciated that diplomacy so much that they brought the attacker to my uncle's tent.

My God, I really thought that my uncle, who was shaking all over and not saying a single word, would kill him on the spot. He was absolutely speechless. Whether my uncle would kill him or spare him was the only thought in the mind of every man present in the tent.

It was a day of trial for all of us members of Al-Sba'a Tribe. The attacker was young and scared to death, and why not. He knew that no one would take revenge for him from Al-Mershed because of what he had done.

During those agonizing moments of silence, the coffee began to be served. Everyone realized that the end was near.

If the young attacker was permitted to drink my uncle's coffee, he was safe; traditionally, a Bedouin would not kill a man who had tasted his food or coffee.

To the astonishment of all, my uncle ordered the servant not to give coffee to the attacker. That order proved to all present that my uncle intended to kill the young man. I almost argued when I heard my uncle's words. *Oh! Please, Uncle spare him, he is the only young man in that family.* Suddenly, there pushed into the Almajles (the men's side of the tent) a horrified, crying woman, shaking and repeating over and over, "Please, Rakan, spare the life of the only son I have!"

My uncle, at that point, lost all of his arrogance, and became more human than ever. He went to his car to drive away, but before the car moved, he called to the coffee server: "Ssob algahwa (pour the coffee)," and ended those agonizing moments in the life of Al-Sba'a Tribe. With that decision, the tribe became happy and united again, and Rakan Ibn Mershed remained its chief.

ψ ψ ψ

In case a Bedouin killed a man from another tribe, the murderer would be defended by his own tribe and need not leave it to ask for protection from a foreign tribe. This would continue until a solution was reached.

During the days under discussion, governmental regulations and laws became more and more applicable to tribes. But they did not eliminate the tribal laws completely. There is a great disintegration going on in nomadic life, but that life has by no means vanished.

Here is another tribal law, about which I found many disagreements between the elders of the tribe. Some claimed it was used in the old days, others disagreed. But it is worth explaining, to show how the thinking of nomadic tribes developed.

If a Bedouin wounds another in the face intentionally, then the law is clear. Upon the wounded person's acceptance of compensation, two elderly men must be chosen to assist in settling the case. They are not judges, because there is no need to have a judge when the law is well-known. They are neutral observers, asked to state only what they see.

When they are ready, the wounded, in front of every man present, wears his headdress as plainly as possible. Now, if the wound is still uncovered, meaning it lies below the middle forehead, the wounded is asked to walk backward. He walks until the two elderly men decide that they cannot see the wound anymore. For every yard, a camel must be paid. Of course, this kind of law is executed only after the wound has healed.

This law is severe in a way, but at the same time, I believe it is beautiful and just. A face wound is a very obvious mark for everyone to see. The wounded must be compensated very well.

ॐ ॐ ॐ

Economically speaking, a Bedouin's income comes mainly from his sheep and camels, or from his services as a shepherd. His basket goods are limited, but usually include ghee from sheep milk, dates, and flour. In the spring season, when sheep and camels give birth, the Bedouin will get his ghee and yoghurt from their milk. He sometimes creates part of his tent from the wool of sheep, goats, or camels. At the end of spring, a Bedouin usually sells his sheep products to get cash. Male lambs, old sheep, old camels, wool, and ghee are the most common sources of cash. He spends his income mainly on food and cloth.

The Bedouin basket goods are changing, and along with this his expenditures are increasing. Some luxury goods are becoming not only accepted but very popular in nomadic life. In the 1960s, the appearance of canned foods, radios, and fashions in clothing were all indicators of the Bedouin's changing tastes and expectations. That change has only continued.

In 1966, I estimated the Bedouin's income from a single sheep. I found that a full-grown sheep, worth about $20.00, would produce an income of about $5.00 per year. Certainly, this estimate assumed the sheep to be pregnant, and that she would successfully give birth to a baby lamb.

In the case of camel ownership, income comes mainly from the sale of the camel itself. Usually, a Bedouin who owns 15 to 20 camels sells one or two camels, as needed, per year, at around $200.00 per camel (1966 prices). Considering that sheep ownership runs into the hundreds, it is clearly more profitable than camel ownership. This is why most Bedouins are now abandoning camel ownership. When camels were still the primary means of transportation, they were much more of a necessity and therefore more valuable.

In a good year, when pasture is abundant, a Bedouin may get more income than he can spend, relative to past consumption. However, the Bedouin has no sense of saving. His lifestyle does not accommodate savings, as the tribe is always in need of something that costs money, and nomadic people are not inclined to seek to carry more with them, wherever they go.

Therefore, he will create extra activities, most of them not essential, to consume his income. He may arrange to marry another woman, force a young son to marry, throw many parties—or, in the 1950s or 1960s, buy a car. If a drought year happened to follow, he would have no savings on which to rely and would probably be reduced to being no more than a dignified beggar.

That was the environment that I, Faisal Ibn Sfouq Ibn Bashir Al-Mershed, was raised in, and was induced to believe in wholly. Everyone was a brother or a cousin, fighting and working hard to preserve and defend the name and the honor of Al-Sba'a Tribe. Selfishness is a natural human trait, but in that environment, the individual was second to the group and the tribe's interest.

It was a lovely and secure life. It had its own established regulations, and we could care less about what was going on beyond the social boundaries of the tribe. In a way, Al-Sba'a Tribe and every tribe nearby, was an independent world within the greater world.

3

—

OXFORD UNIVERSITY IN A TENT

Around 1942, the tents of my uncle and others became less no-madic, compared to the rest of the tribe. They didn't venture as far as before. Nevertheless, my father's tent continued on with the wandering tribe. So, in my early life, I was moving year-round. Being my father's only male child, I was given the utmost attention from almost everyone—except my father. He believed rightly that a child given so much attention would be spoiled in the end.

This did not mean that my father did not love me. On the contrary, I was extremely dear to him, and he showed me all kinds of affection and love in more reserved ways.

He was described as a quiet, secretive, and tolerant leader. He was a man who would not give up easily but persisted in negotiating even when the case appeared unsolvable to most people. Many times, he was chosen by my uncle, his older brother, to arbitrate cases within the tribe, due to the characteristics I described above.

But my uncle, the chief, had the opposite characteristics of my father. One of the most notable differences was that my uncle loved and hated on the spot, but he forgot easily too.

No doubt these strong and contradictory personalities affected me a great deal, especially since I spent the early years of my life with both men equally. I am said to resemble my uncle in impatience when I want something. Either I will get it as soon as possible, or I will forget it forever. My father gave me his tolerance to respect the opinions of others, and to live in a world where differences and disagreements are inevitable.

With this brief background about the socioeconomic and political setup of Al-Sba'a Tribe, let us return to my personal side of this story. When I reached the age of about six, a difficult decision had to be made by my parents. By that time, I had three sisters, one older and two younger than me. Any decision concerning the only boy in the tent was hard to make. My father was of the opinion that I was too young to leave my parents. But my mother insisted that I should go to my uncle's tent, to be in school with my cousins. I found out later that my father's stand was really based on the dread of his only son's departure.

My mother argued well, to get me into the school tent beside my uncle's tent. It was among the tents that moved least in those days. She based her judgment on a well-established tradition in the Al-Mershed family; that every member of that family had the right to be prepared for the leadership of the tribe someday. I remember the day when she told my father in a very emotional voice, "Abu Faisal (a sign of respect meaning "Faisal's father"), I hope that I will not see the day when Faisal receives a letter and has to take it to one of his cousins to read because Faisal is illiterate."

I am sure that sending me away to the school tent was much harder on her than it was on my father. But her conviction that Faisal must be given all available opportunities, to compete with his cousins for the leadership of the tribe, forced her to accept and even encourage my departure. I am very certain now, that if my mother could have visualized how schooling would lead me so far beyond reading and writing a letter, she would have rejected the idea completely. But to her, as well as to my father, the highest level of education would come when I reached that milestone. And why not think that way, when both of them were illiterate to the point that they could not read and write even their own names?

Oh Mother, I love you so much for making that crucial decision. How fortunate for me that you made that decision, which created so much agony in later years. But remember that I missed having you around me everywhere I went.

You accused me later, about not caring much whether I was beside you or not. But dear Mother, believe me, I was deeply sad everywhere I went, every time I imagined you waiting for my uncertain return. Mother, it is this modern urban life, with its beauty and ugliness, that made it impossible for you and I to live side by side. You insisted on staying with my father in the tent, while my profession, which took so many years and so much effort to acquire, has no place in nomadic life. Dear Mother, I did not choose to desert you or the tribe as a whole. Even though time forced me to live in a different environment than you, that tribe is always in my memory.

Don't you remember, my beloved Mother, when I was telling you that someday I would be a lawyer? And you told me to go ahead, dear Son, and do it? Were you expecting me to practice law in a court around our tent? And don't you recall that when I changed to dreaming about being an officer in the Saudi Army with all kinds of decorations, you smiled your approval and admiration? Again, I ask, dear Mother, were you expecting me to command a regiment around our tent?

Of course, today the answer to all those questions is no, but to you, then, it was yes. You wanted Faisal the lawyer, the officer, the chief of the tribe and the minister of everything, around you all the time.

I don't blame you or Father or anyone of the tribe for affectionately calling me "Deserter." But remember this, all you members of that lovely and respected tribe: during those days, I, like every one of you, never entertained the idea that the day would come when I would live away from you. I was thinking of being your leader, who could read and write in addition to displaying all of the usual qualities of a tribal chief. I failed to realize this dream, not because of personal intentions, but rather due to cowardice, when I let myself be dominated by the processes of this ugly modern life. In a way, I was not in control of myself but just drifted. Time alone decided when to stop my drift. And so, my dear Mother, Father, and tribesmen, my educational episode is exactly like that thief in the tale you members of Al-Sba'a Tribe always told:

> Young Bedouin: Father, I caught a thief.
> Father: Bring him!

The young one: I cannot.
The Father: Then leave him.
The young one: He is not letting me go.

Like the young Bedouin in the story, having caught the thief, I was bound to him just as much as he was bound to me. I soon had an education to pursue, but the education pursued me, too. It took hold and would not let me go.

First, I wanted only to learn how to read and write a letter; I was determined then to go back to all of you as an educated man.

But education never let me go. It was so beautiful and opened so many fascinating avenues for me, that I found it very difficult to resist exploring them all.

I walked and enjoyed every step I took, despite the hardships and agonies I faced, and despite the sadness that journey created for all of you. Hopefully now, after reaching that level that not one of you has even heard of, or is indeed able to comprehend, I am almost ready to free myself from that thief.

But forgive me, dear tribesmen, for saying (now that the journey is nearing completion) it has made the prospect of returning to you and living with you full-time very difficult.

Please understand that I have lost my freedom to act in a way that will please all of you. Forgive me, dear tribesmen, for saying these things which you don't like to hear. In my fight for education, I have respected those honorable traditions you taught me to follow. Didn't you teach me to fight until the last? Didn't you raise me in a setting where ambition is the best path to leadership?

These and many other traditions of yours I applied in new surroundings. In a way, our separation has not been through traditions and values, but rather in the space between two environments that can never meet. I know you don't understand this reasoning. But I write for the world to be the judge between you and I. Also, I write for the future when your educated children will realize that I, Faisal, did not leave you by choice, but that a new life, the future life of everyone, forced me to be away from you.

ψ ψ ψ

Learning was a revolutionary development for nomadic tribes in the 1940s.

At that time, it was traditional for the chief of the tribe to have a clerk write his letters to conduct tribal business. Neither Al-Sba'a Tribe nor Al-Mershed family had anyone who was able to read and write. Illiteracy was almost absolute, and sad to say, it was to some extent, respected. Bedouins (Al-Badou) looked down on a person who could read and write as soft and not courageous. It is weird thinking, to say the least, but that was the reality of tribal tradition at that time.

After a long search, mainly in cities, for a clerk who could accept living in the desert and moving with the tribe, Mohammad Jomaa joined us. He was originally from a tribe which became literate by living in cities all over the region. And so, he became the clerk and lived with his family in a tent beside my uncle's tent. When my uncle, my father, or anyone else did not need the service of the clerk, he had nothing to do. And so, the Harvard or Oxford of Al-Sba'a Tribe was established in a tent beside my uncle's tent. I really have no idea how that happened exactly, or who came up with the idea to establish a so-called school. Needless to say, then and now, I was happy to have our great learning institution. And so began my long journey to learn how to read and write.

Looking back at those days, I am amazed that I and a few other children learned to write and read a letter, which was the ultimate goal of that exercise. We found out that our teacher, Mohammad, barely had the equivalent of a ninth-grade education. The teaching methods were very simple. Students were asked to memorize what was in the books and that was all.

When I reached school age, I was judged ready to enter our great school tent by passing the rigid exam administered by my father, who was illiterate. I was accepted. For the record, that famous exam was to count from 1 to 100. If I was able to count without mistakes, then I could go to the tent at the start of the year, when the tribe was around. It was crowded at first, but usually around late fall, when the tribe began to move in search of grazing areas, the dropout rate from our great institution was so high that the tent became almost empty, with only me and a few cousins.

The school tent usually stayed beside my uncle's tent, which moved less frequently, compared to the typical tribal movement. On the other hand, the "CEO", my father, was moving with the tribe from one place to another in the vast desert in search of better grazing areas. That development necessitated my staying in my uncle's tent, and so I missed regularly being around my father, mother, and sisters from an early age. Although my dear uncle and his children, four of them older than me, compensated for the absence of my parents and sisters, in reality no one can compensate for a lost mother's love and those warm hugs. When I first arrived at my uncle's tent, I forgot all the sadness and tears Mother showed when I left her. I assured her that I would come to see her often and that there was no need to cry. I never expected that our separation would last over six months that first year.

Cousins were all around. They were eight boys and four girls, and I began to enjoy them as we played together. Turkiyah, my uncle's eldest daughter, at the age of about 25, became almost my second mother. She took care of me very well. I was a brother to her, a son, and a cousin. To me she came to represent a trusted source of love and affection. I greatly needed such security at that age, and I fought for her interests against everyone. If the occasion arose, I defended her even in front of my uncle and father. When she was married three years later, I tried without success to stop the marriage, thinking that no one would refuse Faisal's wishes. When I failed, I became so desperate that I began to stone the car that took

31

her away. I cried very hard when the car left, taking away my dear Turkiyah, whom I would miss so much. My uncle was so moved that he promised me he would take me often to see her.

The school tent held about 30 boys, from first to fifth grade. Those students who were not cousins were other relatives from the tribe. We had one teacher to take care of the whole school, who as I've mentioned, had only a ninth-grade education. In addition to his responsibility as a teacher, he was also my uncle's secretary. He usually went with my uncle during the time of revenue collection from the tribe, or when my uncle went to cities in Iraq, Syria, or Saudi Arabia. During his absences, which were frequent and sometimes rather lengthy, the fifth graders would become the teachers. I believe that, for two to three months every year, we took care of and taught each other alone. The school year usually lasted only six to eight months.

In the first days of my presence, my uncle told the teacher that Faisal must be given the liberty of deciding whether or not to come to school. I was my uncle's nephew, and so I enjoyed this privilege. This carte blanche idea regarding my attendance was a very difficult one for the teacher to accept. But who would disagree with Rakan ibn Mershed's word during those days?

When the teacher gave me the first-grade book, I refused it on the grounds that my cousin Traad had more and different books from mine. I insisted that I should get books exactly like his. Traad was in fifth grade and about 15 years of age. The teacher tried hard to convince me that I needed at least five more years to reach that level. But I refused his argument and went straight to my uncle to complain.

Within a short time, the teacher was in my uncle's Almajles, trying to convince him that Faisal should be disciplined from then on. My uncle refused his demand and solved the matter by seating me with the fifth graders. The teacher protested but had to accept the decision.

Incidentally, there were no chairs to sit on, or tables to use for writing in that school. We all sat in one circle in the tent, but each class of student usually sat side by side. So, my uncle's decision to allow me to sit with the fifth graders was kind of a triumph.

The first year of my schooling was an experiment in the highest kind of appeasement. I was free to leave school any time I wished, while other students with more valid reasons to go, had to stay. I was envied by almost everyone, but I believe that most people loved me despite this favor. The teacher even became my strongest ally, as he began to realize my potential. He came to be the fourth person, besides my uncle, father, and mother, who greatly influenced my personal development.

ψ ψ ψ

By the end of the school year, around June, I went to see my parents and the tribe camping somewhere in the desert of Syria. Whenever I traveled from my uncle to my parents, I had to traverse the sometimes-great distance between them. City-dwellers find it hard to fathom how a young boy could not only make the journey but find his way back to a family of nomads, who by definition, do not remain in a fixed location.

But it was second nature to me, having grown up the way I did. I knew my way around and was familiar with many landmarks that would help me find my way. But the greatest asset to a Bedouin who went looking for his family, or for anyone in particular, were the other Bedouin tribes who were also circulating in the region. Everyone knew everyone else, and news traveled easily between tribes. The first group of people I came across in my search was likely to know where my family was, or where they had been recently. Or they knew where someone was who would know, and it was a simple matter of seeking them out. Again, the city-dweller has trouble imagining this. But to a Bedouin it makes perfect sense. Following the news of my family's movements was like reading signs on a highway.

Once I returned to my family, I spent all the summer with them. When school recommenced, I was in the first grade. But, by the middle of that year, I was promoted to the second grade and finished the year first in that class.

My uncle was extremely proud when he heard about my achievements that year. He was completely happy, even though this meant I had performed better than his own children. In his eyes, I was more intelligent than any of his sons. When he began to express that belief, almost everyone started to accept the idea that I was the most intelligent child in the whole Al-Mershed family.

In reality, I was no more than an average kid, given exceptional encouragement and inducement to do well. At the same time, my cousins' own father denied them kind words and the slightest encouragement. They grew to fear their father, more than anything else.

Physical beating was a way to discipline kids at that time. My cousins were subjected to that by their father and sometimes by their uncle, my father. I was never beaten by either of them. This double standard in dealing with the children of the same family created my superior image among Al-Mershed boys. In reality, I was given chances that were denied to others.

ψ ψ ψ

The following school year was full of incidents concerning the teacher-student relationship. The students had noticed that the teacher, during my uncle's absence, would vanish from the whole camp for two or three days.

The oldest students investigated the matter and came up with the reason. It happened that our teacher was in love with a girl in another camp about 20 kilometers away.

We began to spread the story. The teacher became so irritated that one day he punished every student from third grade and above.

That punishment caused the permanent exodus of the oldest students. They refused to come back to school, despite the severe punishment they had received from their fathers.

News of the exodus was received with joy and happiness by our teacher. He was in love and realized that he had no more barriers for his freewheeling to pursue that love. But he was too cautious to leave anything to fate. One day, he gave us a lecture about his cat, which was playing in the school tent. He told us that the cat could tell him everything that happened in the school during his absence.

We did not believe a word of what he said. But the next day he shattered all our confidence about the cat's inability to inform him. While the cat was in the tent, he suddenly left. We proceeded to accuse him of everything under the sun. Upon his return, he called the cat and began to repeat what each of us had said. We were astonished, and from then on kept quiet every time he left the tent while the cat was around. No one suspected the teacher of hiding beside the tent and listening to our conversation about him.

By the end of spring season, we felt so much animosity toward that cat that we began calculating how to get rid of it. No one dared to do anything except my brave cousin Mohammad. He kidnapped the cat and took it far away—probably killed it. Our teacher missed the cat and began to investigate its disappearance. Later, Cousin Mohammad had to pay dearly for his heroic act on behalf of the students' welfare.

About one month before the end of the school year, my uncle decided to go see his brother and the rest of the tribe. I went with him, after the teacher agreed there was not much to gain from staying, especially since my standing in third grade was first, as in the year before.

When we reached the tribe, almost everyone was dancing and happy. Camels and sheep were fat and healthy. The lovely Arabian horses were racing each other all over the plains. Everything had the air of freedom and innocence.

I was given a gazelle, about three months old, as a prize for my good achievement in school. But my aspirations were for a much bigger prize. That was my father's mare's offspring. Khulfah (the mare) was pregnant, and everyone around was guessing whether she would bear a male or a female. She came from the most honorable and respected family of Arabian horses (the Alobayah kind) and had proved herself by beating all horses in the tribe. Thus, her pregnancy was a matter worth talking about.

In the middle of one night, the mare gave birth to a lovely female. When I jumped to claim it, my mother told me I was overruled. My father had already given his word to the Aldwaihes family, from which the mare Khulfah originally came. I was sad and so came to accept the gazelle as the best prize I could hope for.

I should say that, traditionally, female Arabian horses are never sold outright. When the price is estimated and agreed on, usually there is an assumption that the first female offspring of the sold mare will go to the family from where it was bought. This practice is a symbol of how honorable it is to have an Arabian horse.

The scenery of plains with sheep, camels, and horses all over compelled my uncle to send for his tent to join his brother (my father) and the tribe. So, we lived together all that year until the fall season. The tribe was about 50 kilometers from its leader's tent. Every one of us felt, I think, the happiness that came from being together.

The big tribe became a single family. It appeared that everyone was rich and happy. And why shouldn't they be, when sheep and camels were so generous in giving milk and yoghurt? The horses were healthy and willing anytime to be ridden just for fun and sport. It was a happy time, to be enjoyed.

It never occurred to me that that happy year would end. I became so fond of seeing my uncle, father, and other members of the tribe together that I hoped to God there would be no more separation. But my hopes vanished in the fall, when everyone began to talk of the necessity to search for areas hit by rain.

Oh! God, where will the tribe and father be this year? Will they be near enough that I can see them often? Will they be in Saudi Arabia, Syria, Iraq—or where, in this vast desert?

By the end of fall, my uncle's tent and some others were left behind. I remember the day when Al-Raheel began. My mother was crying but urged me to be a good and serious student in our school tent. My sisters (four of them) were emotional and wished me luck. The eldest one, named Saitah, convinced me that it was better for the gazelle to stay with them. And so, the tribe, father, mother, and sisters, and even my gazelle, departed without any of us knowing exactly when we would meet again. Madhaheer (a caravan of camels loaded with women, children, food, water, tents, furniture, etc.) of Al-Sba'a tribe were like a black cloud in the sky. Gradually, they became further and further submerged in the mirage of that lovely desert.

Gone were the lovely sounds of camels, sheep, and horses, and gone was the happiness of being together. I looked around and saw no more than about 20 tents left behind. But here and there was evidence of their presence, a small dog, a piece of cloth, or a still-burning fire. They were left as if to remind everyone of what had been in this particular area.

There was always such a dense and frustrating quietness after Al-Raheel. It resembled, to some extent, moments following the end of a battle between two armies. Eventually, the men of the tents that were left behind came to my uncle's Majles and began talking and wishing the tribe all the best of luck.

Almost everyone noticed how sad and quiet I became. If any man mentioned my father's name, tears would come to my eyes like desert rain. I found it unbearable to listen to any conversation. Everything around me appeared to be artificial. And why not, when almost every woman of the remaining tents had been parted from some of her friends? Every boy and girl had seen some of their peers leave with the tribe. But there was no one who sacrificed the love of parents and sisters for the sake of learning how to read and write a letter like Faisal did. Every student of the famous tent at the end of the day had his parents' and sisters' affection, except Faisal.

This did not mean that there was no one to take care of me. On the contrary, my uncle, his wives, and their children were the source of all kinds of love and attention to me. But despite all their love, there was nothing to match that of a mother, father, or sister.

I left the camp and walked to the nearest hill. Thinking, and looking in the direction the tribe went, I began to cry alone.

Oh! lovely family and tribe, does education really deserve all these sacrifices? Does learning how to write and read a letter mean more than being happy with you? Why all this? My uncle is the leader, and he is so despite his inability to read and write a letter.

I decided at that moment that education (reading and writing a letter) was worthless and did not deserve a single day of separation from my family and the tribe.

⚘ ⚘ ⚘

My fourth year of schooling began while I was still the most miserable boy around. Everyone noticed that I continued to be quiet and withdrawn. This affected my outlook on education, which I began to approach with indifference. The teacher noticed the change, and I am sure that he told my uncle.

There were only two choices for my uncle. Either Faisal would stay in the school tent, to get as much as he could, or he would leave school and be almost illiterate forever.

Two months later, my uncle faced this ugly choice. One afternoon, when I was beside my uncle in Almajles, talking as usual, I stopped suddenly. Without looking at my face, my uncle encouraged me to continue. When he heard no response, he looked and saw my tears. Everyone in Almajles was surprised to see my tears. My uncle tried hard to know the reason for them. Finally, I stood, and this time I began crying as I talked. "Uncle, see that lamb in front of the tent. He is running to meet his mother after a day's separation. But where is my mother now?" When my uncle heard that he was unable to say a word. He was so moved that he sent for the driver to take me to my family and the tribe immediately.

A letter to my uncle:

Oh! Dear Uncle, I love you for that decision, the decision you disliked so much. My learning in that year was hopeless, no matter how long I stayed. I respect you, Uncle, despite all your later questionable actions and erratic characteristics. These, fortunately, did not affect me negatively. You were a good leader when such was rare. You fought to defend our tribe's interests against other tribes three or four times larger than ours. Furthermore, you created and maintained our family and tribal name as one of the most respected all through the Arab countries of the Middle East.

When kissing governmental officials' hands was a step for chiefs to further their personal interest, you refused to hurt your dignity and that of Al-Sba'a Tribe. When other tribal chiefs were brought to act against the principles they and their tribe believed in, you, Rakan ibn Mershed, refused to be bought like a commodity in a dirty and corrupt market. Remember, Uncle, that despite all of the difficulties you and the tribe were facing, you created in us children of that tribe the will to fight to the last in an honorable way.

Farewell, dear Uncle. You are old and weak, politically as well as physically. This is life, and there is no escape from life's judgment, no matter how strong the person. Please, don't regret your present position. Compared to chiefs of other tribes, you are one of the few lucky ones. Your present position is not a consequence of deliberate actions on your part.

Rather, it is due to the ugly and inhuman transition from a nomadic to a settled life. Believe me, you did your job with the best results during the glorious days of our tribal life. And he who has such a past has a history which will be remembered and talked about for a long time to come.

Your history is full of honorable incidents. Let me remind you of some.

I am sure you remember when Fawaz Ibn (son) Shaalan, head of Alrwalah tribe, our cousins as part of greater Aneza tribe, tried to force his will on us and take our water wells in Qdaim in the desert of Syria. You mobilized the tribe and stood and refused Fawaz's demands. In that incident, Uncle, you were following well-established traditions in Al-Mershed family and Al-Sba'a tribe—never submit to coercive acts and bullying. In other words, fight and live with dignity, rather than live peacefully like sheep.

Yes, Rakan ibn Mershed, you did it exactly like your uncle Hazaa ibn Mershed (called Abu Shawarb, due to his big moustache) did it before you. He stood with only about 15 horse riders to defend our honor against Ibn Rasheed's elite company to save our white camels, the symbol of Al-Sba'a Tribe's flag and honor.

You remember that incident, Uncle, because then at the age of about six years you were crying out and begging your mother to empty your shoes of the stones that were in them. In reality you felt pieces of gold hidden there. Hazaa ibn Mershed did it, and later, much later, you did it. So, Uncle, we have a long history and a very honorable one. I hope that now God will help us to channel all such energy, for the best development of our lovely country, Saudi Arabia.

ψ ψ ψ

Four students, two cousins, and two children from the tribe graduated in 1951 with fifth-grade certificates. A year later, in 1952, I followed with my fifth-grade certificate, a photo of which is in back of this book. It stated that Faisal Sfouq Al-Mershed, who was born in the desert in 1940, passed his fifth-grade certificate exam.

Where was I to go, after that great achievement of being more than able to read and write a letter? As far as my family and the tribe were concerned, I was to go nowhere. What added to that conclusion was that my two cousins, who graduated the year before me, failed their sixth grade in Aleppo City. And so, it was obvious to those sources of wisdom that it was no use to waste more time in going to school, away from my family and the tribe.

But somehow my uncle was adamant that his children must go back to school. He had a late awakening, so to speak, to the value of education, and that opened the door for me. Almost all people assumed that I would join my cousins—but an incident took place that changed a lot in my personal development, especially my feelings toward my uncle, whom I adored and loved.

He was so good to me, by encouraging me to talk in Almajles especially when he had dignitaries as guests from other tribes or from cities. Even when my father was around, I was with my uncle most of the time. It was a shock to everyone that my uncle forgot to register me in school. That was his excuse, when my father asked him, "Rakan, did you register the boys in school?" When my father heard Uncle's answer, he stood and ordered me to join him to leave.

I never saw my father angry before like he was that night. And he addressed my uncle for everyone in Almajles to hear, by quoting an Arab saying: "The forgotten is useless."

That incident, I believe, pushed my father to insist on me going to school, though most of the time he was not keen for me to continue my education, when my mother was pressing him to let me continue. Next morning, my father registered me in government boarding school in Homs City in Syria, about 50 kilometers from Hama city, where my cousins were in school.

4
Man-Child

In 1951, while I was back with my family, I began to regain my old personality and became freely happy. But I missed my uncle. In a way, I was a boy who wanted the best of two worlds. I wanted education, but I wanted to be with my family. I wanted to be in two places at once.

The grazing area was not good that year, and so, the tribe was obliged to move continuously. During one of these moves, after I had seen how many other boys were riding young camels, I insisted on riding one too. My father tried hard to stop me, but I was determined and eventually rode a young camel alone.

Just as I was telling myself that next time, I would have my own horse, the camel began to move fast. The reason for that sudden change in pace was the valley the camel was crossing. But I got scared and out of fear began to shout orders to the camel. The young camel, upon hearing my shouting, began to make all kinds of noises and increased its pace, as if I was ordering it to move faster.

I managed to maintain some confidence for a few minutes, but finally I began to cry. The camel went hysterical, and every now and then I was sure I would hit the ground. But I did not fall. Fortunately, I was near Aslaf, and one of the men came galloping over on his horse and freed me from my perch atop that camel.

My father was laughing; so was everyone else. My first attempt to be independent, and to have my own camel, ended with my riding behind one of the older men. The next day was Al-Raheel too. But that time I insisted on attempting to ride a young horse.

I rode a lovely white horse of ours, with better luck. Most of the day, I was beside my mother's camel, telling her all kinds of stories.

I am sure she was proud to see her only son riding a horse beside her. While we were talking, I saw a boy riding a camel, and began to chase him, despite my mother's objection. After a while, I returned to my mother's camel, more confident than ever. I began to gallop between the scattered group composing Al-Madhaheer during Al-Raheel.

Unfortunately, the horse saw Aslaf. Its mother was with them. As a result, the horse headed toward them against my will. I tried to stop it, but realized I was not a good enough rider to control the horse. It continued until we reached Aslaf, where the horse stopped beside its mother.

When they saw me coming, everyone in Aslaf was scared that I would fall. But I was safe, though scared to death. Again, my hope to be an independent rider was shattered to pieces.

When Al-Raheel began the following day, my father asked me, smiling, "What is new today, Faisal?" When I told him that I had decided to ride the water camel, he burst out laughing.

That choice was a sign of surrender. Bedouins usually load their water on the quietest and consequently the oldest camel. I believed our water camel was so quiet that even exploding dynamite would not induce him to move faster than his usual slow pace. I continued to ride that quiet old camel for about one month, despite my dissatisfaction.

My experience with the limited freedom provided while riding that quiet camel ended on a very rainy day, when an arrogant camel broke my left leg. My father had decided that our reddish-colored goat, and its two lovely young offspring, recently born, should be carried on a camel. While we were moving, I heard the goat making all kinds of sounds. To help that lovely goat and to prove my usefulness, I left my camel and ran to the other, to see the goat.

My efforts to stop the camel carrying the screaming goat seemed useless. Finally, I decided to hold the camel from the front, because this usually halts a camel immediately. But I was too short, and that arrogant camel walked all over me and broke my left leg.

Despite the need to travel further, to reach a better grazing area, the men of Aslaf decided to stop Al-Raheel. Thus, the broken leg of a boy stopped the whole tribe's movement. Every tribesman offered his advice about how to fix my leg, and everyone appeared to be worried, except my father. At least, he did not show his worry. When he saw me resting in my bed, he said with a smile, "Faisal, this is a Bedouin's life, so learn to be tough. Next time, no camel will dare to walk over you."

Thank you, Father, for that advice. I think you were proud of me four months later, when I was beating everyone around in horse racing, as I rode your lovely horse, Khulfah. And I think you were even more pleased when you saw me ride the most arrogant camel and practice shooting with a big rifle when I was nine or ten years old.

Dear Father, you raised me to be a man! To my astonishment, as later years exposed me to modern theories in childcare, I realized you reared me according to the best theories in modern society. You were illiterate, but you were intelligent enough to know how to take care of a son, whether he had a broken leg or merely bruises from falling off a horse or camel.

But, dear Father, I will not forget one action, seemingly unforgivable at that time. Your decision deprived me of my mother for over a year. Why did you have to do it in that year? The year I sacrificed my education to be happy beside you and her? Father, I understand the reasoning behind your decision now, but I will not forget how sad I was when Mother left the tent in anger.

ψ ψ ψ

To nomadic people, male children are more important than females. My father, up to that year (around 1949), had only Faisal and four daughters. He began to worry about what would happen if some occurrence took Faisal's life. His worries forced him to take the only logical solution in nomadic life. Hoping to have brothers for Faisal, he married another lady, as his brother had many times. So secretly was this done, when my mother heard of it she left the tent in protest, although she was pregnant. She went to her father's tent, somewhere in the desert of Iraq.

Ironically enough, later in that year she gave birth to my first brother. Father called him Abdulaziz. This name was picked because when we received the news, Amir Abdulaziz Al-Sudairy, the ruler of the northern part of Saudi Arabia, was in our tent, collecting taxes (Zakah) for King Abdulaziz ibn Saud.

That marriage influenced me greatly. I began to mistrust my father and to believe more in my uncle. What outraged me most was that everyone in the tribe agreed with my father – that his marriage was the logical solution to his need for more boys. No one ever cared about my or my mother's feelings. Rather, they tried to convince me that the marriage was, in a way, honoring the tribe's traditions.

Down with that particular tradition, which always cared so much about quantity rather than quality. Damn such traditions, because feelings and future problems were never taken into consideration. And down with the tradition that forced me to lose a year of schooling and to sacrifice a mother's love.

My relationship with my father became very tense, and he began to find weak excuses to criticize me. One day I refused to drink water, complaining that it was mud, not water. I remember waiting half an hour, sometimes, just to give the mud time to settle at the bottom. Later, having decided that the process was time-consuming, I began to add yoghurt to that muddy water and to close my eyes while I drank.

Well, no matter how I drank the water, my father did not like the complaints. One day he told me, "Faisal, this is the best water we have. If you don't like it, then go back to your uncle's tent where the water wells are better."

Thus, indirectly, he kicked me out of the tent.

Much later, when my uncle came, I left, full of anger.

ψ ψ ψ

In 1949, while I was in the fourth grade, I interrupted my schooling for about a month during winter to see the tribe and my mother, who had returned. The year proved to be the worst year in the history of Al-Sba'a Tribe. The drought covered the deserts of Saudi Arabia, Iraq, Jordan, and Syria. Our tribe decided that the best way to save the sheep and camels was to move to a rural area. We planned to move to an area between Homs and Hama, two cities in central Syria. But the challenge of how to reach that area persisted. We were camping where the border of Saudi Arabia meets those of Iraq and Jordan. Because of the shortage of water and grazing area, we were obliged to transport the sheep by truck. The Bedouins still refer to that year as the one when "even sheep rode in cars."

It was a turning point in the history of Al-Sba'a Tribe. Most of the camels were replaced by trucks; they were more useful than the glorious camels. Al-Sba'a Tribe forgot all the agonies of the previous seasons, when 1950 proved to be a good year.

Once again, all of us, including the school, were together and on the move again. We wandered all over the lovely, green desert. Schooldays that year were infrequent, and during Al-Raheel there was no chance to study.

Looking back at those days of my early education, I wonder how we students managed to even learn how to read and write a letter. The usual educational facilities were not available, and the tribal environment was an obstacle to education.

The most agonizing question for all of us students was how to study at night. There was no electricity, and kerosene lamps were few. Many times, while I was using the ladies' kerosene lamp, it had to be taken to prepare dinners for unexpected guests. I protested to my father. But to him and the tribe, anything was more important than education, especially when I was already in the fifth grade, the last grade in our school. My father believed strongly that my education should not divert me from being a good Bedouin who might lead the tribe someday. He had many helpers around the tent, but time and again he called on me while I was studying to do something his helpers would have been glad to do. When I protested that kind of interruption, and listed the names of some of the helpers, Father became angry. He insisted he should call me on the grounds that no matter how much education I acquired, my destiny was with the tribe. He said I should behave according to that destiny.

Troubles between my father and I increased day after day. In reality, our disagreements (he was usually the winner) were not personal. I loved him and still do, and I am sure he felt and feels the same.

The problem was a struggle between two conflicting standards, that of a Bedouin's life and the one we were exposed to in school. One morning (a very cold one) I heard my father shouting near my bed. To my astonishment, without explaining what wrong I had done, my father began criticizing me. When I asked him why, he accused me of pretending not to know the reason. "Can't you see, Faisal, how you slept?" When I asked him what was wrong with the way I slept, he exploded, telling me my position was a disgrace for a Bedouin in sleep.

What had happened was this: in Bedouin tradition, a boy or a man should sleep with his head in the direction where the camels sleep (usually toward the front of the tent). In this case, I was sleeping the opposite way. The Bedouins reason that he who sleeps as I did, indicates his disrespect for camels and their ownership. Furthermore, he who sleeps that way will see the last of his camels very soon. I was really not aware of all that witchcraft, which seemed like a fairytale cooked up by my father. But my father never believed me. He insisted that I must ride with the camels, to understand how to take care of them and to learn respect for them. When I protested that my school was open, he said, "Forget school, camels are more important." There was no chance for me to reject his order, especially as it happened that my uncle was absent.

When I tried to wear my shoes, my father began to laugh and forced me to go barefooted. He reasoned that he and my uncle before me had done the same. And he said that I had better accustom my feet to that treatment at an early age, because someday it would be necessary to walk barefoot.

So far, I have not seen such days, except when I was around the tribe. My father was teaching the traditions of a vanishing life, but I was not able to convince him of that. To him I was still a part of that life.

For about 12 days I was with the camels, going from one place to another, riding sometimes, but walking barefoot most of the time, drinking camel's milk and eating only dates. To the astonishment of the regular camel herdsman, I was able to smuggle some books to read while I was with the camels. He tried to convince me to forget studying, but I refused. That man's hatred for books and education increased greatly the next day, when the issue of my books almost caused the death of a man.

That story is a classic now.

It began as I was studying in a very lovely, green field surrounded by sheep, which happened to be in that area. Our herdsman called me to drink some camel milk he had drawn recently. I ran to him, and while I was enjoying the milk, I remembered a book I had left around the sheep. I ran back to get my book, but was shocked to find one of the sheep had already torn the book to pieces. I was so angry that I hit that sheep with a stick and injured one of its eyes. The shepherd caring for those sheep came running, and when he saw what had happened, he slapped me.

Our herdsman had no idea why I had left the milk but was watching closely. When he saw what the shepherd did, he came running with his rifle. Owaid was his name. Good Owaid never waited to ask any questions but immediately hit the shepherd with his rifle. The shepherd fell from the strike and Owaid, shouting, began to load his rifle. I was scared because Owaid was determined to kill the other fellow.

To the scared shepherd, who had no rifle, he shouted, "Do you know who you slapped? This is Faisal, Walad Sfouq Al-Mershed (Faisal the son of Sfouq Al-Mershed), and you will now die."

The shepherd, upon hearing my name, ran toward me and held me tight to his chest, repeating, "Faisal, ana be wajhak. (Faisal, I am in your protection)."

That was the first time in my life I protected a man. I convinced Owaid to leave the man alone, because he was in my wajh. By that time, many other shepherds had gathered around, and each one of them was trying to do the threatened shepherd a favor by killing a lamb in the honor of Faisal ibn Mershed.

Later, I solved the argument by letting my assailant kill a lamb. In a way, I was honoring rather than punishing my adversary of a few minutes ago. This was one of the qualities of leadership in which we were induced to believe. To forgive a person in a weak position is an honorable act.

The shepherd who slapped me, later became one of my dearest friends, until his death. When I returned to our tent, the story of the shepherd and I had spread all over. My father sent for the shepherd, and I thought he was going to punish him. I told Father that the man was in my wajh and I would defend him.

The shepherd arrived in a state of fright, because some people had urged him to flee. But he was in some ways a courageous fellow. To my astonishment, my father received him well and gave him an Abah (a man's cloak), money, and a Thobe (man's dress). Not only that—my mother gave him some dresses for his wife. I realized later that day that my parents' actions were to honor an established tradition. He who slapped one of the Al-Mershed boys should be given prizes by the boy's parents. This act demonstrated that the tribe was supposed to be democratic in nature. It aimed to dramatize the fact that even Al-Mershed boys were subject to punishment by the tribesmen. The idea was that this would keep them from feeling superior in dealing with the tribe's members when they became men, so they say, and I certainly followed it literally toward my tribesmen with love and respect.

ψ ψ ψ

On the night of my return, I stayed awake very late to study and to catch up with classwork. But I encountered difficulties immediately. While I was reading the history book, I found a chapter very difficult to comprehend. I read it several times without luck. Frustration followed, and I quietly began to shed tears as I cursed camels and nomadic life under my breath.

When my father saw me, he was surprised by my tears. When I told him the reason for them, he advised me to sleep and let him tell the teacher I had been with the camels.

I told him his reasoning was more shocking than reassuring, burst out crying, and repeated that the most important thing was to understand the lesson. Excuses were of no use, since eventually I would have to pass an examination.

This incident and many others like it convinced me at an early age that no one was going to help or encourage me if I was faced with difficulties in my schoolwork. Everyone except the teacher was illiterate and would suggest I just stop.

And so, depending on only myself, I was forced to go it alone. Such a realization and dependency on my own will at that early age helped me a great deal later, when I fought alone for higher education. Dependency on myself extended beyond the sphere of education, because of our way of living in that nomadic situation. I was induced and urged to act like a grown man when I was barely ten years old. During the absence of my father, I was the oldest man in the tent and was therefore responsible for such roles as ordering some helper to kill a lamb in honor of a respected guest. Many times, I was obliged to abandon my studies in order to entertain guests, staying with them as long as they wanted to talk about past times of nomadic life, which I had heard many times before. I remember once staying so late that our dear guest advised some of the men in Almajles to persuade me to go to bed. I refused on the grounds that I should fill my father's place and talk with our guest. Early in the morning, I found that I had slept against my will and that one of them had put me in my bed. I was so ashamed that I promised myself that I would not do it again, no matter what.

So, dear reader, you see that I was given little chance to act like a child. As of now, I believe sincerely that I am among the few in this world who did not pass through the childhood stage, acting like a child and playing innocently.

5

GO HOME BEDOUIN

In 1950, two of my cousins left for Aleppo in Syria to study in a boarding school. They were in sixth grade, and I was in the final grade at home, the fifth grade. Scholastically, that year was a disastrous one for all three of us. I was sick most of the year, and so when I insisted on taking the examination at the end of the year, I failed. My two cousins also failed sixth grade, and so we all had to repeat our grades. In the fall of 1952, or the school year 1952–1953, I was prepared to join my cousins in Aleppo, after having passed the fifth-grade major examination. Later, when my father traveled to Syria, he took me with him. He registered me at a boarding school in Homs, far away from my cousins. That year was the end of my two cousins' education, because they proved beyond a doubt that they were not really interested in school.

The first order I received in my new school was to get rid of my Arabic clothes and to wear Western dress. I refused to abandon my dress on the grounds that I was a Bedouin, and it was a disgrace for me to wear pants.

The administration of the school sent for my guardian in the city. He tried to persuade the school to give me a chance to adapt but his plea was refused, and I was forced to wear Western dress for the first time in my life.

I cried a lot the first nights after I set aside my Arabic dress, and I began to hate the principal of the school, who had forced me to abandon it. All over the school, boys began to point their fingers toward me and say, "Look at the Bedouin. He is the son of Ibn Mershed from Al-Sba'a Tribe." I felt alone, but I was determined to be a good student.

So, in addition to being in a real school, alone, and not knowing a single student, I was suddenly in an environment that was alien to my upbringing as a Bedouin. As mentioned earlier, the tribe was referred to in Northern Arabian countries, in particular Syria and Iraq, as the Displaced Arab Tribes. "Displaced from where?" one might ask. But almost everyone knew where Aneza and all its branches came from. They came from Najd, the central region of Saudi Arabia.

Nationality papers, at that time, were not required, nor was a note from the chief of the tribe, most of the time. We were known as part of that Arab nomadic tribe from Najd—and to be fair to the governments of Iraq and Syria, we were treated almost as citizens, by having our chiefs represent us in their houses of Parliament.

Was it the notion of Arabism that led to such democratic representation, or fears of the tribes, who were very powerful then? Or was it a combination of the two? I really do not know.

But in those years of schooling in Syria, and especially in sixth grade, I realized that we were unwelcome in Syria and should go back to the place we came from. This was based on the way I was treated in school.

It was ironic that Al-Sba'a Tribe was not treated nicely, when my uncle and some of the tribesmen fought side by side with the people of Hama for Syria's independence against the French occupation. And fought again, when some of the Syrian indigenous tribes fought with the French.

During that first year I cried most nights in my bed, remembering my mother, and lacking in particular the security I derived from being around my cousins and other children of the tribe.

The tribe was a source of tremendous security, because I was welcome in any tent, to eat and even sleep if I wanted, not because I was from Al-Mershed family, but because sharing was embodied in tribal traditions, from one generation to another. Never had I lived in a city, and so on the weekend, when I went to my guardian's house, I began to explore it. And little by little I relaxed and gained confidence.

About a month or two after entering school, my father came to send me to Riyadh, to enroll in the King Abdulaziz Military Academy. This was on the advice of the governor of the Northern Region of Saudi Arabia, Abdulaziz Al-Sudairy. We had met in 1948, when he was my father's guest to levy the Zakah on Al-Sba'a Tribe.

To entice me more, my father told me that a friend of mine from Motair tribe, whose family lived around us, had already left to enroll in the Academy in Riyadh. Being lonely, missing my family and my cousins, I told my father that all I wanted was to leave school and go back home with him.

Day students created a hostile school environment for me, for being a Bedouin, led by one child in particular, from a prominent and wealthy family in Homs. He hated me so much. I, of course, reciprocated. My father was very sympathetic but convinced me to stay in school until the end of the year, and so, I stayed to face the bullying.

There were many reasons for that hatred, but the main one was that both of us competed to be number two in the class. Why not number one? What happened to ambition? Number one in the class was claimed by a relative of my adversary, who came from the less wealthy side of that prominent family.

I was afraid of that bully, and he never stopped telling me to go back to my country, and that I was not welcome in school, or in Homs. In the desert, with the tribe around, no one would dare tell me that, because of my family position, and because we knew where the tribe came from. My adversary and his group's frequent bullying became like a stigma. And for the first time I felt I did not belong in the environment I was in. The Al-Aatasy boy was bigger than me, and I was sincerely afraid of him.

I tried very hard to coexist with him peacefully. One day, before history period began, my tolerance reached its limit, and I was determined to take some kind of action, regardless of what would happen to me. That boy was a typical example of a spoiled rich boy and disrespected by most of the other boys. In front of everyone in the class, he pointed at me and said, "Look at that dirty Bedouin."

The class began to laugh. I was really outraged.

I replied, "Yes, certainly your clothes are much cleaner than those of a Bedouin, but do you know that we can fight better than you. You city-dwellers are soft, just like ladies."

The boy never expected that kind of reply, but now he moved toward my desk. At that moment, I began to remember my cousins, and wished they were around to beat everyone in that class and show them how Bedouins can fight.

When my adversary reached my desk, I did not wait for him to hit me first but immediately hit him in the face. Unfortunately, just as I hit him, the teacher entered the room.

The boy became a coward when he saw blood running from his nose. The teacher left to call for help, while the entire class gathered around him. When the disciplinary committee met, all but one boy in that class became a witness against me. I recognized later that that boy's family was originally Bedouin and had settled in Homs.

The teacher told the committee what he had seen. He stated that I hit the Al-Aatasy boy, but he was beside my desk. The committee decided wrongly to punish me with three days of suspension from classes and one week's denial of the right to eat or sleep in the school. I told the committee that the verdict was unjust because my adversary was subjecting me to threats all the time, and yet the committee did not punish him.

All my pleas for equal justice were rejected. When I realized that there was no use in arguing, I told the committee that I accepted the suspension from classes, but I would not accept the second part of the punishment. I reasoned that it was a disgrace to prohibit me from eating in the school, as if I were some kind of beggar.

I appealed to the committee to announce the first verdict, but to refrain from announcing the second part. I told the committee that denying food to me meant not punishment but disgrace. I declared, "I am not a beggar, and food in the Bedouin tradition is given to every guest without charge."

All my sensitivity to that issue was rejected by the committee, which had no respect for my background. I was really hurt when I saw the verdict on the bulletin board, to be read by everyone in the school. I left to see my guardian, who came to the school immediately and demanded a retrial. He threatened the committee by saying that my case was judged wrongly, and that he would take it to the Director General of Education in the city.

My guardian was not one to be regarded lightly, because he happened to be a member of the Syrian Parliament. The principal was scared and tried to persuade my guardian to forget the whole case. But all his pleas were rejected, the committee met again, and the verdict was that I had to be suspended for three days from classes—but my adversary was also punished with three days' suspension because he provoked me.

My guardian told me, in front of the committee, "Faisal, you come from a very well-respected family. Do fight for your rights but never step on the rights of others."

Thank you, Guardian, for that advice, and may God bless you in your grave. I followed that advice and later stood up for my rights similarly when I encountered an arrogant and unfair instructor during my college education.

One day, King Saud of Saudi Arabia was on a state visit to Syria and passed by the city of Homs. Students marched in the street to wave flags and so on. My adversary, along with some of his group, pointed to me and said, "That is your king, go back home."

ψ ψ ψ

By the end of the school year, when I returned to the tribe, the relationship between my father and uncle was very bad. They were in conflict over dividing the wealth that had been left by my grandfather. Later that summer, my father decided to just leave everything to my uncle, amounting to about 100 camels and 2,000 sheep. The notables of Al-Sba'a tried to persuade my uncle that it was my father's right to have some of the wealth, but my uncle rejected that argument—so my father was left without a single sheep or camel. The tribe immediately rallied to my father's aid, and in a short time my father was prosperous again and even had his own car.

In that same year, at the end of 1952, my uncle sold all the camels. The rest of us in the tribe said farewell to the camels my grandfather had acquired. Despite the family differences, I do have some fond memories of that summer. It could rightly be called the summer of "Faisal the Doctor."

Since few Bedouins had ever attempted, much less successfully completed, the sixth grade, they all assumed that I was an encyclopedia, having all kinds of knowledge, regardless of subject.

One day, when I was enjoying a conversation in our Majles during my father's absence, an old man called Khaled, who had almost the longest moustache around, came to our tent. Khaled was not from Al-Sba'a Tribe, and he was the kind of person who clings to you like a leech. He also happened to have an eye problem that caused tears to always appear in his eyes. The moment he entered Almajles, he asked for eye drops, claiming that our tent must have what he wanted, because I had just come from the city. I tried to convince him that we really did not have eye drops, but he refused to believe me.

In the face of his obstinate refusal, a clever idea to get rid of him came to my mind. I remembered that I had a small bottle of glue from school. I decided to be a doctor and to use glue as a medicine for Khaled's eyes.

I checked his eyes, as if I were a real doctor, and gave him the usual professional assurance that there was no danger at all. Next, in front of everyone, I asked him to lie down so as to allow the magic substance to be dropped into his eyes.

I realized I should not put glue in his eyes. Instead, I asked him to close his eyes, and I began to put glue all over his eyelids. I also began to irrigate his big moustache and even his eyebrows with glue drops.

When the glue dried, a hysterical scene unfolded. The first result was the immediate lack of tears, because of the drying effect on his skin. The man was exceedingly grateful, and I advised him not to wash his face for at least twenty-four hours for fear that I would be discovered. But what made everyone laugh out loud was what happened to Khaled's moustache. Every two hairs or so twisted together like a stick. So just imagine seeing a moustache that looked as if it had fingers. Khaled trusted Faisal the Doctor so much that when some people later told him what I had done, he never believed them.

Because I did not deny being a doctor, everyone who believed Khaled's story came to see me when they had a physical problem. One day another old tribesman who had lost almost all of his teeth came along. He complained repeatedly about his inability to eat well, insisting over and over again that he was not old enough to lose all his teeth so suddenly. He had reached the conclusion that it wasn't age, but some kind of sickness, that was destroying his teeth.

His name was Rafi. He was really a character. I agreed with his diagnosis and assured him that I would do my best to cure the sickness in his remaining teeth.

I asked him first to open his mouth and stand in the sun bareheaded for about half an hour. After that, I again resorted to my school supplies and brought out all of the watercolor equipment from my painting class. I began to paint each remaining tooth a different color.

Rafi again followed my instructions and sat for about one more hour with his mouth open. Everyone in Almajles realized I was joking and decided that it was best to enjoy it, since there was no harm being done to Rafi's teeth.

The funny thing was that Rafi claimed that his remaining teeth became stronger than before. Maybe this is the proof of the power of suggestion in healing.

While we were enjoying jokes and tricks, and while I was at the peak of my reputation as a doctor, my father returned from his journey and put an end to all those lovely and innocent affairs.

ψ ψ ψ

In 1955, I tasted for the first time as a mature person, the impact of failure. In ninth grade, Syria had a general certificate examination, similar to that in the French system. It was so rigid that if a student failed any one of his courses, he was obliged to repeat the whole year. I passed nearly every course with high marks but failed the English section by one point, and so my destiny was to repeat the entire ninth grade curriculum.

After I failed, I felt so miserable during the summer that I became abnormally quiet and passive, accepting criticism without any protest, and withdrawing to the extent that my dear mother became greatly worried. Some of the tribesmen thought that my failure that year meant the end of all my schooling. Therefore, they more forcefully than ever went about trying to convince me to see that Bedouin life was the only one to take seriously. It was the most miserable period of my life. I realized I was beaten and almost convinced myself that all those around me were happy that I had failed, because they thought that I would give up studying.

Things were even more difficult later in the summer because my mother was not around. She left us when my father married a distant cousin. She went to her family from Shammar Tribe, which was camping around Al-Mosel, a city in the Kingdom of Iraq. My sisters subjected me to a lot of pressure, to convince my father to let me go get my mother. My father was really mad at my mother and was reluctant to let me do so—so the environment in our tent was not pleasant, to say the least.

At last, my father let me go, and it took me about two weeks to get my mother from Iraq, with my youngest brother Sami, and my sister Mayer.

ψ ψ ψ

My father once more began to urge me to go to the King Abdulaziz Military Academy in Riyadh, to be an officer in the Saudi Arabian Army. I refused his suggestion, and, to his amazement, I insisted on trying again in school. To my astonishment, my father straightforwardly stated that he would not support my schooling if I refused his suggestion. And so that summer became a test for me, fighting for my education against an illiterate father who thought that paying about $400 per year was too much for school. My uncle was not interested, so there was no hope of help from his side. Instead, I added fuel to an already explosive situation between my father, my uncle, and me.

One day, I showed disrespect for a tribal head who was our guest, by refusing to greet him due to my dislike for the way he talked about me. My uncle and father immediately ordered me to leave the tent, and relations between us became more tense.

At the end of the summer, my father told me that he was too poor to support my education. I recognized this as an excuse, for his resources that year would have allowed him to send me to any school in the world. I went back to Hama, Syria, to repeat the ninth grade, with the help of my mother, hoping that my father would later change his mind. But I carried with me the displeasure of my father and many of the tribesmen.

ψ ψ ψ

Two of my cousins were already in Hama, and so I joined them. One of them, Thamer, about two years younger than me, was in my ninth-grade class. He was very intelligent, but a less serious and hard-working student. The other was Naif, who proved to be the worst student the family ever had among the children. Nevertheless, he was the likeable and friendly one, who kept our spirits up during that whole miserable year.

My two cousins agreed immediately to share their allowance with me. So, we lived on an allowance of about $1.25 per day, to cover our food and all other everyday expenses. We lived in a hotel, where rent had to be paid by the end of the year. However, the owner of the hotel did not receive what we owed him until two years later. We were poor, miserable, and really angry at our family, which was capable of supporting us with better living conditions than two small meals a day. To this day, I cannot comprehend why our family left us in such circumstances.

I felt a real hatred for my father and uncle that year. I would only ever feel that way one other time, much later in life, when they left me in similar circumstances. They were cruel beyond description, but what agonized me most was that I had no way to support myself. I lived like a parasite on my two cousins' allowance, which was not really enough for them alone. I knew why I was in a bad situation—because my father refused to support me. But I never understood why my two cousins were also treated equally harshly by my uncle. He insisted hypocritically that they should continue their education and then acted blind to the fact that living expenses also had to be paid.

ψ ψ ψ

About one month before the end of the school year, the tribe began to ship its wool to Hama to be sold. One of the tribesmen came to see us. He felt so sorry when he saw our situation that he took me aside and told me that he would be willing to give me $100, to be taken from the sale of my father's wool, for which he was responsible. I refused, on the grounds that my father had not told him to do so. However, I asked him to give me a personal loan of that amount, promising him that I would repay him some day. He would not do this but again tried to persuade me to accept money from the wool sales. I refused again, so he left. When I told my cousins, Naif was miserable about losing the chance to have money. He reasoned that there was nothing wrong with stealing from his father or uncle when they should give us the money anyway. Thamer supported me when he realized my sensitivity toward the issue. Naif tried hard to convince Thamer and I to take the money by describing our difficult situation, as if we were not well aware of it.

Looking back now, I believe Naif, the most pragmatic and realistic of us three, was right. But we argued with Naif that our honor was in jeopardy. In reality, as Naif said, we pushed the issue of honor too far in a desperate situation.

Naif slept quietly that night, after he had reached a decision about a plan he executed the next day. He carried out a masterpiece of action to relieve our misery. He wrote a letter in my name and went to see the Bedouin who had proposed giving me the money. When he found him ready to leave the city, he told him that I was sick and gave him the letter. The poor Bedouin was shocked and tried to cancel his departure. But Naif convinced him that my illness was caused by nothing more than malnutrition, and that I only needed the money. According to plan, the Bedouin gave Naif some money for me to go to the doctor, plus the $100 he had proposed the previous day. When Naif entered our room, he was so elated that he ordered a full meal for all of us from the hotel restaurant. Thamer and I were astonished, and while we were cross-examining Naif about his sudden wealth, the owner of the hotel entered. He told Naif that he would not place the order for the meal because of earlier incidents. On multiple occasions we had ordered food and left the hotel owner obliged to pay because we had no money. Naif tried to convince the hotel owner that this time we had the money—but he could not be persuaded. So Naif was compelled to show him the money.

After we ate, Naif begged me not to get angry, as he told us the story of the money and the forged letter. We laughed so much that we forgot all the so-called honor Thamer and I had upheld on the preceding day. Our laughs were so loud that the hotel manager protested that we were disturbing his customers. Naif was slap-happy, and told him, "Look, I will pay you the rent of every guest who leaves because of our noise." The hotel manager left us, deciding that we were "some kind of nuts."

We regularly ordered our meals on one plate from the restaurant, until Naif and I discovered something. We both noticed that Thamer became abnormally quiet while eating, while Naif joked, and I philosophized. Thamer's conversation consisted of a simple yes or no from time to time.

We challenged him about this sudden change during mealtime, and he insisted that he simply enjoyed listening to our conversation. But Thamer was not telling the truth. What he was enjoying was a larger share of the food. If he didn't talk, he could eat more.

Naif and I took the logical action to deny Thamer that advantage. We began to order our meals on separate plates. Thamer protested, on the grounds that it was a shame to do so in front of people, when we were brothers and cousins. We rejected his argument, and dear Thamer, who had such a healthy appetite, was sometimes obliged to order twice.

Thamer still remembers that discovery and still pays dearly for it every time we meet and talk about those agonizing but lovely times.

☙ ☙ ☙

I passed the general examination for the certificate of the ninth grade, while Thamer failed, only to go through the same experience I had faced the year before. It was tough to have most people against me for going to school, but in the end I passed my exam and was promoted to the tenth grade. By the way, my total grades when

I passed were less than the total when I failed. It was that one lousy point in English that made the difference.

Passing that tough examination was a good experience, though I somewhat regretted the name change that accompanied my certificate.

Upon receiving my certificate my last name became Al-Bashir, based on my grandfather's name, Bashir, instead of Al-Mershed. I protested to my school administration. They minimized the matter and assured me that the name on all my school records was Al-Mershed, which was true.

Who registered me as such? To this day I have no idea. I am sure the Syrian education authority found me registered in their civil records as Al-Bashir. From that day forward I carried Al-Bashir as my last name, until 2000, when I added Al-Mershed to my civil record in Saudi Arabia.

Although I made a big fuss about the name incident, neither my family nor the tribe paid much attention to it. The reason was very simple—everyone assumed that eventually I would come back to settle with them, where everyone knew me very well. A certificate having my grandfather's name as my last name did not matter.

As a result, I became known in documentation as Faisal Al-Bashir, while everyone called me Faisal Al-Mershed. Tribesmen and my family never considered this name a problem. Bashir was to them a virtuous man, and by taking his name, they reasoned, luck might follow for me. Also, they were of the opinion that no matter how many degrees I had, everyone in the tribe would still recognize me as Al-Mershed.

Be that as it may, all my degrees from ninth grade and up carried Al-Bashir instead of Al-Mershed as my surname. I could still rectify that error any moment I like, but this would require changing documents all the way through multiple degrees from institutions of higher education.

Later, I reasoned, what is in a name? I am really just as happy carrying my grandfather's name as my family one. But in 2020, I added my last name, Al-Mershed, to my academic record with the University of Arizona in the United States, where I eventually earned my PhD.

ψ ψ ψ

One year, my father became ill. It wasn't too serious, but his walking was restricted, and he became less able to supervise the care of his sheep. He began making frequent journeys to doctors, and some of them said he had to go to Paris for an examination. Others contradicted this advice; one doctor in Beirut, Lebanon, told him there was no need to go to Paris at all. My father returned, and on the way home paid a visit to me in school. I was going through the midyear examination of the tenth grade.

When I finished, my father took me to the tribe, which was camping in the northern part of Saudi Arabia. While I was enjoying my spring vacation away from school, my father told me, in front of all our tribesmen in Almajles, "Faisal, son, you are grown up now, and I am a sick man. Leave school to help me keep our name and the tent in good order."

I listened to Father, and let him continue his talk.

"Faisal, no matter how far you go in education, at the end you will come to this tent and the tribe. But what is the use of education if, when you come back, there will not be a tent to lead from and a tribe to advise?"

While my father was talking and hitting me in a very sensitive spot, I almost reached the decision to quit school forever. He was really in a bad position, and needed my presence urgently, not to help so much, because he had many helpers around, but rather just to be around for reassurance. Parents' love and emotion concerning their only grown son never becomes so clear and defined as when they begin thinking that the end of life is near. The presence of the son is the most important thing in their minds and hearts.

For the first time, my mother was on my father's side, forcefully urging me to leave school and stay beside them.

"Faisal," she said, "dear son, it will be a disgrace for you to leave for school while your father is in this state of health. What if you leave for school and your father dies? Then you have no choice except to stay in the tent, to advise, to help, and to guide your mother, sisters, and brothers, because you are the only man we have."

I agreed with every word she said, but at the same time I prayed to God to save Father and keep me in school.

While everyone insisted that I had to quit school, I argued that my uncle would not leave his brother, no matter what, and that my presence would be much less useful than they all anticipated. There was an agreement that neither my uncle nor the tribe would leave my father in need of anything—but they also argued correctly that what my father needed was not material, but rather something intangible they could not supply.

Those beloved, illiterate tribesmen tormented me with arguments that I should go and see my father and pushed me into a very critical position. I realized that all that I had learned in school was not enough to defend me against their demands that I see their beloved, sick leader, Sfouq Al-Mershed.

Yes, tribesmen, you were right. What Father needed most during those critical days was of more value than all the sheep you owned, and worth more than all your hard work could produce. He was sick and felt the need to see his son every day and every moment before the death he felt was approaching.

And so, dear reader, imagine the dilemma of a boy at the age of sixteen or seventeen, facing two such conflicting alternatives. Imagine the pressure they exerted on me, those people I loved so dearly and wanted so much to respect me.

I could leave school, to stay with a stricken father, and say farewell to all the effort I had put into education in order to better my life, or I could go to school with all the anxiety and agony of leaving my father in need of my presence. Stuck with that choice, I was miserable beyond description, confused and distressed, left alone to make a decision determining my whole future direction, without consultation with an unbiased person.

I believe now that I grew older very quickly that spring vacation. I became so old that all the happy days and joys of teenage life seemed far behind me. When the day of departure approached, I told Father in Almajles that I had to go to school. I wished him a speedy recovery.

My father kept quiet for a while, as everyone listened to the silence.

Later, he said, "Faisal, I wish you luck. The road you are walking over is, to you, the right one. To me it is not. It appears that you are convinced about your new endeavor. And so, son, go ahead. But remember that you are the most selfish and stubborn boy the family ever had."

I kissed his hands and bid him goodbye. When I tried to shake hands with other tribesmen, I realized that no one wanted to bid me farewell. Even my dearest mother, sisters, and brothers refused to talk to me. For the first time in my life, I felt guilty and that I did not deserve the affection of my father, mother, sisters, brothers, and fellow tribesmen. I was like a man who suddenly feels like he has no relatives at all.

Yes, Father, I was selfish, cruel, and stubborn. But please forgive me for what I did. I was a young boy who had tasted what more knowledge can give, and who realized that sooner or later nomadic life would vanish. I was looking forward to a new kind of life, much different from the only one you and the Al-Sba'a Tribe ever saw. It has proved to be the right life for every human being who believes in the essentiality of continual change and adaptability.

ψ ψ ψ

My education, from 1957 to 1959, continued to come under constant attack. Financial support was often cut without explanation. I was obliged many times to borrow money, hoping to pay my debts in the future. In a way, I was a dependent and independent individual at the same time, alternatingly secure and insecure. Every day I was wary of a final blow which would end my schooling forever.

During those years, I lived hoping that a magical power would prevent me from ending my education. Although I was poor most of the time (not even able to buy my writing pads), only a few intimate friends from the school ever realized my plight. It became necessary for me to confine myself to my lousy room even on weekends, for fear that I would be seen by one of those to whom I was indebted

The strange thing is that with all those difficulties I kept up a front of joy and happiness. What helped me do so was purely some kind of secret hope that the end of all those difficulties would surely come someday.

What amazes me most about all those hard years is that I never felt lasting hatred toward my family or the tribe. I reasoned that all the difficulties I faced were due to my own decision to continue getting educated, and they had nothing to do with that. Psychologists may call this kind of realization proof of my maturity, but I assure them that there was no need to judge whether or not I was mature. As I said before, from the age of nine I was required to act like a mature person. And this is a critical distinction between the nomadic life and an urban one. An identifiable childhood stage, excluding its physical nature, is not well-known in Bedouin society.

I paid dearly for education, from the angle of health and my feelings, clouded by worry and insecurity. But I always went back to my family and the tribe when school closed in summer. In a way I was sure I should pay dearly for not obeying the suggestion of all who loved me so much. Every time I was with the tribe, I tried to help as much as I could and avoided mentioning my education. As a result, a sort of peaceful coexistence was established between young Faisal, the tribe, and my family.

That was not enough to stop all my worry. This was especially true as I came to realize that even the high school diploma would not satisfy me, and that I had to continue on to college.

But how was I to go to college, when there was so much insecurity concerning support from my father even for high school? My agonies increased gradually as the high school exam grew closer. I had much anxiety about what would happen after that. I lived for the present only, knowing nothing about my future beyond the conferment of that piece of paper. I lived exactly like that Bedouin in the fall season, who has no way of knowing whether winter will be the end of his sheep or a blessing to him.

ψ ψ ψ

The summer of 1958 followed the pattern of the happy summers I enjoyed before 1955, when everyone dear was around and my father was healthy. That summer, my dear father regained his health, and his sickness was cured. A sense of pride in my accomplishments in school began to appear in him. I encouraged this feeling when I showed him some of the prizes awarded to me for my achievements in the tenth and eleventh grades.

Ironically enough, with all that education behind me, I was for the first time tested in the role of playing Faisal the Shepherd, as one of our shepherds had been fired by my father. However, finding an acceptable replacement would take time. Everyone volunteered to help take care of our sheep until my father found a permanent shepherd. But my father refused all offers, saying he already knew a good one. He was smiling, and I never suspected that he was going to pull one of his tricks on me.

Oh Father, you were so lovely when you were happy. In front of everyone, he said, "Faisal will be the shepherd."

I laughed when I heard that, because I did not believe him. I told him, "Father, you will regret that, because you know I will lose all the sheep."

He smiled and said, "Well, let me just try you for a time."

For about one month, I proved to be a good shepherd, on those hot days of the summer of 1958. Everyone tried to persuade Father that it was a disgrace to the tribe to let Faisal act as a shepherd, while most of them had nothing to do except sip coffee and recite poetry and old tales. My father kept insisting that I should taste a shepherd's life.

My release from that job followed a mistake I made. Although it was an accident, I am glad it took place.

We discovered that some sheep had been stolen; every shepherd was warned to be on the alert. My father told me that in case of a thief in the dark the best way to position a gun was to point the rifle or the .45-caliber pistol in the direction indicated between the two ears of the good dog that was with me. I followed this advice on one cold night, when I awoke to hear the dog barking violently. I thought for sure that there was a thief around.

Remembering the position my father taught me, I loaded my rifle and took the ears of the dog as my instrument of direction. I waited for identification, in case one of my friends was coming to visit me, but silence followed, and eventually I fired.

The poor dog ran like lightning and suddenly dropped. When I reached it, it was dead, and the next day Faisal's career as a shepherd ended forever.

ψ ψ ψ

In 1959, I was in my last year in high school and I was sure it would be my last year in schooling, whether I passed the tough exam or not. I was preparing for my rigorous baccalaureate examination (high school diploma), the education system's yardstick for excellence, and I promised myself that failure would end my education. I felt unable to accept any more of the harsh life, coupled with the anxiety I had been experiencing.

I took the examination in great fear, hoping not to repeat my failure in ninth grade, while realizing that only 20 to 30 percent usually passed. But God felt sympathy for my agonies and the consequences of failure. With his support and much hard work, I passed with above-average grades.

And with that I became the first to receive a diploma from Al-Mershed family, or even my tribe (Al-Sba'a). And what is better than success to induce happiness in a human being?

The summer of 1959 was the hardest summer Al-Sba'a could remember. Most of the sheep had died in the harsh drought of the preceding winter, and the whole tribe was reduced to no more than one camp, with few resources on which to live. I remember that even our tent reached the stage where it was extremely difficult to afford a bushel of wheat. If this was true in our tent, then many tents of the tribe were in terrible conditions beyond imagination.

Despite all that misery, we felt that we were relatively happy because we were together. That warmth, created by togetherness, was our only source of assurance that God would be generous in the coming years.

That summer caused some major changes that became historically significant in the Al-Sba'a Tribe. Many tents did not recover, and others only barely made it through the adverse times.

Nevertheless, the news of my success was received with joy and happiness. Cousin Nouri was the carrier of that good news. One night, while I was listening to my mother's conversation, he came running and said, "Faisal, I have good news! Promise to give me what I want."

I accepted his offer, and so he gave me the newspaper containing the names of students who had passed. I was so happy that I gave my wristwatch to Nouri as a gift.

In the morning, as the news spread all over the camp, I heard sporadic shooting. It reminded me of the good old days, when shooting for fun would break out spontaneously. While we were listening to the shooting, men began to gather and move toward our tent. When they reached the tent, they were in groups of three, five, ten, or more. More than 100 Al-Sba'a tribesmen came to congratulate Faisal, the winner. They came to celebrate and enjoy the success of their son. And who could say, or believe, that my success was not the success of everyone in that tribe? They came despite their poverty, to congratulate the young man who became the first among them to have a high school diploma.

Oh my God, I felt dismayed that I had nothing to offer those beloved tribesmen. I was not even able to provide the huge feast required by tradition on such a happy day. But the dear tribesmen were not looking for a material show. Rather, they were sincere in their happiness, just to hear good news, such as Faisal's success. Some of them killed the sheep they had left in celebration. Others emptied their rifles and pistols of their only bullets.

Singing and dancing began, only to continue for three days in honor of a lousy high school diploma. Damn you, life! I had not accomplished anything to eliminate the miseries of my tribe. Damn you, diploma! You were not enough for me to deserve all that respect and love.

These thoughts were not due to modesty or humility, but rather, they were my true feelings when those poor men were celebrating the good news. I told my friends that I was sad, and I expressed how much I wished that the news came in a time very different from the summer of 1959.

It was true, what one Arabic poet said in the old times, that illiterate and ignorant people will feel happy even on miserable days, while the educated will feel sad even on happy days. The latter live not on yesterday's and today's achievements. Instead, they worry about tomorrow and the days after tomorrow.

That was exactly the situation between my tribesmen and myself at that moment. My dilemmas increased proportionally every time I thought about how much my high school diploma was going to help me and my tribe. While every tribesman thought the results of my success would be unlimited, I thought to the contrary. Everyone reasoned that I had to go to see Ibn Saud (the King of Saudi Arabia), whom they thought would do whatever I wanted.

Poor tribesmen, your expectations were too high. None among them ever thought I was planning to go on with my education. To them, the high school diploma was the upper limit, the twilight of all education.

ψ ψ ψ

And so, for almost five days, Al-Sba'a tribesmen, who were camping in Gdaim, celebrated my having a high school diploma by dancing, horse racing, and shooting, etc., despite their misery from the drought.

I was very happy, of course, but inside I was very sad. I missed my father, who was not around to share my success. He was leading what was left of his tribesmen with the sheep, to greener areas in the mountains of Syria. I wished he were present, despite his past actions of trying to stop me from continuing my education.

The other source of my sadness was about what I could do for those people who were sincerely celebrating my success. I knew the answer was nothing, and it hurts to show happiness when a person is torn inside. I participated in the festivities, regardless of my sadness.

6

City Boy or Nomad?

While 1952 marked the beginning of my more formal academic education, it was also the first time I lived in an urban environment during the school year. This resulted in my being, mentally and physically, almost simultaneously, in two different and opposing environments. They were so different that I found no common ground between them. One was urban life and schooling, and the other was my background of tribalism and nomadic tradition.

ψ ψ ψ

During that time, and especially from the beginning of the 1950s, most national governments in Syria and Iraq became hostile to the Displaced Arab Tribes. Such feelings increased in particular when a bloody coup took place in Iraq, which overthrew the monarchy. One of the reasons for such hostilities was that the tribes indeed did not belong, and many said that they should not be allowed to stay as a fifth column for a foreign country.

I was impacted by this hostility to tribes when, early in my time in Syria, I read in the governing party's newspaper about the most horrible attack on Al-Sba'a Tribe. The party was called The People's Party, and the prime minister of Syria in those days was the head of the party. The attack was direct, done by the head of a Syrian indigenous tribe whom we had continuous quarrels with, mostly about land.

The paper stated that Al-Sba'a Tribe from Aneza was part of the so-called Displaced Arab Tribes who came from Najd in Saudi Arabia. It continued that they should go back to where they originally came from. It was the first time I ever read such a statement in print in a major Syrian newspaper. That attack, and similar ones from different sources, came while my uncle was in the Syrian parliament representing the tribe, with other heads of Aneza subtribes. Usually, a tribesman's loyalty was first and foremost to the tribe. The concept of loyalty to a country was not rooted in their traditions at that time.

ψ ψ ψ

While I was in the eleventh grade, in 1958, a merger between Syria and Egypt took place. A new country emerged under the name of the United Arab Republic (UAR), led by the charismatic leader Jamal Abdel Nasser. At that time, he was adored by most Arab people, including the leadership of Saudi Arabia. He visited Syria in 1958, post-unification, and passed through almost every city, making speeches along the way.

We, the students, assembled to greet him in Hama square in front of the local government building. We were very happy to see President Nasser addressing the crowd from the balcony.

We listened to President Nasser address the people about the unity between Egypt and Syria. He mentioned the name of the country, the United Arab Republic (UAR), and we went hysterical. We were so happy. It took us time to cool off, and once we did, one of the students in our group was so emotionally charged that he began to scream. He cried out that it was the first time in Arab history that the word "Arab" was part of a country's name.

I tried to correct him and add more truth and reality to his statement. I reminded this student and everyone listening that Saudi Arabia included that honorable word since 1932.

He was insulted and answered me by saying that the word in the name of Saudi Arabia refers to "Al-Badeu" (the nomads), and he was supported by most of the students.

At that moment, I realized that according to some Arabs that word was very selective in its meaning, based on whether the person was

75

urban or not. And so, our previously united student group disintegrated into a shouting match between us. We said goodbye to our Arab brotherly unity.

It was a prelude to what happened a few years later, when the two countries who formed the UAR decided to go in different directions and separated. It proved that strong emotions may ignite the formation of a country at the beginning, but to sustain its permanency and prosper, people need bread and butter, so to speak, more than they need slogans.

ﷲ ﷲ ﷲ

This notion of tribes and nomadism among most urban Arabs leads me to say that we Arabs had and continue to face a problem with our personalities and characteristics.

For example, we Arabs, whether settled or nomadic, usually identify someone by saying he comes from such and such a tribe. While we look down at nomadism and tribalism, most Arabs try to relate their roots to tribes all the same. Even President Nasser of Egypt claimed to trace his roots to a tribe in Yemen. Yet he and his propaganda organs brainwashed his listeners on a daily basis, telling them that the main obstacle to bettering their lives was tribalism.

This phenomena of relating one's roots to a tribe is more dominant in the Arabian Peninsula than elsewhere. Most educated Arabs present themselves as above this backward notion of tribalism; they look down at tribes and nomadic peoples, and describe them as backward, as far as they are concerned. Yet to the urban, educated people, who disdain tribes and nomadism, nomadic people are known for their generosity, bravery, and other noble characteristics. So, this kind of ambivalence, as well as clear aggression, sometimes oscillating between respect and disdain, I believe leads to an imbalanced personality, and contradictory ideas and beliefs.

Tribes would reciprocate the disdain of urban people and disrespect them. What annoyed them most was that urban people changed their minds frequently. To a nomadic tribesman, when one believes in something, he should not change his mind easily. This kind of character, in my opinion, led urban people to the famous saying that tribesmen are rough, rigid, and undiplomatic.

I am sure many people disagree with my analysis, especially those who never lived in environments of both urbanization and tribal nomadism.

ψ ψ ψ

In the mid-1950s, a long drought hit the Middle East, leading to the deaths of many tribal herds, mostly sheep. My tribe, Al-Sba'a, suffered a lot. With the passage of time, many members of the tribe were forced to settle in their tents in a place called Gdaim, in the desert, about 200 kilometers east of Homs and Hama cities.

The drought was so severe, the young men of the tribe had to look for jobs throughout the Arab countries of the Middle East. And so began the exodus of young men of the Displaced Arab Tribes to Kuwait and, in particular, to Saudi Arabia.

And why not Saudi Arabia? Didn't we claim that we came from Najd, and didn't those who labeled us as displaced, in print as well as in unfriendly acts in Syria and Iraq, urge us to go back to the place we came from?

We were not in any doubt that we would be welcome in Saudi Arabia, especially, because some Aneza tribes, and in particular Al-Sba'a, were living in villages in the Al-Qassim region of Najd. And didn't we help anyone from Saudi Arabia, regardless of their tribal association, to gain employment in Iraq and Syria when we were powerful?

So went the reasoning. The sad thing was that when the exodus started, Saudi Arabia was not in a prosperous position, economically speaking, which came as a shock to most young men of Aneza and its subtribes.

ψ ψ ψ

So, for me, the years from October 1952 to June 1959 were years of trial and adjustment. Upon entering school in 1952, in Homs, I began to move away from loyalty to the tribe and began to form some loyalty to a country. In subtle, gradual ways, I was becoming a city-dweller. And most of my classmates refrained from reminding me that although I was from the nomadic Al-Sba'a Tribe, eventually I would go back to my country, Saudi Arabia.

I was going to school in an environment very different from the one in which I was born. It was an environment where most contacts were based on a business-like relationship, rather than on personal, familial ones. It was a permanent and stable environment, compared to the nomadic environment and the ways of living I had known.

All around me, people were working at trying to better their lives. They were doing it regardless of their family background or blood relationships. In that environment, education and not the family position in a tribe was the first step to a better life and high regard.

That urban environment convinced me beyond a doubt of the disadvantages of being a Bedouin and moving from one place to another. Nomadic life was gradually beginning to diminish. Truth be told, tribes began to stay longer in one place, but diehard believers did not seem to notice. That realization forced me to question every value I had learned in tribal life.

The first thing I questioned was why nomadic life did not change, or why it changed so little with the passage of time. Why did we live almost exactly like our ancestors? Why did we not settle while we had sufficient wealth to be city-dwellers or villagers?

When I had a school vacation, I usually searched for my father's tent, which moved with the tribe, whether in the desert of Jordan, Iraq, Syria, or Saudi Arabia. Communication was by word-of-mouth, and at that time was very efficient, because borders were open for nomadic tribes.

Within the two to three weeks of vacation time I lived by the tradition of my tribe, and then went back to urban life and schooling. Little by little, with the passage of time, the divergence between my two opposing personalities became so great that I was forced to choose which one I would like to follow.

At first, I was a good actor, playing it safe with my family and the tribe. I never discussed these questions with any of them directly. But over time, with smaller groups of tribesmen, I began to spread revolutionary ideas, as far as they were concerned—that nomadic life was doomed and would end someday, and that the tribe had to adjust before it was too late. I reached the conclusion that to live decently in this fast-changing world one had to abandon nomadic life. Furthermore, that education was my only means to acquire a decent life in urban society.

During those years of questioning, I was already entering the second cycle of my personality development. The first cycle included my being left to go to school while the tribal traditions were still the ones most deeply rooted in me and the ones I respected most. In a way, my first cycle had all the characteristics of the early life of my father, uncle, or any member of Al-Sba'a Tribe. It was different only in one aspect, but a very minor one during those days. It was that I learned to read and write within that nomadic environment.

But my second cycle was so different that it forced me to recognize the disappearance of nomadic life and to search for new ways of living. Despite all my clever acting, hiding my real intentions and desires, it became obvious that I was going to eventually depart from my family's way of life and that of the tribe.

And so, step by step, I was almost labeled insane to think that way. To the tribesmen, it was inconceivable to imagine that nomadic life would vanish. Al-Sba'a inherited that way of life over hundreds of years and generation after generation. And so it would continue—according to Al-Sba'a Tribe of Greater Aneza. I did not blame them, because none of them experienced living in a different environment, and so the perpetuation of nomadic ways of life and tradition was taken for granted.

Later, when I failed my ninth-grade exam and had to repeat the whole year, many thought that was the end of my schooling. And so, Faisal would return to his roots and forget all those crazy ideas, such as nomadism and tribalism being doomed to vanish.

My relationship with those around me, especially with my father and uncle, began to deteriorate. The first major attack I waged was against the kind of leadership my family gave the tribe. I began to criticize, directly or indirectly, the quality of their leadership, as they were not leading the tribe to adjust to new ways of life. One incident in particular stands out.

ψ ψ ψ

With advancement in age, my uncle became less tolerant of those around him. He began to treat Al-Sba'a tribesmen as if they were not respected and free men. In 1953–1954, he made one of the biggest mistakes of his leadership, when he forced part of Al-Sba'a Tribe to leave a water well in the summer, on the grounds that they had attacked another tribe without consultation with him. The incident was a minor one, and not unusual, when Bedouins realize that water is too short to meet the demands of all. But my uncle was so unreasonable and unfair, that he created a big mess out of the affair that affected his leadership for about three years.

I never heard of any other time when Al-Sba'a Tribe, or even a part of it, was forced to move in summer against their will. But that summer, that lovely part of Al-Sba'a, which happened to include the closest relatives to Al-Mershed family, was forced by their leader to start Al-Raheel and to search for water wells in that intense heat. What amazed me more than anything else was that not one of Al-Mershed family or the tribe ever tried to tell my uncle directly that he was wrong. My father was the biggest hypocrite, because he tried to convince the tribe that what his brother did was right, though he himself did not really believe in the justice of that action. To me, that kind of double-standard wheeling and dealing was not the way to treat any part of Al-Sba'a Tribe, especially that part which collected (two short months before this incident) more than $50,000 for my uncle when they realized he was in need of money. That incident induced me to openly criticize my immediate family, especially my uncle.

Also, during those days, I argued with my eldest cousin that the leadership we (the family) provided, was not for the good of the tribe. I emphasized that we had better start adapting our leadership to the changing times. I was arguing sincerely that sooner or later nomadic life would vanish, and that it was the responsibility of leaders to convince the tribe to think along the lines of settling permanently. My respect for every member of that beloved tribe convinced most people that I would be the future leader of Al-Sba'a.

My criticism of my uncle's leadership reached him, and he began to degrade me in front of anyone: "Faisal and his like want to undermine the family tradition," was a typical argument my dear uncle repeated again and again. He didn't realize I was already convinced that when I finished school there would not be a leadership worth fighting for. He was a traditionalist, a stubborn and dignified man, who never thought that the glory of nomadic life would come to an end so soon. My crusade of ideas that nomadic life would vanish someday was never accepted by any of the tribesmen at that time. They all believed that Bedouin life would indefinitely continue into the future as it came from out of the past. They wouldn't have dreamt their way of life would disappear someday.

While I was respected for my sincerity in dealing with Al-Sba'a tribesmen, I grew to be distrusted for my modern beliefs concerning the tribe. But life went on and I stood firmly alone with this idea.

7

HELLO RIYADH

A round September of 1959, my father and I met Mohammad ibn Ahmad Al-Sudairy, the man who had helped me so much and whom I will remember forever. Mohammad was a very influential person in Saudi Arabia, as the former Governor of the Northern Region, and he happened to be a relative of the royal family through marriage. The moment he saw us, he told my father that Faisal must go to the capital city, Riyadh, and choose whether to get a job, to go on a scholarship for higher education, or to enroll in Riyadh University. He gave me a personal letter to the Minister of Education in Riyadh, who happened to be Prince Fahad (later King Fahad). I left immediately for Riyadh and saw that city for the first time in my life.

So about two weeks after the tribe celebrated my graduation, I vanished, without a word to the mother I loved or the sisters and brothers I adored, who waited almost seven years to see me again. The only person who knew was my father, who had urged me to go to Riyadh in 1952, when I was in sixth grade.

My father's ex-driver, Salhoub, worked as a taxi driver in Arar in the Northern Region of Saudi Arabia. He came to Syria to take me to Arar. We left Syria in the evening with Mr. Mohammad Al-Sudairy's letter of introduction. It was the only document I used to enter Saudi Arabia. I had no passport and no ID, except that letter, and have never held any other country's passport or ID in my life.

On arrival in Arar, I stayed in Salhoub's house, where I found his older brother, Saleem, who was my uncle's driver. The next morning, I visited the governor's office, to pay my respects to the governor and to introduce myself.

About a week later, I was ready to travel to Riyadh and had no idea how. But the two brothers, Salhoub and Saleem, took care of that, and one afternoon took me to a station of heavy trucks loaded with goods to Riyadh.

When I entered the truck, beside the driver, Salhoub froze. He quietly shed tears. When the truck started to move, Saleem started running and told the truck driver to look after me well, as if his previous talk with the driver had not been enough.

I can never forget that scene and the loyalty of those two brothers. Both were born and raised around Al-Mershed tents, especially my uncle's and my father's. Originally, their father, Aman, was from Skaka in the Aljouf Region of Saudi Arabia, and he took refuge with Al-Sba'a Tribe after he lost his left arm in battle. He was very reserved, but despite that he became a part of my family, in his tent beside us. I never heard how he lost his left arm.

It took the truck three days to cross the Al-Nofoud Desert and reach Riyadh. Once there, I looked for a man from Otaibah Tribe, and when I found him, he greeted me enthusiastically. He knew my family from a long time ago, and knew other Otaibah Tribe families around us, during our time in Syria.

His name was Salal Ibn Ghareeb Al-Otaibi. He left his daily con-tracting business to take care of me, by introducing me to some tribal chiefs in Riyadh, from Otaibah, Motair, and Harb. They knew my family and my tribe from before I was born. And all of them honored me in the traditional ways of welcoming a guest from a notable family.

Salal took me and introduced me to the Governor of Riyadh, Prince Salman (the present King), and other officials, including the Deputy Minister of Education, in the absence of Prince Fahad, who was at an Arab League meeting in Morocco. Salal did more than a friend of my family was supposed to do. He went, as far as I am concerned, beyond the call of duty, when it comes to hospitality. I am in debt to him for making my stay in Riyadh, a city I knew no one in until then, a very comfortable one.

☙ ☙ ☙

I was well-received by every prince I met. Each one of them asked about my family and the tribe, and I tried my best to give the clearest possible description of our tribe's desperate situation. Regarding myself, I stressed hard that what I was looking for at that stage was not a government job but the opportunity to further my education. My love for education became my supreme interest, while the needs of the tribe became secondary. This was not because I did not want to help the tribe, but due to my growing realization of the limited help each prince could offer.

Eventually, I submitted my application for a scholarship to the Ministry of Education. As mentioned earlier, the minister, Prince Fahad, to my misfortune, was absent. I spent much time going back and forth to the Ministry to make inquiries, as it took one month to hear the final decision.

It was bad news, in the end. The only excuse the Ministry gave was that I had applied too late. I did not question that statement.

Next, I went to see Prince Salman, who happened to be Prince Fahad's full brother. He was immediately interested in my case and encouraged me to go to the University of Riyadh. I was really not enthusiastic to attend that university, and when I met the Acting President, a valid excuse emerged. The university had not yet established an economics department, and economics had drawn my interest strongly.

I went back to Prince Salman and told him the story, after getting an official statement from the university to support what I said.

The Prince asked which school in the world I would like to attend. My answer was any English-speaking university, regardless of location. The Prince promptly suggested the American University in

Beirut, Lebanon. I concurred with his suggestion and felt so happy that at last my college education would become a reality.

When the Prince began to look for his personal secretary, to settle the matter, he did not find him. The Prince told me to return on Saturday, as that was a Thursday, and the following day, Friday, was a holy day in Saudi Arabia. No one would be working.

It did not occur to me that, between 1:00 p.m. on Thursday and 10:00 a.m. on Saturday, everything would change, and that the absence of a lousy secretary could cost me so much money or decide my future. On Saturday the Prince was a different person. He told me that he had no authority to send me to college.

I did not argue with him, but I was shocked to hear the bad news. I realized that someone had changed the Prince's mind over the weekend. The Prince was young and easily swayed by others.

I thanked the Prince, but before I left, and in front of everyone in his office, I told him, "Your Royal Highness, I came in search of education. I will fulfill my goal even if it must be without the help of anyone."

I uttered that statement out of anger, based on my belief that my education was not up for negotiation, and was not to be dismissed upon my first such disappointment.

I spent that night thinking about what should be done to fulfill my goal. I felt scared and weak. The future began to appear darker than ever. I knew that neither my father nor the tribe would help me with a single penny for further education. And I knew, definitively, for the first time in my life, that there was no one to depend on except myself. Despite all my agonies, I repeated a philosopher's saying: life without hope is not worth living. Hope kept me spiritually alive. I refused to accept the Prince or the Ministry of Education's decisions as the final outcome. I convinced myself to try another channel.

I went straight to King Saud himself. The King in those days was the eldest son of King Abdulaziz, the founder of the Kingdom, and it was the tradition of the royal family to have no barriers for citizens wishing to see them. Every citizen, even during the reign of King Faisal later on, was entitled to deal directly with the King on appointed days.

I was introduced by one of his aides. The King became so interested in what I told him that he immediately ordered his secretary that I should see him at 10:00 a.m. the next day in his private palace.

His decision was going to fulfill my desires for sure. Everyone could see that the King was interested, for otherwise there was no need to see him in his private palace.

I spent the night thinking about all the happy days that would follow my meeting with the King. The next morning, I was in the palace one hour ahead of time. When 10:00 o'clock approached, I told the secretary, whom the King had spoken with the previous day, my wish to see the King.

The secretary was a man who encouraged a desire to hit him in the face even if you did not know him. He created some kind of false atmosphere of importance, to rival that of the King. He looked me up and down as if he were surprised to see a young man speak to him without hesitation. Never did he say anything except, "Wait." I waited until noon.

The secretary complicated the matter impossibly, because it was getting too late to see the King. It was said, by a Westerner who spent most of his life in the Arab world, that it was easy to deal directly with King Abdulaziz ibn Saud, because he was precise and straightforward—but that dealing with his so-called educated aides would complicate rather than facilitate any issue. That was exactly what happened when I encountered that selfish, ignorant, and proud secretary.

In the end, the secretary gave me the letter I had presented to the King the previous day and asked me to have the head of the King's Private Bureau, who happened to be the son of the King, sign it.

When I reached the bureau in that big palace, I found to my surprise that the Prince I sought was absent. He, in fact, was outside of the country, and no one knew when he would return. An old man in the bureau told me that the secretary knew very well that the Prince was not around, and that he was using this tactic of delay to stop me from seeing the King.

Returning to the first waiting area, I told the secretary that the Prince was absent. He told me to await his return. I protested, on the grounds that the Prince might not come soon, and that I could miss a year of college by the delay. Gibraltar was not moved by my protest but remained firm and quiet. Finally, the great pharaoh uttered the words, "Come tomorrow."

Tomorrow became many days, until I abandoned the whole matter without ever seeing the King. I am sure that, had I not encountered such personalities, I would have been in school that year. The Prince and the King were sincere in what they said, but my troubles came from those middlemen who had no function except to delay everything and to be jealous of everyone who came near to a member of the royal family. That kind of experience with people around big personalities hardened my feelings toward them forever. I began to look at any aides with disrespect and suspicion.

I thought those experiences would be the last of their kind. But time proved me wrong, much later, when I encountered another such person, without expectation or planning.

ψ ψ ψ

I left Riyadh convinced that my college education must be postponed for the time being, because the channels currently open were not worth attempting anymore. From October 1959 to June

1960, I remained with the tribe, performing my role, but always hoping and dreaming I could go to college.

I realized, during that year, that if I wanted to go to college, I had to work for it—no king, prince, father, or tribe was going to hand it to me or even help me.

In June 1960, I was in the Eastern Province of Saudi Arabia (the oil area), looking for a job. I hoped to work at the Arabian American Oil Company (ARAMCO). I went straight to the company's office of employment.

I was told to come "tomorrow" to fill out the application. I was astonished, because I was under the impression that the now familiar word was not in the vocabulary of an efficient company such as ARAMCO. But "tomorrow" once more became many days, until finally I was allowed to fill in the magical forms in search of a job with ARAMCO. The beautiful ARAMCO, the efficient ARAMCO, which loved to have Saudi Arabian citizens who were holders of high school diplomas. ARAMCO the promising, ARAMCO ... Oh, please take me, ARAMCO!

I went through much brainwashing of that kind, until I reached a stage when I felt that life without ARAMCO was "not worth a dime." Twenty days passed before I was even allowed to take the examination. It was in the English language, and mostly covered mathematics.

The examiner told me that I did a good job, especially when I refrained from answering questions I did not understand. In reality, the examination was very elementary, but it was the first I ever took in English.

An American in charge of employment asked about my plans for the future. When he realized that I would like to be an economist someday, he decided that the accounting department was the place to go. There I went through all kinds of cross-examinations and received promises. When I asked how much my monthly pay would be, I was shocked to hear that it amounted to about $65.00 per month. I rejected the offer immediately, on the grounds that ARAMCO usually paid at least $200.00 per month for a high school graduate.

The next day, I tried my luck with the mass media department of ARAMCO, and I ended up in the office of the manager of the ARAMCO television station. It was the first time in my life I had seen a television, much less a television station. I was amazed to see so much unfamiliar equipment. When the manager asked me to go through some testing, I was really shaken. I told him that I had never seen such things in my life, and that it would be useless to give any test, as it could not possibly reflect my true potential.

I tried to convince him to let me observe for at least a week, to get accustomed to the work, but he refused. Instead, I was ushered to the announcer's room and was asked to read in Arabic while an American movie played. My voice was shaking, and I knew I would flunk the test—and I did.

The manager was not interested in Faisal's trembling voice. But out of "mercy," he told me that if I accepted $65.00 as monthly pay, he would find me a job. I then recognized that an offer of $65.00 was a sort of gentlemanly rejection. I left the television department as I had the accounting department. I was really angry, especially with the television man who would not even give me a chance to get adjusted to a new thing. Maybe he thought I was one of Bob Hope's children, or one of Ed Sullivan's protégés, or at least a person who had grown up knowing all those television stars. He never seemed to accept the fact that I was Faisal the Bedouin, son of Sfouq the Bedouin, who had never been exposed to this thing called "TV." And so, I realized that all the ARAMCO advertisements in Saudi newspapers were for local consumption, not for action. I did not blame ARAMCO for rejecting me or any one of those many other young citizens who must have come along. But I felt bitter, because ARAMCO was not courageous enough to tell young people they had no openings for them. So, I left that "paradise" after I was stopped at its main gate.

Farewell, ARAMCO the Promising. It was nice knowing you without makeup or artificial beautification.

ψ ψ ψ

Eventually, in August 1960, I was employed by a travel agency in Dhahran International Airport. My monthly payment for the trial period was $166.00 a month, plus free accommodations. Two months later, the salary was raised to $200.00 a month with accommodations. I was happy with that job, regardless of its financial aspects, because for one thing, it introduced me to a modern and sophisticated environment where English was the main language. I took advantage of my situation and worked hard to improve my English.

Secondly, I was able to travel anywhere in the world, on an almost free ticket, once every year. With foresight, I reasoned that this last opportunity would be important, if my college education was to become a reality someday.

Dhahran Airport was oriented toward the American way of life. And there were many Americans with whom I practiced the English language every time I was given the slightest chance. I was born in an environment where the son was required to perpetuate his father's profession. But in that airport, I experienced life in an open environment, urban in tone and fast in pace. The family name or tribal association meant little if anything in this impersonal, business-oriented, and modern place. Hard work, and nothing else, mattered.

I caught on easily, and within four months of my employment was promoted to full traffic officer with $244.00 a month plus free transportation and accommodations. The manager of that agency began to depend on me, especially as he realized my sincerity and potential. In addition to my job as traffic officer, he assigned me to be in charge of the Personnel Department. One of my colleagues was an Indian who had a B.S. in Chemistry from Delhi University. I convinced him that we should live together in one apartment, and so Abdul Karim Al Deen became one of my closest friends ever, up to then. He helped me immensely with my English, and I was able to speak English in my dwelling and at the airport. I was encouraged by Abdul Karim to read all kinds of stories in English, and that experience helped give me confidence that my English was really improving.

During my entire employment in that agency, I only came late to work once, though the hours were irregular. Hours were geared to the arrival and departure of the agency airlines which included Scandinavian Airlines System (SAS), Swissair, United Arab Airlines, Middle East Airlines, and others. The manager was aware of my consistency and began to entertain the idea of making me his deputy.

He told me once that he did not understand why some businessmen always stated that Bedouins were the least stable in employment. I told him that it was hard to generalize, because nomadic life was in reality a shifting and unpredictable one. However, I said that I did not believe an educated Bedouin was less stable than an urban person.

I teased him, saying that the day might come when I would have to leave his agency. He never believed me, and thought it was one of my jokes, especially because he realized that I was happy with my pay and my chance to perform in English. It never occurred to that kind and friendly man that I was not satisfied with the job as a profession. He never thought that I was unimpressed with the suggestion of being his deputy. To him it seemed out of the question that Faisal the Bedouin would leave a secure job to fight for something less certain. Receiving aircrafts to me was only a means for subsistence, and a position from which to jump to something else. I did not blame my manager for thinking along the lines he did, because even my father, hearing about my pay, thought the same. Neither could conceive that I would abandon that job to fight a battle with results hidden far in the future.

Never did I tell anyone, not even my roommate, about my intention to go to college. I reasoned that silence on this subject would be better for my position in the agency, and that some people might try to persuade me to do otherwise if I talked. But I secretly began to plan my future, with such refined details that, at this moment, I am astonished at its success.

My plan was simple and precise. It was based on the idea that I must save every penny and see how much I could accumulate.

My first lesson in economics began before I took a single course in that field. I decided that to increase my savings, I should invest all I had in something with assured returns. I was lucky to encounter a dull, small-time businessman who agreed to borrow all of my savings at a rate of 6 percent interest. I presumed this meant per year, while he interpreted it to mean per month. However, I never corrected him when he repeated the terms of the agreement, "Faisal, it is 6 percent per month."

I said, "Of course."

That simple person never realized his blunder until the day when he paid me all my money. I did not feel guilty about that mistake, because I reasoned that I had been nice to everyone, but when it came to my education almost everyone was against me. Why should I remain soft and generous in a world I had come to learn was hard and selfish? To live in this so-called modern world, I reasoned that I must play according to its rules. I abandoned some of my straightforwardness and purity, and some ideas of fairness that I had learned in my tribe. I became a greedy individual, ready to take almost any step to fulfill my goal of going to college.

❁ ❁ ❁

During the winter of 1961, I became addicted to reading. I read every book by Hemingway that was available in Arabic. I read in Arabic, *Ghosts in the Dark* by Colin Wilson, *Gone with the Wind*, and *The Individuals*. Even Perry Mason detective stories in English made my reading list.

While I was reading so much, I developed a desire to write in Arabic. I published my first article in Guraish newspaper in the Western Province of Saudi Arabia under a false name, "M." I based the article on my experience trying to find a job. The theme was how hard it was for an educated Saudi young man to find work, despite all the advertisements companies published.

The article generated a great deal of follow-up discussion in that paper. I felt especially good when a big construction company published the list of all of its employees, to show that it had numerous Saudi Arabs. I was so happy with the impact of that first article that I began to entertain the idea of writing regularly to newspapers in my free time. And so, my second article was published, also under a false name, in Riyadh's *Al-Qassim* newspaper. That article was economic in nature, and even after all my training, today I feel that it was not bad at all. Especially for someone who had not taken a single course in economics. It proves to me that economics is a science of common sense and good judgment.

In that article, I accused Saudi Arabian industrialists of not establishing industries the country needed most. I argued that establishing a shoe factory or a date-packing plant, to use the available raw materials in the Kingdom, would be much better than establishing Pepsi-Cola factories, even if the product was the "hospitality drink," and even if it gave us admittance to the "Pepsi generation."

My third article was as much a surprise to me as to everyone else, because it was published in the *Al-Khalij Al-Araby* (Arabian Gulf) newspaper in the Eastern Province under my full name, though I had asked the editor to publish it under my false name.

The subject of that article was about the thing nearest to my heart. I was forced to write it after I cried through almost an entire night. What ignited my feelings was seeing a woman begging while she carried two children after Friday prayer in front of a mosque. When I gave her some money and talked to her, I realized that she was a Bedouin.

Later, alone in our apartment, I began to visualize all kinds of images. What if my mother was begging somewhere in the north of Saudi Arabia? What if every woman of that beloved tribe was begging all over the Kingdom? For the first time since June 1960, I began to think about my family and the tribe.

Damn you, modern life! You even forced me to forget my beloved family and the tribe.

I cried until 4:00 a.m., when I wrote an article emphasizing that it was a disgrace for Saudi Arabia, with all its oil revenue, to leave a beggar in the street. At that time, the government had no social security program, and I suggested private donations to eliminate the poverty of the Kingdom.

No one paid much attention to my grand scheme, and so I wrote my fourth article in the same newspaper. That time, I attacked newspapermen directly. My accusation was that they wrote in a style that only the highly educated could understand. I argued that a newspaper's mission was social in nature, and that it should be designed to reach the most classes of society possible.

After that article I stopped writing, despite all my friends' protests. My writing in newspapers diverted me, I realized, from concentrating on my life goal of pursuing a college education. I convinced myself to concentrate all my energies on that goal.

☙ ☙ ☙

I heard from many Americans I met in that airport, that life in the United States was very expensive, and that I had better accumulate at least one year's expenses before I left Saudi Arabia. Most of the time, I thought I was dreaming, but I asked myself, "What is wrong or bad about dreaming?"

To add some substance to my dream, I tried very hard to find just one story of a Saudi Arabian student who had been poor and without a scholarship, but in the end, made it in a United States college. I failed to find that assurance.

Up to that time, the winter of 1961, I was not sure I would go to the United States, or even that my English was adequate to study there. One test of my English ability came very soon, with rather embarrassing results.

I was always fascinated by the use of the phrase "never mind" when I heard people talking. I decided to use it when the chance arose. One wintry night, I was waiting for one of the agency's flights scheduled to arrive from London via Beirut. It was a Middle East Airlines flight, and an American asked me about the arrival of the aircraft. I told him that so far, we had heard no news, although the flight was over three hours behind schedule. The man was worried, and so I walked with him, just to chat. When I asked him why he was so interested in the flight, he said that his wife and two children were supposed to arrive on it from London. He expressed particular concern about the weather being so bad.

At that stage of the conversation, I decided this was the opportune moment for my reserved and ready expression. Sympathetically, I patted him on the shoulder and said, "Well, never mind."

In an astonished tone, the man demanded, "What do you mean, never mind! I have all my family in jeopardy."

I was really surprised and realized that I had used the expression in the wrong place. The American guessed what had happened when he saw my face, and proceeded to lecture me on the usage of "never mind."

I was skeptical at that stage, and almost attempted using "never mind" in reference to his lecture.

After that embarrassment, I decided to work hard on my English. Instead of reading books to help me in English, I ended up buying a book called *American Colleges*. I spent many nights trying to figure out all the abbreviations and the costs for each college or university. The term which gave me the hardest time was "co-ed," which appeared after almost every college's name. My roommate, Abdel Karim, would have been able to tell me what it meant. But I avoided asking, in order to keep my secret.

From reading that book, I was convinced beyond a doubt that United States colleges were atrociously expensive. I decided that I had better start collecting financial help from a source outside of Saudi Arabia.

My encounters in Riyadh, with aides surrounding influential personalities, did not stop me from dreaming that somewhere in this world someone was going to help.

To begin with, I thought of writing to United States officials. The first name that came to my mind was that of Senator William Fulbright, the chairman of the Foreign Relations Committee in the United States Senate. I had heard often about Fulbright Scholarships. Without trying to find out any details about them, I wrote the senator, asking for help, doubtful that he would answer. I was almost sure that Fulbright would be too busy to care about Faisal's case.

But that human senator wrote me a letter, telling me about the scholarship, saying that he had nothing to do with it except his name, because he was the senator who introduced the bill to the Senate after the end of World War II.

Well, the first attempt to solicit American help had failed, and I realized that I had missed the target again. But I am glad that I contacted that senator, whom I later respected as an individual, despite my disagreement with some of his thinking concerning the domestic ills of United States's society. I wish I had kept a copy of that letter, but it is gone.

Nonetheless I remember—and thank you, Senator, for giving me proof that even a busy senator must have the time to guide and advise a young stranger, even one who is a foreigner.

I tried very hard to stop writing anyone, but I failed to convince myself before one more try. That was a letter directed to President John F. Kennedy.

My letter to the president was long and full of many irrelevant points. I stressed my goal, emphasizing that my aim was not just to get educated but to help my country. Also, I told the president that despite our two countries' occasional disagreements, I believed that helping me was worthwhile. I really had a big mouth in that letter, even stressing my opposition to some of the United States's foreign policy. I wrote as if I were the head of an independent state, rather than a young man seeking help. But at the time I thought all those arguments were very persuasive.

Surprisingly enough, that great president took Faisal the Bedouin's letter seriously. About a month later, I received a letter from the U.S. Embassy in Jeddah, Saudi Arabia.

At first sight, I did not care much about the letter, because I could not recall ever contacting the embassy. But when I opened the letter and saw the president's name, I grew elated, even before reading the whole thing. I congratulated myself, thinking, "Faisal, this time you made it in." I didn't yet realize that in diplomatic correspondence the first one or two paragraphs are almost invariably encouraging, with only the last statement before "Respectfully yours" or "Faithfully" (etc.) being the substance of the note. Therefore, my elated reaction vanished only when I read the last paragraph. There I was advised to write directly to the universities for a scholarship.

Farewell, correspondence with big personalities—and farewell to any correspondence to solicit any help from anyone in this world.

⚘ ⚘ ⚘

I applied to different universities in the United States, emphasizing that my goal was to major in economics and that I would start in this area as a freshman. I described my financial position.

I received three acceptances, one from the University of California, Berkeley, the second from Howard University, in Washington, D.C., and the last from the University of Washington, in Seattle. Without knowing how to evaluate these schools, I picked Howard University. The reason is simple. Howard University is in the capital of the United States. Because of the pattern of good universities being mostly in capital cities in the Middle East, I thought a university in the capital of the United States must be better than one located in Berkeley or Seattle.

I wrote Howard a letter, stating that I would begin studies there by February 1962.

Up to the spring of 1961, no one, including my dear friend Abdel Karim, knew what I was up to. Later, when I told him, he advised and helped me greatly. Alone, I realized that the first thing to do was to minimize the cost of reaching the United States as much as possible.

I told my manager at the agency about my intention. He did not believe me at first, but later he respected my decision. This was especially so when I told him that, financially speaking, I was sure I would not gain from going to college, because my salary at the agency was already that of a college graduate. As a matter of fact, counting transportation as well as accommodation expenses, I was making a little more than many college graduates.

I stressed to that manager, furthermore, that I knew I would face difficulties in the United States. But, my dear manager, I was trying to meet a challenge forced upon me by my feelings and future hopes. I was trying to fulfil my goal without the financial help of all those who were dearest to me.

The truth, I told the manager, was that I looked at a college degree as more of a matter of honor than a calculation of how many dollars it might earn me.

In the end, I closed every avenue for further negotiation, when I told the manager that even if he promoted me to be his deputy, I would not hesitate to reject that offer and go to college. The manager realized my determination, and so he told me that he would help me as much as he could. He was a man who kept his word, and despite all of his shortcomings he was a sincere and faithful friend. I told him that what I wanted from him was nothing more than a free ticket to the United States. He laughed when I stressed it need only be one-way.

He gave me a free ticket to London, and greatly reduced rates from London to New York, after taking many steps to avoid red tape in that agency and with the airlines.

Thank you very much, dear manager, Safwat Al-Sheikh, from Egypt.

Time, at last I am getting even with you.

Officials of this world, I am going to fulfill my goal despite all of your objections and policies of offering no help.

Dear Father, and tribesmen, I am going to college even though I have not received a penny from you.

Yes, I am going to do it at last, in the farthest country from Saudi Arabia. I will be going to the United States, the country to which not one of you tribesmen ever thought to go.

My father's tent (1968)

My elementary school diploma

Representing Saudi Arabia at the United Nations Conference on Trade and Development (UNCTAD) in New Delhi (1968)

Greeting the King of Belgium, Baudouin (1975)

Attending meetings with Anwar Sadat, President of Egypt, during his visit to the Ministry of Planning (1976)

Attending meetings with Anwar Sadat, President of Egypt, during his visit to the Ministry of Planning (1976)

*At the Saudi- American Joint Economic meeting
in Washington, DC (1977)*

*Participating in Muammar Gaddafi's (with head turned)
visit to the Ministry of Planning (late 70's/early 80's)*

*King Juan Carlos and Queen Sofia during their visit to
the Ministry of Planning (late 70's/early 80's)*

*Governor of Riyadh HRH Prince Salman (now King Salman)
visiting the Ministry of Planning (late 70's/early 80's)*

President Valery Giscard d'Estaing of France meeting with Crown Prince (and future king) Fahad at the Ministry of Planning (late 70's/early 80's)

President Valery Giscard d'Estaing of France meeting with Crown Prince (and future king) Fahad at the Ministry of Planning (late 70's/early 80's)

Above & Below: Pierre Trudeau, Prime Minister of Canada, and father of current Prime Minister Justin Trudeau, at the Ministry of Planning (1980)

ψ

PART TWO

—

INTO THE GREAT UNKNOWN

I began to count the days. Abdel Karim was so dear that sometimes he asked how much time was left, because he didn't want to see me go.

I was always precise and able to say, for example, eight months and twenty-one days, or three months and five days. I was happy, so very happy, as time went on. I felt confident, and taller than anyone, because I was going to college on my own. I began to enjoy the fruits of my not-yet-fulfilled goal very early.

My friends and colleagues pressed me to tell them why my behavior had changed suddenly. I began to leak the news that I was going to the United States for my college education.

Everyone asked the same question, "Do you have a scholarship?" When I said no, people thought I was just dreaming, and many, fearing I would end up lost and frustrated, advised me to abandon the whole idea.

I cannot forget the advice I got from a low-grade governmental official who, by luck, went to New York for a week when Trans World Airlines inaugurated a route to Dhahran Airport. He told me that it was impossible for me to go on my own and went overboard stressing only the bad things he saw in New York City.

An American Air Force captain heard of my plan, and one day dropped by my office to see me. He was straightforward, and his advice was the best that I received. He told me, "Faisal, life in the United States is very different from that in Saudi Arabia. People work fast, eat fast, talk fast, and generally the pace of everything is very fast. If you are going hoping that someone in the United States will help you, then, dear friend, forget the whole idea and stay in your own country. But if you are determined to depend on yourself and willing to fight hard to get through college, then go and don't wait. Faisal, you and no one else are the only one able to see that your goal is fulfilled."

Thank you, Captain, you really were a sincere person, who described living in the United States very well.

The news of my intention to go to the United States traveled fast. It created a kind of uproar within my family and the tribe. Almost all the dignitaries in the tribe insisted that my action was not traditional in nature. (I was definitely sure of that, and for a change we agreed on something.) And they insisted that my father should stop me from going to that "what-was-its-name" country.

Their arguments centered on the idea that in the end I would be lost—literally. Also, they considered my present job good enough.

To my surprise, around November 1961, I found my father and two of the tribesmen waiting for me in the agency's office in Al Khobar. I was overjoyed to see them and to hear the latest news about the tribe. Especially when my father made it clear that he had come to the Eastern Province because he needed some spare parts for his car. That statement assured me that my father was not going to intervene with my going to the United States.

But soon I began to suspect that this was subterfuge. After two days, we finally sat together, to debate the obvious question and the real aim of their sudden visit.

Well, I won, and my father wished me luck. I gave my November salary to him, and some other money to each of the two tribesmen. They left me, but not happily, especially the other two men. My father reasoned that I was man enough to make the right decision. But the other two were intensely afraid that I would get lost. They thought that Faisal was some kind of a sheep, or camel.

Sometime after my father's departure, my dear cousin Thamer arrived. After two years' delay, he had passed his high school diploma examinations, and then decided to follow Faisal in abandoning nomadic life forever. Dear Thamer went to Riyadh and came back disappointed in the same way I was before him. When I asked him why my uncle did not finance his college education, Thamer just said, "Please, forget depending on the family."

At that moment I realized that my cousin also felt bitter toward his family, as I had toward mine. The main problem between us and our families was not financial in nature only; rather, it was due to different beliefs and ways of thinking. Our families and the tribe thought that nomadic life would continue to be the most honorable way of life. Thamer and I believed, on the contrary, that nomadic life would vanish and that it was much better for us (the young) to search for a new life.

By mid-December 1961, I had collected my money and fixed my date of departure. I would reach the United States with about $1,800 to my name.

One night, around the last week of December, I was one of the passengers leaving Dhahran for Cairo. It was one of the hardest nights I ever faced. Dear Thamer was around. Before departure, he took my pocket calendar (for 1962) and wrote a few words—which I did not read, on his request, until the aircraft took off.

"Dear Cousin Faisal," he wrote, "the road you just began to walk on is new for all of us. It is dangerous, but it's an endless success. Remember that you are a member of Al-Mershed family. Fight to honor that name by success and hard work. Remember again, dear cousin, that you are fighting for all of us, the young and future generation of that family. May God keep you safe and let success be your companion. Thamer Al-Mershed."

I cried upon reading those words of Thamer's. And I felt especially miserable since Thamer was still looking for a job when I left. But I reasoned that he who had helped me find a job would not let

Thamer down. Thus, I left Dhahran and said farewell to my beloved country for the time being.

"Saudi Arabia," I said, "I will come back to serve you despite all the difficulties I encountered within your borders in my fight for a college education. I will come back to find a dear and generous mother. And I will come back a well-equipped citizen, ready to fight for your development and progress."

✤ ✤ ✤

In Cairo, I drifted for a few days, knowing nothing except that my long journey to fight for a college education had just started.

In London, I saw a non-Arab society for the first time in my life. I was really scared to see that the relaxed pace of an Arab society had no place in London. Everyone appeared to be walking fast and alone. Many times, I stood alongside a street, just to watch how people went by. To me, everything seemed arranged perfectly, in comparison to the country I came from. The traffic was moving in a routinized way. The people were formal—in reality, too formal. Almost everyone had an umbrella, as if it were a disgrace to walk without one.

I thought, "Is this the life I will live, this systematic way of life?"

I prayed to God that the United States would be different from London, the city that scared me so much.

✤ ✤ ✤

At 6:30 p.m. on January 7, 1962, a BOAC flight from London to New York landed in Idlewild Airport (now JFK). Aboard that flight was Faisal the Bedouin, bound to be the first member of Al-Sba'a Tribe who ever dared to undertake such an endeavor. I am sure that no one recognized that great personality, but I was happy, confident, and determined to follow the road I took until I achieved my goal.

About two hours later, I realized that if London's people were walking fast compared to Arabs, the New Yorkers were flying. Everything appeared to me as if some madness was pushing it. This impression was strengthened at the station, where the airport bus unloaded passengers. I tried many times to get a taxi but failed at every attempt. One old man noticed me and told me in his New York accent, "Look, fellow, you will not get a taxi all night if you continue to behave this way."

Well, he was right—and so I did as New Yorkers did. I lined up all my baggage on the curb, and the moment a taxi pulled up I threw my bags in it. God! It was as if we were drilling for evacuation. The taxi drivers usually had no time to wait, or even to get out of the car if a passenger wanted help. I realized later that taxi drivers in New York did not consider helping a passenger load his baggage their responsibility. Maybe this duty was not stated clearly in the labor laws, and so they refused to follow an unclear practice. It may require a Supreme Court decision, to make it more definite.

The next day, I was in the Saudi Arabian Consulate, to register my address at Howard University, Washington, D.C. All staff members who realized that I had no scholarship shared their pessimistic views about my future—except one. When I went to leave, he took me to his office. After encouraging me to fight for my education, he told me to go to see King Saud, who was in Boston for medical treatment. I said, "Not again, please. I had enough bad luck in Riyadh in 1959."

He convinced me that it wouldn't hurt to try. And Saudi Arabia had a law in place that said every Saudi student who studied at his own expense in the United States would receive $500.00 per year in assistance.

I left for Boston in search of better luck with the King. In the limousine from Boston Airport to the city, the taxi driver told the passengers with a laugh that, the previous day, King Saud had given each nurse in the hospital $500 and an expensive watch. I did not have the slightest idea whether this was true or not. But I hoped that, if it were true, my luck would at least equal that of a nurse who was treating the King.

Well Faisal, I thought, now you will see whether some of those smart fellows around the King will give you the chance to be as lucky as a nurse. I began to dream, but some inner feeling told me that there would be no opportunity for me. On the other hand, I was sure that if I were given that chance, all my financial problems would vanish on the spot—and so I waited to see.

At the reception area of the Sheraton Hotel, where the King was staying, the following conversation took place:

> Faisal: I want to see the Saudi Ambassador.
> The clerk: Which Saudi ambassador?
> Faisal: As far as I know, Saudi Arabia has only one ambassador.
> The clerk: This hotel has at least 16 Saudi ambassadors in it.
> Faisal: But this is impossible!
> The clerk: We have the Saudi ambassador from the United States, Saudi ambassadors from Europe, Saudi ambassadors from Latin America, Saudi ambassadors from …
> Faisal: Oh, no! I want the Saudi Ambassador to the United States.

The conversation ended after I realized that all our ambassadors had left their posts to see the King. I am sure the clerk was happy to see me enter the elevator, on my way to see the Saudi Arabian ambassador to the United States, and out of his sight.

On the second floor there was an Arabic-speaking person. Without even introducing himself, he began to ask me questions. I told him that I was a Saudi student who had just arrived in the United States.

"Tabaa'n (of course), you have a scholarship," he said.

When I said no, he became suspicious, for no reason that I could comprehend. He asked me to give him my passport. I almost laughed, thinking, what on earth happened to make him think that I was stupid enough to give him my passport?

He tried desperately to get my passport, while the elevator took several journeys up and down. But I refused. That "great diplomat" did not realize that I had no idea who he was, and that I therefore couldn't care less about his orders.

Well, at one of the elevator stops, another Arabic-speaking person entered. And when he heard what was going on, he said, "Your Excellency, leave the matter to me."

I was relieved when I followed that person to his room, but I felt that my encounter had been with a big personality because of the use of the title "excellency."

Mohammad Ali Al-Shwaihi, the man who had intervened, later became one of the dearest and most helpful friends I ever had. When I entered his room, Mohammad said, "Don't you know with whom you were arguing?"

I said, "How would I know, when His Excellency did not introduce himself?"

Mohammad smiled and told me that it was the Saudi Arabian Ambassador to the United States.

Oh God, not again! Another misfortune to prevent me from seeing the King!

Well, Mohammad told me that I better forget seeing the King, because the ambassador was the one I had to convince first. And so, on Mohammad's advice, I simply wrote the King a letter, telling him my story. Mohammad promised to submit it through the appropriate channels.

Thus, Faisal's last try to see the King for a scholarship ended. This time it ended with less frustration and argument. It ended as quickly as the New Yorkers' pace of life.

There was nothing left to do, so I departed for Washington, D.C. My encounter with the ambassador immediately took me back to those officials in Riyadh. To the secretaries of the King and the Prince. To all those aides around big personalities, those aides who had nothing to do except shield a leader from seeing and discussing the problems of his citizens. Even if one of those citizens happens to be in a strange country, such as the United States.

I realized many times that my failure was due to my own stubbornness to obey those aides. But I thought and continue to think that I was right, and they were wrong. Dammit! Every time I was near to ending my misery, some aide would block the way.

Faisal, you have no one to depend on except yourself. Forget trying to fulfill your goal the easy way.

Big aides, I will get even with you someday!

ψ ψ ψ

When I arrived at National Airport in Washington, D.C., I took a taxi to the city. The driver was friendly. He became something of a tour guide the moment we left the airport. He drove me to see the monuments, the heart of the city, and took me to Howard University, where I was set to begin my studies.

When I asked my tour guide, the taxi driver, where I might go to live for a while, he mentioned the International Student House at 1825 R Street, NW. He took me right there, and I was lucky to get accommodations for three days, until I could move into a Howard University dormitory.

The house secretary was a British lady named Monica. She gave me numerous instructions about the house regulations, and a key to the front door in case I stayed out after 11:00 p.m.

I left the house immediately, to see more of Washington, D.C., the city in which I expected to live for a long time to come. I was impatient, and so I tried to get to know the whole city at once. I walked its streets, observed the people, and saw things on foot that I had marveled at from my tour guide's taxi.

Everything was big. So many things were magnificent. How I wished that school would start the next day!

When I came back to the house, I realized that I had already missed dinner. But good Monica went ahead and brought me some chicken, after she realized that I did not eat the pork that was on the menu that evening. While I was eating alone, an American girl named Ann, from Florida, left the group with which she was talking and joined me.

I disappointed her, as far as conversation was concerned. I was hopelessly rigid, due to the environment in which I had grown up and lived. I was afraid to try to be friendly with girls, until the time when I knew that I would be an important participant in the conversation.

ψ ψ ψ

After three days, I left the house to live in a freshman dormitory at Howard University. I remember that at one point I looked around at all the people on campus and felt that I had been misled.

I had watched movies about the United States. Those movies all starred Rock Hudson and Doris Day, or actors who looked and sounded much like one another—white people, blonde people.

Everyone in the vicinity of Howard was Black. I did not expect that. And I wasn't disappointed—just surprised to find that the image of the United States that I had been given was so unlike the way it appeared in the flesh.

Mr. Wilson, the foreign student advisor, and his secretary, Mrs. Green, told me to deposit every dollar I had with the university cashier. So I did.

I realized, eventually, that the school's spring semester would not start before the third of February 1962. While I waited for classes to start, I spent most of my time in the Foreign Student Advisor's office. That office became like a home to go to every time I felt lonely. I later saw many other foreign student offices at United States universities, but due to Mr. Wilson and Mrs. Green, the Howard University office proved to be the best. How I wished later that every department and bureau at Howard University did its job so well. I had no doubt that, if that were the case, Howard University would be one of the best schools in the United States.

What amazed me most was Mr. Wilson's knowledge of foreign student problems on an individual basis. There were about 800 foreign students that year. And I swear that Mr. Wilson knew each one, down to their first name and major field of study. Mr. Wilson proved to be the best-equipped man for the job. Time after time, he proved he would fight to the end for the rights of a foreign student, including me.

One day, around the end of January 1962, Mrs. Green called me to her office. She said she had a registered letter, addressed to me. I told her I was sure that some misunderstanding had occurred. None of the letters I sent back home could have reached Saudi Arabia yet, so how could it be possible? Well, Mrs. Green, in the presence of Mr. Wilson, produced the letter.

I opened it reluctantly, and read aloud, "Pay to Mr. Faisal S. Bashir the amount of $1,000."

I almost jumped for joy, and this caused Mr. Wilson and Mrs. Green to laugh, on and on.

"Well, young man, you have already increased your deposit by $1,000," Mr. Wilson said.

I read the accompanying letter, which was signed by dear Mohammad Ali Al-Shwaihi, who had presented my letter to the King in Boston.

Thank you, Mohammad. You proved that you were different from all those other aides, who only tried to obstruct my progress.

❧ ❧ ❧

The day of registration, on the third of February 1962, turned out to be one of the most difficult days I ever experienced. First, I received about eleven cards I had to fill in, all with the same required information. Why American universities had so many cards I never even tried to find out. Looking back, I am sure that some students thought I was some kind of an idiot when, as a result, every time someone asked me a question I said, "My name is Faisal S. Bashir, freshman, economics major." Those cards seemed to me like eleven stages of drilling, to ensure I did not forget my name and address.

The second problem was my interpretation of my major. I thought it meant that all my courses should be in economics. Therefore, I went straight to the economics registration desk and asked for departmental approval of my selections. The man in charge told me, "You cannot register in economics now."

I said, "Why? I am an economics major."

"But" he said, "you are a freshman who is required to take other courses. You will be lucky if you take any economic courses before completing one year."

I protested and left, saying I would return to show him who was right.

It took Mr. Wilson a great deal of time to convince me the man was right, with a long lecture on the American system of college education. Later, I visited the so-called "trouble office" so many times that I believe I beat any previous record. Seven hectic hours passed before my registration was complete.

My first encounter with college education was indeed not a pleasant one. Application to an American university and the subsequent registration are almost too much for a foreigner to comprehend.

In my case, the difficulties increased because I was a Bedouin. Some questions were (and remain) hard to answer, because all application and registration materials were geared toward American students. It took me a long time, once, to prove to a university that my answers on the application form were real and not jokes. Still, I am not sure that the university's admission office ever believed me.

Some of the questions which raised the university's suspicions were as follows:

> *Question 1: Write your full name (Christian, middle, and surname).*
> *Answer: I never heard of a Christian or surname.*

I was obliged to write a long paragraph, on a separate sheet of paper, to explain my answer. First, I said, I have no Christian name, but I have a Muslim one (thinking that by "Christian" they meant the religion). For my surname I wrote that I did not understand what that meant. But I added my family name was Al-Bashir.

> *Question 2: Did either of your parents ever attend the University?*
> *Answer: No.*
> *Question 3: Are your parents college graduates?*
> *Answer: They are illiterate. They cannot even read or write their own names in their own language.*

The university thought I was joking about that, but this was the truth of the matter. Some admission officers apparently think that no one will succeed in college unless one of his parents is an Oxford or Harvard graduate.

> *Question 4: What is your parental address?*
> *Answer: The desert of Saudi Arabia.*

University officials thought I was out of my mind when I insisted that my parents had no address except the one I had stated. They found it hard to comprehend, but for me it was as logical as the validity of life and death. Sfouq and his wife, the parents of Faisal S. Bashir, never had any other address.

One form insisted that I give their zip code. I wrote, "Sorry, this is all I have."

> *Question 5: Were you ever a member of a Greek house (fraternity or sorority)?*
>
> *Answer: I am a member of Al-Sba'a Tribe, that is all. What is a Greek house?*

Again, some admission officials were astonished.

> *Question 6: Are you or your parents active in your city affairs?*
>
> *Answer: We have no city. My parents and I are nomadic. One day we are in X location. One week later in Y location. Please do understand my problems.*

After all my trouble with those questions, I came to the conclusion that American universities should have some materials applicable for foreigners as well as for Americans. I am sure that my case was somewhat special, but many other foreigners also found the university application and registration materials difficult to answer.

♆ ♆ ♆

The first thing that caught my attention in freshman classes was that I was almost the oldest student there. At the age of 21, I was supposed to be at least a senior by American standards. My age, compared to my classmates, no doubt gave me some sense of unease. But every time I discussed something with them, I realized that I was ahead of almost all of them. The educational level of a Howard University freshman, seemed equivalent to mine when I was in the eleventh grade in high school. And I believe that was the case for most American freshmen. However, what sometimes made my classmates' performance better than mine was their superior English ability, and their preparation for the examinations we had to take, which were supposedly objective, and which were alien to me.

Those exams were a stumbling block. I tried very hard to convince the Office of Admissions that courses such as general social science, college mathematics, and general physics, etc., were courses I already had taken in high school. To me, it seemed better that I occupy my time with something more useful. My mathematics teacher strongly supported me, when she realized that I was doing almost perfect work. I always failed to convince Howard University officials of this, however, because a so-called objective test was the only way for them to evaluate my ability.

That kind of examination, as far as I am concerned, was (and remains) the worst means to measure a student's ability, but mass education needs it, and so the American education system sticks to it. I argued many times that in objective tests answers were always available. The student need write nothing more than yes or no. In my eyes, this was a disgraceful system of examination. And I believe I paid dearly in grades, because I was so often forced to take that kind of test, which I had never seen or been subject to in my life.

My lack of respect for that kind of test increased every time some professor gave a short essay examination, in which I usually came out on top. With an objective test I was always around average, no matter what I did or how hard I worked.

9
—
BEDOUIN PLAYBOY

In my first semester at Howard University, social life was un-known to me. During that entire semester, from February 3 to June 15, 1962, only once did I leave the campus to wander in the city. That was a mistake. It was due to my timidity, and my realization that I had no time to waste on entertainment.

One day I happened to see the dome of the Capitol Building and thought it was within walking distance. When I reached the Capitol, I continued to walk without knowing where I was going. In the end I was so exhausted that I entered a movie house. The movie was typically American. Doris Day played the heroine.

The Foreign Students Office tried to help with my nonexistent social life—but I was uncooperative, and so life went on. I was as lonely as a Bedouin in the vast desert of Saudi Arabia.

I recognized early on that the student body at Howard University was predominantly black. Almost completely financed by the federal government, Howard was also the only federal university in the United States.

Being at a predominantly African American university did not affect me in any way. However, I began to notice the race issue for the first time in my life. From talking with students and officials of that university, the race issue in the United States, with all its ugliness, became very clear.

Later, eventually, when I had made friends, I came face-to-face with segregation. I was with a group, mostly of young women who were students at Howard. We went to a restaurant we had been to many times without incident, and somehow, for whatever reason, the proprietor tried to turn them away, saying it was because they were black.

I would not stand for that. I knew the building was on federal property, and I knew the law did not allow for discrimination. I said as much to him, and he backed down. It was a small victory.

What amazed me most was that among the black students there was some kind of division. Those Black students with relatively lighter skin clustered together, while those with darker skin established their own groups. This was especially apparent in the university cafeteria.

I will not forget the frustration of a single girl at Howard due to the race issue. She was as blonde as Marilyn Monroe, white in all aspects of her features, but in some way that was unclear to me, she was African American. I never saw that girl date or even walk with a Black boy, nor did I see her chatting with a White boy. Her circle in the cafeteria was composed mostly of girls with very light skin who were also Black. She was frustrated and lonely, but she put on an artificial act to show everyone that she did not care.

I realized later that she was a "swinger" behind the scenes, but in public, she wasn't specifically associated with any particular group. In a way, I did not blame her. If she walked with a White student, she was subject to being called by all kinds of bad names by African Americans who knew her. If she walked with a Black student, she would be accused by the White students. As a result, that girl lived in her own world, on an isolated island between Black and White races.

One day, she and her group of two other girls joined my table. I think they did it because they realized that no harm would come from being seen with a student who almost never talked to any girl, regardless of her race.

After dinner, Her Highness (the blonde girl) took out a cigarette and waited for me to light it for her. Well, I told her that I was sorry, I did not smoke, and I had no match. After that the conversation continued and one girl asked me if I drank. I said, "No."

Then came, "Do you dance?"

Again, I said "No."

I am sure those girls were shocked and began to wonder what kind of human being I was.

To break the ice, so to speak, I asked them why they did not ask me the last and most logical question. All of them waited to hear what I wanted to say.

I said the final question should be, "Why am I alive?"

When I uttered those words, all three of the girls went into hysterics. We laughed so much that some students began to wonder what had happened.

The blonde and her group became my closest friends in the cafeteria after that encounter, but I made no move to date any one of them. I believe they liked that arrangement.

ψ ψ ψ

My grades that first semester were above average. No one felt as happy about that as Mr. Wilson, who encouraged me all the way.

I enrolled in the summer session of 1962, but I moved from the dormitory to live permanently at the International Student House. I was the only student from Saudi Arabia living there. Most of the others were graduates, especially the girls. There were about 33 students from all over the world. I believe that I was the only freshman, but I was still older than almost all of the graduate girls.

Nevertheless, I convinced myself that dating them would be unthinkable, as I believed that a graduate girl would not accept a date with an old freshman.

Such feelings never led me to withdraw from lively discussions in the house. On the contrary, I was actively involved in most of the social activities there, and I believe that I was generally liked by most people in the house.

The girls began to accuse me of rigidity, due to not dating any girl. They never realized that my restraint from dating was due to my inferiority complex, stemming from my classification as a freshman. My lack of action in this regard began to be interpreted as some kind of superiority complex, as if I thought no girl in the house was worth dating.

I was very happy, in a way, to hear what was circulating about me among the girls. Their attacks increased when they realized that I came from a nomadic tribe where women were not considered equal to men, although this was certainly not my own view. They took the respectful distance I kept from them to mean something it did not really mean.

Life in the house continued, with an undeclared war between Faisal and most of the girls, until Mrs. Becker, director of the house, who had been an instructor of sociology at the University of Wisconsin, noticed what was going on. One day, she told me, "Faisal, you are sociable, friendly, and have a good sense of humor, but I have not seen you date any girls."

I gave her all kinds of excuses, but not the true one concerning how I felt to be a freshman at that age. I stressed that I was the least secure in the house financially, and that besides, I did not have the time to date. Mrs. Becker lectured me on the advantages of dating as a means of socializing, and as a safety valve to free my mind from my personal problems.

Mrs. Becker was right—and let me emphasize here, for the credit of that dear lady, that she never intervened in our personal lives in that house. I noticed that she understood my problems at an early stage and began to offer help. My relationship with that woman developed into a wonderful friendship. I began to consider her as the next best thing to a mother that I had.

Dear Mrs. Becker (Mrs. Curti, now), thank you very much for all the help you offered to develop my personality and to utilize its potential in very constructive ways. I believe that you were a great lady and a dignified one, who was the best-equipped to be the director of that international house.

𝔴 𝔴 𝔴

Living in that small house was quite an experience for me, and for everyone else in it. Residents there had many social as well as educational activities to choose from. The house, as far as I was concerned, became like a laboratory, in which I learned much and was introduced to many great personalities, such as Supreme Court justices, senators, ambassadors and ministers.

In addition to all those advantages of living in the house, there was one disadvantage. Because the house was small, rumors (especially personal ones) spread all over, as if a gossip machine existed somewhere within it.

"Miss X is going steady with Mr. Y, who is determined to marry her," one rumor said.

"Mr. Z almost committed suicide last night because Miss M refused to date him anymore," another rumor went.

I once told a British student, who was living in the house, that our quiet place was going to explode someday from those rumors. They began to scare me, although I was the least affected by them.

I began to wonder what would happen if I dated a girl. Might not someone start rumors around an innocent date? I was ready to accept those which were true, but what if a false personal rumor started around me?

Life went on, despite all those rumors, and I drifted on the edges of the mainstream. I always tried to avoid being a target for gossip. To live in peace one has to convince others to let him do so. No

matter what an individual's intentions, his actions must be accepted by others to symbolize his desire to be left alone and to live the
life he likes.

☙ ☙ ☙

Very soon (the middle of the fall semester, 1962–1963, to be exact), I realized that no matter what I did, my dear friends in the
house would not accept my policy of peaceful coexistence with
everyone.

One day, while Mrs. Becker and I were discussing some international problems. I changed the topic to tell her how much I loved
the house and how much I wished rumors were not a part of it.

Mrs. Becker was aware of what was going on. She told me, "Faisal,
this is life. We have to accept it the way it exists, and try to modify
it and adjust it, if we can, to serve a happy world."

That was the advice which encouraged Faisal the Bedouin to jump
deep into social life, including dating. That was the advice which
gave me much satisfaction and made me a more balanced person.
That was the advice which, when I pushed it to the extreme, almost
completely destroyed me, and with me the goal that I left my family, country, and tribe to fulfill.

I was very deliberate about my full entry into social life at the International House.

I decided first to make myself a target for rumors. Accordingly, I
began employing tactics to prove to everyone that I was capable of
dating girls.

Competition among the boys in that house was very high—and,
I have to make clear, I joined while I was in a disadvantageous position. Most boys were graduates, and (this is not the "modesty of
the artist") I was the least handsome among them. But I decided
that with a little bit of luck and good tactics I should prove myself
at receiving girls' attention.

127

I was frank in my discussions, and a teaser at the highest level. These two characteristics helped me greatly and threw many girls off-balance when they were trying to judge what kind of a person I was.

Many times, I voiced my objections to equality between men and women, in a joking fashion. However, many girls thought that I was serious, and they described me as the only student in the house who really disrespected women. On the contrary, other girls thought that I was the most friendly and sociable person in the whole house. I let those two impressions of my character spread among the boys as well as the girls, while I was planning my future moves.

Dear reader, I have to certify now that I did not make a single date without projecting what kind of consequences, reputation-wise, I would get from it. I have to admit now that I did not date a single girl without pre planning or without wanting to prove to others that I was capable of dating any girl around. I was indeed very deliberate as I went about this.

There was only one date in my life (much later, around August 1964) where no planning was made and every aspect of it was innocent. It happened that I never dated any other girl after that date—and I will describe it later.

But one day an American girl came and sat beside me. She was called Elizabeth, and was the roommate of Ibtisam, an Iraqi girl who lived in the house. Elizabeth was an intelligent college graduate, and very good-looking. She began the conversation by asking me, because I was an Arab, why Ibtisam did not go out on dates.

I told her that the background Ibtisam came from, and the environment she lived in, did not encourage dating. I said that Ibtisam was acting according to the traditions of an Iraqi environment.

Elizabeth was, in a way, moved by my friendly explanation that avoided attacking Ibtisam. She said, "You talk rationally about Ibtisam, while she says so much against you."

I let Elizabeth continue talking, listening carefully. Soon I realized that Ibtisam considered me to be the least desirable student to date, or even to know as an acquaintance.

When Elizabeth finished talking, she was astonished to find me smiling. To her amazement, I added that I agreed with what Ibtisam had said. I went ahead to tell Elizabeth that I was the least secure financially in the house, a Bedouin, and an undergraduate. I added that, in the final analysis, I couldn't care less about Ibtisam—"period."

I left the whole matter at that stage and waited.

From all the boys in the house, I began to hear that Ibtisam was the only girl who did not date anyone. According to them, the cleverest boy would be the one who could date her first.

And so I established my plan to prove to everyone that Ibtisam was not immune to dating, despite the way she acted.

One Sunday afternoon, most of the Arab students and students of other nationalities gathered in a small group in the house. The discussion eventually reached the status of women in Arab society.

Ibtisam was passionate about this, and she spoke on the subject freely. But she was so arrogant in her arguments that she became blind and unobjective. She all but concluded, in discussing the subject, that all blame for how things were must be laid at the feet of Arab men, and that women were doing their best to upgrade their social position. She presented the matter as a state of constant warfare between the sexes, in which men were always winning, and women were always losing.

A Syrian graduate student, who was majoring in linguistics, tried to persuade Ibtisam to be more objective in her accusations against

Arab men. But she was too stubborn to even listen, and continued to blame men in Arab society for all social ills. Ibtisam almost dominated the whole discussion, and I sincerely felt that she was just trying to impress non-Arab listeners.

At that stage, I decided to participate and even to counter Ibtisam, regardless of consequences.

The first thing I said was that it was unobjective and useless to lay all the blame on either men or women, regarding the status of women in the Arab world.

I told Ibtisam that she ought to blame the women as well as the men. I went on to state examples of how environmental effects on men and women hindered, in a way, the establishment of a healthy Arab society that respected women and upgraded their status.

Everyone except Ibtisam was interested in what I said, and quiet prevailed at that point in the discussion. Then I realized that I had to disturb Ibtisam, either to catch her interest or to force her to make a fool of herself in front of everyone.

I told Ibtisam, "Look at yourself. What have you done so far to be a positive factor in establishing a better relationship between males and females in the house? You Arab women, and especially the educated ones, have very little to offer. Most of your offerings are no more than superficial appearances, mostly negative in consequence, and yet you insist that the Arab man should and must respect you for them. Ibtisam, you are living in the United States, and you will go back to Iraq eventually. I bet you will say that you want Iraqi men to respect you and treat you as an equal. In reality, you will not have brought from the United States anything except a certificate and the idea that the status of women in the United States is much better than in the Arab world.

"I am sure that you will expect all that upon your return, forgetting how long it took women in the United States to reach this status.

Up to this day, I have not seen you going out, even with a group to have a cup of coffee in a cafe and to chat innocently. I don't blame you for that, because you educated Arab women always think that a man is no more than a monster who must not be trusted.

"I don't blame you personally, but I blame the environment which affected all of us so much. But I was expecting a much better analysis than that which you gave, because you are not only educated but also, to some extent, free from the Arab environment's effects and restrictions for the time being.

"What you lack, Ibtisam, is the same thing every other Arab girl lacks. You need to establish some confidence in yourself so that you can stand alone and fight against the so-called monstrous creation: man."

I was calculating as I said this. I was trying to get a certain reaction from Ibtisam and coax her onto the social scene she had avoided— but I was also sincere about every word I said.

Ibtisam, preparing to leave, began to accuse me personally. She even stated that because I was a Bedouin, and from Saudi Arabia, I was the least prepared to participate in such a discussion.

In other words, my strategy worked, Ibtisam made a fool of herself, and left the discussion boiling with anger.

As far as I was concerned, I believed that educated Arab women were the least active about the social ills of their society. They always complained and compared their miserable status to that of Western women, but when it came to concrete contributions to society's development, they shied away and vanished behind all the latest fashions and philosophical ideas they'd picked up somewhere from the surface of the Western world.

To me, the unobjective thinking of educated Arab women, coupled with the rigidity of the society's social structure (dominated by men), were the greatest obstacles to the establishment of a healthy and modern society in the Arab world.

Most of the non-Arab students agreed with me and respected what I said to Ibtisam. However, my "Arab brothers" thought that I was very harsh with her, and I suppose they were right. However, by then, her talking about me behind my back, and reductive thinking about the Arab world, had gotten under my skin.

I realized that most of those boys wanted to create the impression that they disagreed with me in order to win Ibtisam's friendship, but I reasoned, "Who cares?" I assumed that day there was no point for me to try to compete for a date with Ibtisam, or even for friendship with her.

Ibtisam was not a bad-looking girl. As a matter of fact, many people thought she was very attractive. There was no doubt that she had great style, and I am sure that she would have received high marks in any contest for the best-dressed woman. She was a brunette, about three years my senior.

Understandably, my relationship with Ibtisam after that encounter never led to more than a "Hello," and "How are you?" I felt that if I played my cards right, after the storm subsided, Ibtisam would be easy to date despite what she thought of me.

Thus, the struggle began, without telling anyone about my plan.

The first move I made was to go on a date with Elizabeth, Ibtisam's roommate, who was blonde and more attractive than Ibtisam. I planned my date carefully so that Ibtisam would be in the room when I came to take Elizabeth out.

After that, I dated another American girl and waited a while to let my reputation spread. My dating continued until I went out with every girl I thought worth dating except the Rock of Gibraltar (Ibtisam).

Girls who became friendly with me realized one thing about my character. What they told me about the others would be kept secret forever. So in addition to being the one who dated most of them, I became the keeper of their secrets. The knowledge I acquired about the feelings of each girl toward the others in the International Student House helped me immensely as I planned my moves.

"Mr. X thinks that because he is a Yale graduate, he must be entitled to date every girl," one girl told me.

Another girl confessed, "Ibtisam thinks that because she never dated anyone, she is more respectable than all the other girls."

Life went on until one day Ibtisam stopped me in a friendly way to tell me how much I had changed. She told me that I had become the first playboy in the history of the house. I laughed and told her I was glad to hear that, as long as being a playboy did not affect my studies.

I left her standing there, once I realized that at last I had aroused Gibraltar's interest.

In the evening, while we were at the dinner table, Ibtisam asked how to fill out the cards required annually of foreigners by the United States Immigration Office. I took the card, since I was sitting beside her. When I saw "Mr., Mrs., Miss" before the word "name," I told her quietly that I had no doubt that she would write her name preceded by "Mr."

She was really shocked by that at first. Her face changed color—but when she saw me smiling, she realized I was joking.

It was an undiplomatic joke, if I may say so myself, but it worked. I got the reaction from her that I had been looking for.

Day after day, Ibtisam showed more interest in going out, but I did not jump to ask her for a date. I restrained myself, to let Ibtisam get more and more frank about what she wanted. Throughout those days, I projected the impression that I was not interested at all in dating her. Many Arab students asked me about her, but I convinced all of them that I had nothing to do with Ibtisam.

One Sunday morning, while I was chatting with other girls at the breakfast table, Ibtisam came along. I invited her to join us, and after hesitating she accepted.

Ibtisam noticed in one of the newspapers that *West Side Story* was running at one of the movie houses in Washington, D.C. She said that she had not seen it although she had heard much about it. Everyone encouraged her to go to see it. I joined in by saying that I had seen it twice and that I also recommended it. When I left the breakfast table, I realized that an opportunity had arrived to ask her for a date. I really did not think she would accept, but I planned to try.

Sunday lunch in the house was usually a special time, and often outsiders came to dine with the residents. As I drank my juice before lunch, I noticed Ibtisam was alone and looking attractive. After a little hesitation, I joined her, to the astonishment of every house resident.

After a few moments, I raised my voice so nearby people would hear, and I said, "Ibtisam, today is the last day of *West Side Story* in Washington, D.C. You should see it. I am willing to take you and to keep you company. Ibtisam, this is an Arabic invitation, it is not a date." Before I finished, I said, "If you don't trust me, then call Elizabeth to go with us."

I left her standing alone as before. My last statement, I believe, somewhat aroused her jealousy.

While we were waiting for the bell to invite us to lunch, the telephone rang. Ibtisam answered it. The call was for me, from a Danish girl who insisted that I should join her for lunch. I accepted the offer, and left the house happy, because Ibtisam had received the call. Furthermore, I saw her smiling with curiosity the moment the "playboy" left the house.

"Faisal," I told myself, "you are really enlarging your circle of activity beyond the borders of the house. Watch out, fellow, and remember your studies." I reasoned later that, so far, my studies were going all right, and that there was no harm in enjoying life with young, beautiful, and sophisticated people. I lunched that day with the beautiful Danish girl in her apartment in one of the most exclusive buildings located at the end of Massachusetts Avenue across from American University. It was a very enjoyable occasion. I felt good and happy.

Before sunset, the Danish girl brought me home in her car. I went straight to bed, having forgotten all about my proposal to Ibtisam to take her to *West Side Story,* if she agreed to go. While I was asleep, one of the students called me to answer a telephone call. It was from Ibtisam, who thought she would not be able to go to the movie. I thanked her for telling me and went back to bed.

About half an hour later, I was disturbed by another telephone call. Again, it was from Ibtisam, who this time told me that she and Elizabeth had agreed to go if it was not too late. I said, "Oh, no. Be ready at 7:30 p.m. in the entrance hall."

At the appointed time, Faisal the Bedouin left the house, accompanied by two girls, a blonde and a brunette. I imagined that I looked exactly like a rich sheikh who had his harem with him. Elizabeth and Ibtisam looked fantastically well-dressed and beautiful, as if they were going to a party at the White House.

The movie impressed Ibtisam. She tried repeatedly to talk with me in Arabic, but I discouraged her on the grounds that Elizabeth would not understand.

Afterwards, Faisal and his harem left, laughing and chatting. We were really enjoying our time. Elizabeth was amazed to see Ibtisam acting in such a human way. She told me that she never thought Ibtisam would agree to join us. I smiled and said, "Wait for the day when Ibtisam will be a real swinger."

Around 12:30 a.m., we entered the house and found a British student standing in the hall. The moment he talked, I realized that he was up high somewhere. He said, "Really, Faisal, you look exactly like an Arab surrounded by his harem. Here you have the two most lovely girls in the house, while most of us were not able to take out anyone." I assured him that going with the two lovely girls was disadvantageous in a way, but I really enjoyed their company. We left our poor British fellow drunk in the hall, speaking out about the injustice of the world, which gave Faisal a chance to go out with two girls when he could not manage to have one.

In the morning, the whole episode was all over the house. "Ibtisam went out with Faisal last night." Some even forgot to mention that we were not alone.

I had scored a direct hit, and my prestige among boys as well as girls rose. Boys became suspicious of my secrecy, especially the British one, who every weekend would say, "Watch that Bedouin. Whom will he date this week?"

The next day, Ibtisam came to thank me for the enjoyable evening. I told her in a kidding way, "See, even a Bedouin will not attack you."

She laughed and apologized for all past accusations.

No one was more jealous of my going with Ibtisam than my "Arab brothers," especially an Iraqi student who was a failure in school. They accused me of cheating them by not telling them about my true intentions toward Ibtisam; I countered that Ibtisam was free to date whom she wanted, and that every boy in that house was also free to ask any girl for a date. Furthermore, I told the Arab students that my date was mainly for Elizabeth and not for Ibtisam.

In a way, I misled the Arab students into thinking that I had used Ibtisam as a cover to convince Elizabeth, with whom I happened to have had some disagreement, to go with me. I planned all that deceptive talk in hopes that it would reach Ibtisam and increase her desire to date me alone.

The Iraqi fellow did what I expected and told Ibtisam. She played it down and showed him no sign of hatred toward me and my Machiavellian approaches.

After that night, Ibtisam and I were sometimes seen alone in the main hall, talking. The news of this spread until it reached the Iraqi Embassy, which warned Ibtisam directly to keep from getting involved with me.

When she told me about the warning, I was not impressed. I told her to assure everyone that, first of all, I never went out with her except once, accompanied by another girl. Second, that I was not in a position to get involved seriously with any girl before I finished my college degree, which might take longer than average, due to my financial insecurity.

I was so direct with her that I annoyed her. When I finished, she was just as direct in response. She told me that in reality she was not interested in me, and that I should always keep that in mind.

And so there followed a period of coolness between us. Nevertheless, she was always watching me, and later she became furious when I began to date Elizabeth steadily. One day, she stopped me to reveal all the things the Iraqi student told her about me. She added that, as a matter of fact, she had come to realize exactly what kind of a person I was—not only a cheater, but also a deceiver, and a tricky one.

Boy, that was the first blast I received from her, but it was a good and reassuring one. After I heard it, I was sure that she would agree instantly if I asked her to date me steadily. That conclusion was later confirmed.

10

THE GREAT SALESMAN

In the middle of the spring semester of 1963, I realized to my discomfort that I had only a few dollars left for my education. I began to worry, and at the same time reduced my going out on the weekends. This was not because those occasions were costing me great sums of money, but rather was due to my realization that I would not enjoy the time I spent going out.

I started to write letters to my family, asking for help. But all I received was $400.00 from my oldest cousin Traad.

That made me happy, especially when it was used to settle my account with the house. I continued to write to the family, emphasizing that life was extremely expensive in the United States—but no more help ever came.

I was compelled to shift my target, and so I began to write the Saudi Arabian Educational Mission in New York City. No help or assistance followed. It seemed there was no chance of a scholarship, despite my good grade point average. By June 15, 1963, I faced the reality that school was financially inaccessible in the summer session. Faisal began to look for a job, to earn a living and to get educated.

Ibtisam's mother came from Iraq around April 1963, and so the girl left the house to live with her in a nearby apartment. Her visits to the house became rare, but she called me more on the telephone.

I went many times to see her and her mother, but Ibtisam noticed many old qualities were missing. Gone was my sense of humor, and almost gone was my confidence about the future. Worried expressions appeared on my face every time I talked about it. I told them about my financial problems, and how it was a necessity for me to try to find a job. Ibtisam was very considerate and told me she felt everything would be all right.

That feeling took a long time to materialize. I told Mrs. Becker about my financial problems and asked her to postpone the payment of my monthly bill until I found a job. She agreed and encouraged me not to feel so depressed. I looked for any job available but failed to secure one.

One morning, when I was reading the ads in *The Washington Post,* I saw, "$400.00 a month guaranteed for college students regardless of their qualifications." I went straight to the advertised address, only to end up in the Washington, D.C., office of the publisher of an encyclopedia.

I was surprised to find about 40 students listening to a man who was lecturing and shouting. When the lecturer recognized me as a foreigner, he said for everyone to hear, "Oh boy, you are going to make a lot of money, because Americans like to hear a foreign accent."

I had no idea what he was talking about.

That lecturer, who called himself Harper (later, we found out this was not his real name), was an absolute nut, a master of all the Madison Avenue gimmicks and of double-talking. He threw out all kinds of promises and supported them with fabricated incidents from the past: John from Cornell made $3,000 in two months' sales; William from UCLA was not so determined a fellow; he did not work the whole summer, but he made about $2,000 dollars in one month; he lost a big opportunity to collect more bucks; he had a good future as a salesman.

The great lecturer continued while all of us listened and dreamed how we would make our first thousand "bucks." Boy, it is really easy to earn money in the United States, I told myself.

However, our great, big-mouthed lecturer never gave us the chance to cool off and to try to examine what he was saying. He continued to show us pictures of students who had made such and such thousands. This is Peterson, who bought that sporty car beside him within two months of work. Not only that, but he also earned some extra "dough."

Harper even had a commentary directly relating to me. "Faisal, look at this picture. It is a Turkish fellow who saved $3,000 to go to school and bought a very dependable secondhand car with an additional $2,000. All this from the work of just one summer. Faisal, remember that the Turkish fellow did all that while his English was worse than yours."

I felt like I was up in the sky, and so did all those other students from all over the United States. My first day in that laboratory of brainwashing was full of dreams. I was sure that I would get rich in a maximum of three months, and that my school expenses would take only a small percentage of my total earnings. It never occurred to me, during those early days, that what I heard was no more than sales talk and promises, supported with data that were mostly lies or exaggeration.

For three days, we were drilled to be the best salesmen the United States had ever had. And Harper was sure that most of us were going to be the foundation of the most progressive sales activities that the company had ever seen.

By the last day of our drillings, I was so impatient that I asked Harper when we were going to "hit the road." That question, to my dismay, gave our great lecturer a take-off point for at least one more hour's talk.

He began by using me as an example. "This is a man who is ready and really hungry to get started. This is the young man who is going to make such and such thousands of dollars. He is the man, because he is already beginning to use the language of great salesmen, when we hit the road." At the end of his lecture he announced that "We will hit the road when each one of you signs these documents." He passed out the contracts, which everyone signed without even reading the terms.

ψ ψ ψ

The great salesmen of the future gathered the next day, ready for action. We were so formal that we appeared as if we were going to a board meeting of the Bank of America. Formal suits, ties, and black briefcases dominated the scene, though Washington's weather that day was very humid and warm. A British diplomat was right to describe his transfer to Washington, D.C., as a shift to tropical Africa. I cannot understand why the Americans picked that lousy location (as far as weather is concerned) as their capital.

In the summer of 1963, however, it was too late to change it. We salesmen had no choice but to comply with the regulations of our great company and to suffer, wearing those formal suits.

The next thing that caught my attention was the kind of cars we rode in. The field leader of my group drove a new convertible Lincoln Continental. He told us it was his and that it took him only two months of work in the field to pay for it. Other cars included a convertible Pontiac and a brand-new Cadillac.

The way our leaders spent money in restaurants was also impressive, a sign of wealth and therefore good sales. Every time we showed some puzzlement concerning money-handling, our leaders would tell us, "Money is no problem, as you will see very soon."

I began to entertain the idea that "very soon" I would be able to own a sports car and drive to school instead of riding the bus. Dreams, dreams, dreams—but they were all I had in those early days of my great adventure in becoming a successful salesman.

After three days in the field, training to watch how the leader recited the "presentation" we memorized, I was on my own.

I was the first to be dropped off from the Lincoln Continental beside a nice suburb of Virginia. It was around 4:00 p.m., but I was told not to start making calls until 5:00 p.m., when most people would be home from work. I would be picked up from the highway at 9:00 p.m.

And so, the soon-to-be greatest salesman that door-to-door sales ever saw started his work. Faisal S. Bashir (the Howard University admissions office had omitted the 'Al' in front of Bashir, on the grounds that almost every Arab's last name had it), the Bedouin from Saudi Arabia, once more became nomadic.

"Suburbia, U.S.A., blow your horns and welcome the marching Bedouin!"

As I crossed the distance between the main highway and the suburb, I thought about how many orders I would place for sets of encyclopaedias. I assured myself that it was possible there might not be any sales on my first night, but at least I was determined to make some presentations. Harper said, and I told myself, that great salesmen always started without selling anything the first day or even week of their great profession.

I realized I had already reached the town, so I rang the bell of the first house. When no one answered, I noted the address for a return call.

The second house had a car in front of it, which gave me a firm feeling that its occupants were present. A lady answered the bell, and according to the guidelines for our great profession, the thing to do in this case was to ask for the man of the house. Promptly I said, "Is the man of the house in?" When she answered with the affirmative, I told her to call him. She was so naïve that she asked me to come in. I entered and found the "man of the house" in the living room. He received me cordially, and this encouraged me to start right in with my presentation. Immediately, while both husband and wife were listening, I was asked what I would like to drink. But our guidebook said a salesman should refrain from drinking until he places an order.

As a result, I continued like a machine gun. The presentation was written so it began by giving the impression that we were giving publicity for a new product. But in the last paragraph it was clear that we were selling encyclopedias. As I opened my briefcase, to show the cover of the set, I said, "All this lovely set plus these gifts will cost you no more than five cents a day. Furthermore, we will be glad to give you the box for the coins free of charge." And I presented them with that change box.

At that point, the man of the house jumped and said, "Are you a salesman?" According to our manual I should have said, "No, I was just advertising," but I realized it was too late to deny that and so I replied simply, "Yes." He told me that they were not interested, and so I left that first house feeling good that I had at least completed my presentation. I had succeeded in keeping their interest until the last word.

This is the sign of great salesmanship, I thought. Harper said so.

At the third house I called upon, a man answered. When he saw me he laughed, and the following conversation took place:

> The man: We are not interested.
> Faisal: In what?
> The man: In whatever you have to sell.
> Faisal: Who said I am selling?
> The man: Then why are you here?
> Faisal: I am here to acquaint you with the best product you will ever hear of.
> The man: Then you are a salesman.
> Faisal: No, I am an advertiser.
> The man: It is the same.
> Faisal: Well, if you classify a salesman as one who advertises things freely (and I stressed freely), then your terminology

is mixed up. (Then I remembered that we were advised to be tough with such characters, and I left.)

The man: Hey, hold it. Come on and let us talk.

Thus, I entered the second house of my first working day. The man of the house was pressing me very hard to show him what I had in my briefcase. I refrained, until his wife joined us.

The presentation proceeded beautifully until the end. At that point the man realized that I truly was a salesman. He kicked me out of the house, amid his wife's protests and my insistence that I was not a salesman.

Well, Faisal, don't be discouraged. Somewhere in one of those lovely houses, your commission of sixty-five dollars is waiting for you.

I continued until 9:00 p.m., without a pause. When I went back to my pickup point, I thought that each of my colleagues must have placed at least one set while I sold nothing. I found the car waiting, and I reported to the leader that I had made two complete presentations. The leader was so happy that he congratulated me, telling me I was the luckiest one. Most of my colleagues had not even entered a single house.

I reached the International Student House around 11:00 p.m. on my first day of work. I told Mrs. Becker about my job. She was skeptical about it, but later agreed that $400.00, the guaranteed amount, was not bad.

And so, life continued. I usually started work around 1:00 p.m., and came back to the house sometime between 11:00 p.m. and 1:00 a.m. Our working hours depended heavily on where the leaders decided to drop us that day.

I began to imagine us future great salesmen as airborne troops parachuted in to disturb the tranquility of each suburb around the capital.

I was dropped off many times in West Virginia, Virginia, Maryland, and the District of Columbia. Eventually, the dreams of thousands of dollars began to evaporate behind slamming doors and the shouting of the man of the house, who realized that I was no more than a low-down door-to-door salesman. Every time I got discouraged, Harper, the great lecturer, would elevate my spirit by insisting that luck was just around the corner. I began to realize that the damn company was not losing a single penny in keeping the troops working for it, because the month was not yet ended so I could claim the guaranteed $400.00. My colleagues also began to show their anxieties, and some of them regretted not having taken jobs paying two dollars an hour.

Little by little, all us college students came to realize that we were no more than sheep, cheated by the promises of quickly getting all the money we needed. My confidence began to vanish with the end of each working day, until the moment arrived that revived every hope I had during the first, glorious days of dreaming.

While I was walking in a suburb of Baltimore, I saw a home with two Cadillacs in the driveway. I rang the bell, and a lady answered. When I asked her about the man of the house, she informed me that he had left for San Francisco, but that she was ready to answer all my questions. At that moment, I was really thirsty, and so I accepted her offer. She felt very sorry for me, and when she asked whether I was a salesman or not, I answered in the affirmative. I let her open my briefcase freely, without even trying any sales talk.

In the end, after a little discussion with her two high school-aged sons, she gave me a check for the price of a set. In return, I gave her a receipt and my grateful thanks. I had violated all principles of our so-called presentation—not talking to the lady of the house, and not admitting I was a salesman.

Before I received that check, I was determined to leave the job the moment the month ended, and I received my $400.00. After the check came in, though, I began to believe maybe my luck had just begun.

Upon reaching my pickup point, I was really happy. When I greeted the troops in the car the atmosphere was tense. Harper, who happened to be in the field that night, insisted that the failures of my colleagues were due to their lack of aggression. He did not even bother to ask the results of my efforts until the car began to move. When he heard what I said, he stopped the car immediately to congratulate me. He was more than pleased when he saw the check.

Overnight, Faisal the Bedouin broke a new record. Harper told everyone that even he had never gotten the whole price of a set in cash as I had done. The second set, ordered with only a small down payment, seemed just a minor detail at that point. The next day I received $165.00. The regular commission for two sales was $130.00; the balance was a bonus for getting one set's price in one shot.

Boy, I was really a hero. Harper and the manager of the company used me as an example to revive the spirit of the troops.

"Faisal, how did you do it?" the manager asked me in front of the class.

"It was easy, sir," I said.

"Yes, it is easy for all of you gentlemen to do exactly what Faisal did, if you just have the guts," the manager informed the class.

All those cheaters realized I was alive again. Harper took me aside and said, "Faisal, you did it. But if you want to do it every night, then shave off your moustache."

That moustache was so dear to me that I had stuck to it despite all my dear girl friends' encouragement to get rid of it. It was as much a part of me as the umbrella on the arm of a British gentleman in the rainy weather of London.

But if my moustache was the only obstacle to being a great sales-man, the hell with it. There went the moustache of Faisal S. Bashir, to serve the cause of great salesmanship.

ψ ψ ψ

My next working day was in Maryland again. At about 8:30 p.m., I rang the bell of an old lady who was disturbed to see me at that hour of the night.

She called the police. I ended up facing a justice of the peace, for disturbing the peace of her suburb and for trespassing without au-thorization.

Before I was picked up, a professor at the University of Maryland had advised me to quit the job on the grounds that it would not provide a good financial return. He was really sincere, but I was unconvinced.

In the police car, I almost laughed when I remembered the profes-sor's advice, and I heard the policeman say into his radio, "Chief, we got the fellow. He is no more than an arrogant door-to-door salesman without a permit."

At the police station, I insisted that I was an advertiser and not a salesman. One policeman was so perturbed by my denial that he begged the justice of the peace to put me behind bars. Well, I was allowed to call Harper, and he came and paid the fine.

On the way to Washington, I told Harper that I would never again go to an area where I was subject to possible arrest. I told him that my whole college education would be ruined if I got in trouble with the police. I might end up being deported from the United States. He agreed and promised to assign me to areas where the company really had permits.

Harper and his clique tried to stop news of my arrest from spread-ing among the troops, because the other students had also begun to worry about encounters with the police. After any such incident, the management would tell the individual involved that that one suburb in Maryland was a little touchy. Furthermore, they insisted that the company actually had a permit to work all over the eastern United States. That was a big lie, but who had the courage to say so when the end of the month was so near?

By some strange coincidence, another incident proved beyond a doubt that I was working illegally, and that I had better get out of the encyclopedia sales business before it was too late.

I was dropped off in Virginia and told to try calling on a Navy base. I asked our leader about the permit, and he assured me that the company had one for that location.

The first call I made was on the home of a Navy officer, who told me I had better get off the base or I would be subject to arrest. I told him that the company had a permit, but he insisted. I realized he was going to call the police, and so I vanished from the west side of the base to the east side, hoping I could find a way out.

Unfortunately for me, the military police were so fast that I was picked up again for the second time in 24 hours. The two military policemen were really impressed by my fast pace. One of them said, "Boy, you are really moving at the speed of a jet fighter." I laughed and told him that I was a Bedouin, trained to chase camels all over the desert.

The two policemen did not believe what I said until we reached the officer in charge. One of the policemen introduced me as follows: "This is the salesman who trespassed on the base, and who now claims that he was originally a camel driver." We laughed, and then I told them that the camel story was true, but that my company had falsely told me they had a permit for the base.

The officer in charge was very kind. He wrote a warning to the company and ordered the policemen to drop me off on the highway.

I continued to work hard until the end of the month. When I asked for my guaranteed $400.00, I received nothing. In answer to my protest, the manager offered me $50.00, which I rejected. I blasted each one of them in that office and promised to sue them in court. But later I realized that lawyer fees were too high for me. I was really in a desperate situation. One month of hard work, under the sun most of the time, produced no more than $165.00. That was really cheap labor, even by the standard wages of India. For the first time in my life, I realized that I had been cheated, and that really hurt me. I blamed no one more than myself and my stupid beliefs in such big promises.

Faisal S. Bashir, after one month of trial and error, attempting to be a great salesman, ended up as a big failure. The promises of thousands of dollars and a sporty car vanished. Neither the hard work, nor even the shaving of my moustache, averted the obvious conclusion that the soon-to-be rich and great salesman was destined to end up broke and unemployed.

ψ ψ ψ

During that whole month of hard work, Ibtisam kept in touch with me. She was happy to have her mother around, but at the same time she was at her greatest stage of frustration. Although she wanted me around her during all my free time, she lacked the courage to tell me why she desired my presence.

I did not help her, because I refused to accept half a solution. I was selfish to the highest degree, forced to be that way because of the hypocrisy of that girl who loved me so much but thought it was a disgrace to tell me so. I did not love her, but I continued to court her, due to my arrogance and stubborn determination to prove that Gibraltar was not impossible to conquer.

I wanted it known that Ibtisam was a hypocrite, and a good actress, who only projected herself as a confident girl, and who couldn't have cared less about any young man in the world. In a way we were like a pair of antagonists, neither one giving the other a chance to quit the fight without a total surrender.

Ibtisam was an ideal case for a psychologist who wanted to study a split personality. In front of people, she acted as if she did not care about me. But every night she would call to ask about me, and to stress how much she would like to see me. So, life went on and I found myself fighting on two fronts. One was Ibtisam and the other was the effort to find a job.

At the end of July 1963, while I was still job hunting, Ibtisam decided to invite all the Arab students of the house for an Arabian dinner. The moment I received the invitation, I decided to spoil Ibtisam's plan, which was obviously to force me to stay late after the other guests left. Cunningly, I called one of my old-time girlfriends from Boston. I asked her to call Ibtisam's apartment at a specific time if she wanted to have a date. She agreed.

By 5:30 p.m., the guests had arrived at Ibtisam's apartment. She was a good, gracious hostess and looked beautiful. The moment she saw me she came to chat with me.

All the Arab boys began to accuse me of some hidden motive in being so quiet, and Ibtisam joined their side. When they confronted me, I countered by saying that all of them had financial security, which I lacked. They were all sympathetic, and so the evening went on.

The moment we finished dinner, around 6:30 p.m., the telephone rang. Ibtisam's face changed and she handed me the receiver with a shaky hand. After a brief phone conversation, I excused myself, saying I had to leave.

Ibtisam insisted on seeing me off at the end of the corridor. I tried to persuade her to stay, maintaining that there was no need for that gesture. She refused to listen. I realized that Ibtisam was hurt and determined to give me a piece of her mind. We walked silently to our destination, and then she looked me straight in the eyes.

She was on the verge of crying. I immediately regretted my action, feeling sorry for her for the first time.

She broke the stillness by asking me whether this was another one of my tricks. I decided to be defensive, to avoid creating a mess while her guests were still in the apartment. I told her no and said that the girl who had called had first called the house to ask for me. The house, knowing where most of the Arab students were, gave this girl the telephone number. At the end of this explanation, I told her, "Well, I have to go."

Ibtisam was silent for a while, but when she spoke she was calmer than before. She said, "Faisal, either you are playing tricks, or you are intentionally avoiding an understanding of our situation. Faisal, can't you see that I am trying to divide myself between you and my mother? Don't you see how much I am trying to meet the two demands?"

I told her cruelly that as far as I was concerned, I had no part in her story. In response, she told me that I was pretending not to know, while in reality I knew what she meant. She was right, but I was too stubborn to accept anything except her total surrender.

At that point I decided to face her squarely and asked her, "Are you in love with me?"

That hypocritical girl said, "No, but I like you very much, and how much I wish that you were a graduate student."

At that moment I hated her intensely and decided to shock her. I told her, first of all, that I was not a graduate student and, secondly, that I was not her lover. So why should I involve myself in her problems?

Before I left, I told her she'd better begin looking for a rich graduate student and refrain from using cheap expressions such as "I like" when in reality she was lying about her true feelings. I left her standing alone, shaking and defeated.

๙ ๙ ๙

Before the first of August, I responded to an advertisement of "a 33 percent commission for all those who would like productive hard work and wanted to meet their urgent needs." It was signed, "Fuller Brush Company, McLean, Virginia." I had never heard of Fuller Brush in my life, and I thought this might be an indoor job. But when I reached the company, I realized I would be doing the same lousy door-to-door work as before.

Having no other choice, I accepted the position. The evening of that same day, my field manager came to the house with all the samples I needed. He was in his late forties, and a very friendly person, as a good salesman should be. Mac was his name, and his face often flashed a smile. As far as I was concerned, salesmen's faces were made of plastic, to stretch and retract according to the situation. I began to hate their smiles, their big talk, and their promises.

When Mac began to give me the same damn promises, and to employ gimmicks identical to what I had heard with the encyclopedia brainwashing, I interrupted him. I told him, "Mac, what I want is not to get rich in one month but only to collect sufficient money to cover fees for the fall semester. Mac, please don't give me all those damn promises, because I am fed up with them."

He was astonished but watched me quietly and let me continue. To convince him that I had really been brainwashed, I recited the encyclopedia presentation without a mistake. I was really emotional while doing so, because it was proof of my failure and stupidity.

I had once believed that all those lies were true. This time I was extremely careful not to be hooked again. At the end of all that acting in front of Mac, including imaginary moves, to open my briefcase, I said, "See, Mac, I was cheated once, but I am determined not to be so stupid again."

It turned out that Mac was an honest and sincere person. He realized I was in a desperate situation, and that I was ready to live at a mere subsistence level while I was going to college. After that, he never tried to tell me anything except the formal details about my future job. The next morning, he came to show me how to sell, assuring me that his company's products were in demand, in contrast to the encyclopedia. He told me that sales were no problem at all.

I kept quiet and walked beside him, again wearing my formal suit in that humid weather of Washington, D.C. He was perspiring heavily, and when he looked at me he was amazed. I looked perfectly cool and clean-cut.

Mac protested by saying, "Faisal, don't you feel this damn heat?"

I said, "Yes. But you have to recognize that I was born in and lived many years in the desert of Saudi Arabia, where God gave us plentiful heat as well as oil. That helps me resist the heat more than you."

He laughed and assured me I would be a great Fuller Brush man. I let that statement pass without any comment.

While we were walking, Mac repeated over and over that he would place the first order within ten minutes and that I had better watch carefully.

When he rang the bell of the first home, a woman opened the door. Mac said, "Hi, I am your Fuller Brush man, just happened to pass..." Before he completed his sentence, the door slammed in our faces.

I almost laughed, but I controlled myself so as not to hurt Mac, who was really angry. His only comment was that he was sure that the woman had fought with her husband at breakfast.

The next house was the second test. "Hi, I am your Fuller Brush Man and I happened to be passing this area and I remembered you as one of my good, old clients. So, I said to myself, why not stop to see whether you are in need of our good Fuller Brush products?"

At least he completed his presentation and had a chance to show his flashy smiles. They vanished as the lady slammed her door, exclaiming that she never used Fuller Brush products and couldn't care less about having them.

To make a long story short, we finished calling on almost all the houses on that street without placing an order. Mac's confidence began to slip with every door's slam and each potential customer's rough words. His last comment before he left me was, "Jesus, what happened to this world? No one wants good Fuller Brush products? Maybe this neighborhood is full of ladies who wear wigs instead of natural hair."

I laughed, and Mac left me to fight it alone without the benefit of having seen him place a single order. What a living, to be a door-to-door salesman!

ꖛ ꖛ ꖛ

Carrying my fancy briefcase, I headed back to the International Student House.

The evening of my first day with Fuller Brush, I was luckier than Mac. The lady at the first house I called upon was polite. When I said, "Hi, I am your Fuller Brush man," she interrupted me and said, "Oh, yes, come in." Well, she placed an order worth about $15.00. I promised delivery within one week and left.

Immediately, I calculated my share of the first order. I continued this practice every time I made a sale for good Fuller Brush products.

At sunset, after having worked two and a half hours, I calculated my total sales as about $60.00. I felt happy when I realized that my share would be around $20.00. Recalling my encyclopedia work, I regretted more than ever all that wasted time. How I wished that I had started with Fuller Brush from the beginning.

My main area of work was to the west, south, and north of Connecticut Avenue. However, I passed the area between 14th Street and Connecticut Avenue many times. I realized that the district was poor and had the lowest volume of sales, compared to the walking that was required.

Being a Fuller Brush man, I entered every kind of house in Washington, D.C. I was really amazed by the differences in living standards from one house to another. I realized for the first time that the United States was not only the shiny buildings of New York City and wide, clean streets such as Connecticut Avenue in Washington, D. C.

To me, at that time, the United States became more like every other country in the world. It has the rich, the very rich, the middle class, and the very poor. I was really shocked to notice that not only did poverty exist in the United States, but that it existed in the capital of that great nation.

Some lived in big houses where the cost of maintaining a pet exceeded the cost of living for a person in some apartment houses. The phrase, "I cannot afford to have a Fuller Brush broom to clean the house," began to ring in my ears. The echo might hardly have died before I next received a fat order for a single item, such as a shaving brush, worth $25.00.

I saw that the society of the United States, like other societies, is full of hypocrites. Some of the non-customers who declared that they could not afford a broom to clean their houses, had empty whisky bottles all around them. Others offering the same excuse went ahead and placed orders worth much more than the equivalent of ten brooms for cosmetics and other beauty items.

My door-to-door sales experience introduced me for the first time to the reality that poverty and uneven income distribution do exist in the United States. And while these qualities are present all over the world, many other countries are poor. The United States is a rich country that can afford to relieve its poverty, economically speaking, with very little capital, compared to other expenditures.

One department in the United States government at that time spent at least $70 billion a year. Considering this, it seems amazing that part of its population is living at the poverty level.

☙ ☙ ☙

Fuller Brush work was easy, compared to the encyclopedia trade. But the challenge was with how to distribute the goods to my customers. I did not have a car, and so I was obliged to carry the goods on my shoulders. I refused to pay for taxis, because that means of distribution was too expensive for me.

My reputation among my customers was great, mainly because I kept my promises about delivery dates, most of the time. Life went on, full of interesting incidents and new experiences. Once, I decided to invade the diplomatic area around Massachusetts Avenue. The first house I approached belonged to a Latin American diplomat. The servant, seeing my briefcase and formal dress, ushered me to his employer immediately.

His boss was at ease, enjoying a drink in his backyard. The great diplomat was shocked to see me because he was wearing only Bermuda shorts. He began to talk with his servant in Spanish, which I did not understand.

What had helped me enter, in addition to my diplomatic appearance, was the servant's assumption that I was some kind of Latin American citizen. People in D.C. often mistook me for either a Spaniard or a Latin American. The diplomat offered me a seat and tried to persuade me to have a drink with him, but I refused. I realized that his English was extremely bad, and that communicating with him would prove to be a challenge. Nevertheless, he was interested in my conversation, because I repeated the words "Fuller Brush" so often. I am sure he thought that "Fuller Brush" was some kind of secret code that he should recognize. But when I opened my briefcase and offered him the catalog, he was shocked to see it full of cosmetic product names.

Immediately, he asked me to leave, and was so angry that he went with me to the door to make sure that I left the house.

After walking about 200 yards, I looked back, only to see the diplomat still watching me. I believe now that he did not believe I was a salesman. He probably suspected that I was some kind of secret agent, perhaps even a "007." I laughed inside, and began to repeat, "Oh, my dear diplomats, it is not only you who look well-groomed and have flashy smiles. We salesmen are like you. We all have one thing in common, putting on an artificial image to reach a fixed target."

I decided I had better terminate my work for the day. I turned toward the house, but while I was walking around Dupont Circle, I decided to call on a few apartments along the way. On the second floor of one of the apartment buildings, I saw a sign on the door, "Enter at Your Own Risk." Well, I entered and found a lovely young woman crying. She was stunned and asked how I had entered. I said, "Well, the door was open and the sign was a clear invitation." After learning who I was, she placed an order worth about $10.00. Before I left the apartment, I asked her why she had been crying.

She said, "My stupid boyfriend just decided to break up with me after I came all the way to Washington especially to be with him." She was really a lovely girl, but I decided to leave, because she was not in a mood to date anyone, not even Faisal the great Fuller Brush man.

☙ ☙ ☙

Back at the International Student House, I got the idea that it would be nice to take a date to see the film *Lawrence of Arabia*.

It was my third time seeing that movie, which was absolutely first-class as far as sound, music, and scenery were concerned. Even so, I felt sick every time I saw how Hollywood changed the historical facts and Arab traditions for modern consumption.

I derived this feeling from many aspects of the film, and I could go into detail about them. But what struck me this time was the way in which the region I called home was depicted as a uniformly vast desert, a landscape of rolling dunes. The reality is, parts of Saudi Arabia do look that way, and I recognized the environment of the film from my youth.

But the whole region is not composed strictly of sand dunes. Some of the mountains look like Switzerland. I remember, later, when I returned to Saudi Arabia, meeting a South Korean executive who could not believe his eyes, could not believe that those mountains were in Saudi Arabia, a country that also boasted the largest dam in the Middle East.

It was a complicated thing, to watch *Lawrence of Arabia*, a film depicting my home, as I sat in a movie theater in the United States. It was false, but it was beautiful, and as soon as my third viewing of it was over, I knew I would go out and see it again.

11

—

THE PAUPER PRINCE

I heard that all the residents of the house had been invited for dinner at the Hecht Company, a department store on 7th Street. I joined the crowd, hoping that somehow, I would get a date. Ibtisam was not on my mind, and I had almost forgotten her since our encounter after her own dinner. As far as the Hecht Company affair was concerned, I was sure that she was not invited because, a) she was not a resident of the house, and b) she could not leave her mother too long at night.

At any rate, I was wrong. While I was talking to some of the Hecht Company people, I saw Ibtisam come directly to join the group I was with. I was really surprised to see her behaving so friendly, and I gave numerous excuses when she asked why I did not see her and her mother as before.

When dinner was served, Ibtisam and I sat at a separate table with the company people with whom we had been talking. I realized immediately that I was stuck with Ibtisam, and that if I wanted a date I had better move fast and solicit the consent of one of the girls at another table.

While we were drinking coffee, I excused myself and went straight to a table where many boys were surrounding a few girls. Among them was a lovely and beautiful girl from the state of Maine with whom I had a casual acquaintance. My approach to her was to take the empty sugar bag she had used for her coffee and to write on it: *Lawrence of Arabia*. She read it and, with a smile, agreed to the date. The other boys were really surprised to see what happened, because most of them were waiting for the right moment to ask her for a date themselves. Well, they were too late, and I went very happily to the former group, which included Ibtisam.

Ibtisam saw my movements and grew suspicious as to what had transpired.

After the dinner, the company officials began to show us their establishment, floor by floor. On the third floor, I decided to find someone who would distract Ibtisam and free me from her, so I could go on my date. I was lucky to find a Syrian boy whom I trusted, and I begged him to try to talk with Ibtisam because I had a movie date. When he heard what I said, he replied, "Do you mean that Ibtisam wants to have a date with you, and you don't want it?"

I told him that he stretched his imagination too far and that Ibtisam had given me no such indication. Well, my friend joined Ibtisam, and I vanished.

Kathy, my date, was astonished when I told her we'd better get out of the building as soon as possible. I told her the reason, but she did not believe that Ibtisam might spoil our evening.

Despite my precautions, when we reached the ground floor and went to get a taxi, there was Ibtisam, standing alone. Each one of us saw the other, and so I told Kathy we were really hooked.

Kathy said, "I bet if you invite her, she will refuse."

I said, "Well, I would not count on it."

When we reached the smiling Gibraltar, I said, "We are going to see the film *Lawrence of Arabia*. Would you like to join us?""

To my surprise, and Kathy's too, Ibtisam said, "Oh yes! Why not?"

And so, we went straight to the film without saying a word to each other. Kathy was really shocked, but I told her secretly that it was too late. I realized immediately that all my expectations to have a lovely and enjoyable night were spoiled because of Ibtisam. I was really angry at Ibtisam and her insincere motives.

The film ended showing the Arabs frustrated and unsuccessful in the accomplishment of the final goal of uniting the Arabs, due to the disagreements between the victors. That was in 1917, but the same sad traits of suspicion, mistrust, and jealousy have remained the greatest obstacles to any achievement the Arab nation aspires to.

Likewise, my night ended with mistrust and disrespect for Ibtisam. We dropped her off at her apartment around 1:00 a.m., and Kathy and I went to the house. Kathy was a smart girl who respected my quietness, and she left me to think alone.

The only statement she made was that I was right about Ibtisam, and she was wrong. We bade each other goodnight, and I went to my room feeling as empty as I felt when I started out from the Hecht Company. Concern centered on how much I spent that night to entertain two beautiful, young women. I laughed at myself when I visualized my role as no more than a bodyguard, protecting them from intruders on their beauty and peace.

In the morning, I got up late, taking into consideration that my work did not start until late in the afternoon. While I was reading the daily newspapers in the hall, along came Ibtisam. The conversation that followed was so harsh that it ended with tears running down Ibtisam's face.

I took the offensive approach immediately, telling her that she had to decide what was best for her feelings. She had to stop being a coward and leading herself to disrespectful behavior.

Furthermore, I made an example of the *Lawrence of Arabia* incident. Ibtisam realized at last that I was able to analyze every move she made, and that there was no use in trying to defend herself. She began to cry, and with that I stopped my attack and refrained from more accusations.

I did not see Ibtisam or receive any calls from her until one week later.

That occasion was a lecture given by the NBC TV station's famous commentator, David Brinkley. I was sitting on a big sofa, and an American girl had seated herself beside me. That girl was a resident of the house who had left it for about one year and had just come back. I was not planning to date anyone that night, and especially not that girl, whom I had heard would be engaged soon.

About ten minutes after the lecture began, Ibtisam and her mother arrived. Ibtisam smiled at me, and I was amazed that she constantly watched me during the lecture. After the presentation, when everyone was talking, I found myself surrounded by American students. They disagreed with my interpretation of the United States's mass media coverage of Middle Eastern events. Most of those American students were my cousins by our ties to the prophets Abraham and Ismael, his son. An exception was Bev, the American girl sitting beside me, who was majoring in International Relations with an emphasis on the Middle East.

I was forced to interrupt the discussion when Ibtisam and her mother came forward and greeted me. When I went to see them off, Ibtisam happily thought that I would go all the way to their apartment. But to her astonishment, I bade them good night at the front door of the house and went back to continue the discussion.

While we were arguing, a British student came to ask Bev for a date, but she refused. A second student from India was also met with a refusal. I overheard it all while the arguing continued, but I pretended I did not. At the close of the discussion, Bev asked whether I had heard her private exchanges with the other students. I lied by saying no, but I realized that Bev was indirectly asking me for a date. Consequently, I pulled out one of my best fabricated tales to show Bev that I was already thinking of dating her, and that a refusal would be like an insult to me.

What I told Bev was this: a girl who sits beside a boy, in the Arab tradition, cannot accept an invitation without giving the boy beside her the first chance. According to that great tradition, I deserved that chance.

I am sure that smart Bev did not believe what I said, but she pretended she did. It was beautiful to have a lovely and smart girl for a date, and so Faisal and Bev left the house together.

The Indian student met us along the street beside the house. He refused to let Bev and me pass without a comment. He said, "Faisal, you better go back to Arabia."

I said, with a smile, "After I finish my degree."

While Bev and I were enjoying the dances and music of a cafe lounge on Connecticut Avenue, Ibtisam and her mother entered. They saw us, but we did not greet each other this time. Bev began to talk about Ibtisam and how frustrated she was. To my surprise, I realized that the two girls hated each other intensely.

ψ ψ ψ

During that entire summer of 1963, I was writing an average of two letters a week to the Saudi Arabian Educational Mission in New York City. I was asking for assistance or a scholarship. It was my right to claim assistance.

The law was clear: every Saudi student who studied at his own expense in the United States was entitled to $500.00 of assistance per year. I had not received anything up to that date.

The day after the post-lecture incident, I placed Fuller Brush orders worth $75.00. I was really happy. When I entered the house, I found a letter from the Educational Mission awaiting me. Upon opening it, my happiness was gone, and I was badly hurt.

It read, based on Law No. 50 of the Ministry of Education, I was not entitled to a scholarship. However, it said that the office would be ready to pay my way back to Saudi Arabia if I could prove I was truly in bad financial shape.

What a nice letter! But what about that damn Law No. 50?

Listen, Faisal, the dear and sincere counselor is even ready to ship you back to Saudi Arabia, exactly like when one dies in some other Arab countries. He will be shipped free of charge by the municipality to his place of birth. So, Faisal, in the great counselor's eyes, you are reduced to no more than a dead person. What a way to go!

While I was visualizing all that, I wrote to the Counselor in strong language. In a way I told him to go and jump in the sea, if he had nothing to offer a desperate student except to ship him off like a piece of luggage.

When the fall semester of 1963–64 commenced, I registered for 16 credit hours, the full load for an undergraduate student. After I paid my fees and bought the textbooks I needed, I was left with only $150.00. I was so irrational that I almost paid what was left to the house toward my debt, which was about $450.00.

If I had been thinking straight, the first thing I would have done was to find a secure job and then register at the university. But so far, I had lived my entire life with insecurity, especially with respect to my education. If I had thought "reasonably" from the beginning, I would be back home beside my mother and father and the tribe. "Faisal, you were always an adventurer and a dreamer with high goals. So, continue to be so, and your adventurism will pay off in the end, because your goal is an honorable one." I told myself this as I quit the Fuller Brush business—because, first, I had exhausted all of the feasible market, and second, my school obligations required a lot of time.

One day, after the fall semester began, I received a telephone call from dear Mohammad Ali Al-Shwaihi, of the Saudi Arabian Embassy. I went to see him, and I believe I told him everything except the real magnitude of my financial crisis. I did not need to, because Mohammad was a smart man who realized my problems without those specific details.

About five days later, Mohammad asked me to see him at the embassy again. In his office, he began to lecture me about the necessity of the citizens of a country helping each other. I didn't recognize what Mohammad was driving at, by his lengthy introduction.

He handed me an envelope as we talked. I hesitated to open it in his presence, but upon his insistence I did.

The envelope contained money. My first reaction was, "Please, dear Mohammad, I will accept almost anything for the sake of my college education, but no charity, please."

Dear Mohammad, a humane and sensitive person, insisted that it was not charity, and that he believed that someday I would pay him back. So far, I have not, but dear Mohammad, I am grateful, and I hope that my respect for you has repaid some of that debt.

Mohammad, to change the subject, asked what had happened with concern to my scholarship requests. I told him about the famous letter from the Counselor, and he was really mad. The first action he took was to call the Cultural Attaché in New York City. He was the second person in charge, after the Counselor. Mohammad insisted on the telephone that if the Saudi Arabian Educational Mission had written a fair letter to the Ministry, Faisal would have a scholarship by now.

Mohammad was really in the fighting spirit. He told the Attaché, "Faisal is entitled to a scholarship based on his grades as well as his legal rights." Before he ended his conversation, he told the Attaché that I was entitled to the $500.00 per year assistance even without consulting the Ministry of Education. Dear Mohammad instructed me to immediately send my grades with all the letters to the Cultural Attaché, and not to deal with the Counselor anymore.

♆ ♆ ♆

I did not conceal my real financial problems from my family, but I received no aid or even excuses from them. What I did receive was a letter telling me about a mass marriage they held, that made me sick and angry. Three of my sisters had been married to three of my cousins.

Furthermore, I was stunned to learn that my brother Abdulaziz, who was born in 1948, had been forced to marry a cousin who was 12 years his senior. When I received the shocking news, I realized that my brother's marriage was carried through on the grounds that it was better to force him to leave school than to take the chance he might follow Faisal's example.

I was considered lost.

My father and uncle, I was told, spent at least $15,000 on that mass marriage. They were prosperous enough for that much ceremony but refused to send me even $1,000 as aid to get educated.

Despite all that, some loyal and good tribesmen did not forget Faisal as his family did. They went ahead and began to collect money for me. One of the tribe's members was so moved that he sold his rifle so he could contribute to my education.

However, those innocent and dear tribesmen made one mistake. They delivered their collection of about $2,000 to my father, to be sent to me. He never did as they asked, and I ended up with nothing except sadness, anger, and frustration.

My fear of eventual failure, due to financial reasons, increased when I began to think about the possible consequences for my brothers and their peers in our lovely tribe.

I began to ask myself so many questions. *What will happen to all of the tribe's children after my unsuccessful venture? Will my father ever let my other brothers, Abdel Razaq, Abdel Mehsen, Abdel Hadi, and Sami get educated beyond the fifth grade?* His decision to cut Abdulaziz's education short in favor of marriage was already a fact, and I was afraid that my other brothers would face the same treatment.

My agonies increased when I imagined that my brothers and others like them would be illiterate in a world where education is valued so much, in a society that is so different from that of my father's and his brother's younger days. Certainly, I reasoned, my failure would be used as an excuse by almost every tribesman to cut short his child's education.

I began to see my failure as a plague that would affect many innocent children of the tribe. I was sure my failure would not be judged objectively. No one would stand up and say that Faisal failed because of inadequate financial resources. Rather, everyone would reason that I failed because I had wasted my money and time in chasing women, drinking, and dancing.

Bedouins will think along these lines about everyone who lives in a city, whether that city is in the Arab world or elsewhere.

Trying to put family out of my mind, I went ahead and wrote the Cultural Attaché, as Mohammad Ali Al-Shwaihi had suggested. At the same time, I started looking for an indoor part-time job. A restaurant owner offered me work, but when he recognized my desperate situation and tried to exploit me, I refused his offer. A department store owner also offered me a job, but after three hours he asked me to leave, without any explanation.

The search for work continued without success. Much of my time was wasted in search of a job by which to live. While I was in that desperate situation, I decided to go and see the Saudi Arabian Ambassador, with whom I had had the famous "elevator incident" in Boston, in January 1962. I was sure that a letter from him would secure me a scholarship. And I thought my encounter with him in Boston was probably forgotten by then.

To ensure seeing His Excellency immediately, I decided to play a trick.

I went to the embassy without an appointment or previous arrangement, as was required by diplomatic protocol. Employing all the false confidence which I had learned from door-to-door sales, I told the receptionist I wanted to see the ambassador. The girl hesitated and asked whether I had an appointment. Without answering her question, I told her, "Just tell His Excellency that Faisal would like to see him."

I am sure that His Excellency and the receptionist thought that Faisal was one of the big personalities in Saudi Arabia. And so, I was promptly ushered in to see the great man.

He was really astonished to see that this Faisal was no more than that stubborn student he had met in the elevator in Boston.

I told him my story and asked him to help. He answered by saying that it was none of his business to interfere in such a matter, because he was administratively connected with the Ministry of Foreign Affairs.

I refused to let his argument pass without saying, "But, your Excellency, you represent the government of Saudi Arabia, not only the Ministry of Foreign Affairs."

When he heard that, he really lost his temper, breaking the always cool image of the great diplomat, and kicked me out of his office.

Well, "dear" Ambassador, I was trying to define your job as broadly as possible, but you proved to be the narrow-minded diplomat who associates himself only with the Ministry.

In the end, all my scheming to see him resulted in doing nothing except adding fuel to our previous animosity. It proved that there was no middle ground for the honorable ambassador and the great door-to-door salesman of the Fuller Brush Company. I began to recall articles claiming that most great diplomats were no more than salesmen of ideas who try to coexist politically with adverse factors. Supplementarily, that encounter proved to me that salesmanship was nothing without the backing of power politics, which I lacked to the utmost degree.

ψ ψ ψ

In the midst of all my financial problems and study demands, Ibtisam came into the picture again. It was on a Sunday afternoon around 4:00 p.m. She came to the house for the tea hour.

After greeting her other acquaintances, she came straight to me and said she wanted to speak to me, as if she were afraid she'd forgotten to mention it. At that time, I was really not in a mood to fight for or even care about any girl in this world, so I let her take the lead.

Ibtisam was self-confident at that hour, and decided we'd better go somewhere out of the house to talk. And so, Faisal and Ibtisam left the house alone for the first time. In a small coffee shop on Connecticut Avenue, we sat to discuss the issue on her mind. She first reminded me of many past incidents and said how much she liked me—but she then accused me of being too stubborn to accept half-solutions to any situation. I agreed with that.

In the end, Ibtisam offered to be my girlfriend, provided I did not go out with other girls. She was frank, sincere, and in love. But at that moment, some inner feeling emerged that made my fight to prove I was capable of dating Ibtisam lose its meaning. When she finished, she was embarrassed to see me quiet and unexcited about the proposal. Then I became sincere with her for the first time.

I decided that it would be best for me to let down Ibtisam as humanely as possible. I told her it was no time for me to get involved with any girl, because I had too many problems distracting me. Even if I had agreed that we should be in a relationship—which I might have done out of a live-and-let-live policy—I would not have been a good boyfriend or even a worthwhile companion. I really went all the way to pressure her into forgetting me, and instead finding a boy without problems like mine. I emphasized that she was going to finish her master's degree within six months. And, eventually, she had to leave for Iraq.

"Ibtisam," I said, "remember that I am still Faisal the undergraduate, the Bedouin you hated so much, and whom you think does not respect women."

But she refused all my arguments. She blocked every escape I attempted at that meeting. She contradicted every point I made and refused to accept what I had to say.

Finally, Ibtisam and I reached the relationship we had worked toward for almost a year. People who did not know us thought we were married. Our friends never doubted that we would marry very soon, although marriage was the last thing on my mind.

Anyway, I drifted with her sincere feelings and began to do what she liked. I hesitated many times, reasoning that some kind of disaster in my schooling would result from wasting so much time with her. In reality, that outcome was destined to come even if I had stopped seeing her.

Ibtisam benefited greatly from that relationship. She became more confident, secure, and relaxed. She was absolutely blindly in love, though she refused to admit it. To her, love meant marriage only.

But what did I get in return?

First, I found in Ibtisam the concerned and loyal girl I could always go to, to discuss my problems. She served exactly as a safety valve for the many problems that dominated my thinking, even while I was in classes.

Even so, the negative aspect of our relationship, as far as I was concerned, was greater than the positive one. I had at last proved to everyone that Ibtisam was my girl. But so what? What followed after that false victory reminded me exactly of that military commander who refuses to surrender despite his realization that an inevitable disaster will take place.

—

12

A College Student for Sale

A disaster took place at school, caused by my financial problems, my encounter with an instructor at Howard University,
and my relationship with Ibtisam. All those factors, coupled with
my sense of defeat and hopelessness, led to a bad performance in
that fall semester of 1963. I ended up on the probation list for the
first and last time in my college endeavors.

My episode with Instructor William (a pseudonym) was the most
frustrating incident of my life. It was a classic example of the behavior of an individual in a position of authority who believed he was
always right.

Instructor William was a young African American, who had received his bachelor's and master's degree in economics from Howard, with honors. By 1963, he had published one or two articles in
respected economic journals. As far as the record was concerned,
he was very well-qualified. But one's record is not the only measure
of having the ability to succeed at a given task.

The head of the economics department had decided that William
would teach the Junior Economic Theory class, which had only
one section. Thus, all economics majors had no alternative for an
instructor in that subject. He lectured so fast that even the American students found it hard to keep up. In addition, he did not seem
to be capable of facing an intellectual challenge. Every time a student tried to reason with him, his answer was almost like that of a
military commander, implying that what he said must be right and
was not open to question.

Many students contained their frustration, since there was no other section into which they could transfer. I did not ask him for a single explanation, when I realized what kind of person he was. I kept

regularly delivering my assignments, to avoid any clash with the Hitler of the Junior Economic Theory class at Howard University.

One day, a student from Trinidad dared to ask William for an explanation. The class was really shocked when the instructor's reply to the argument was to kick the student out of the class for good. The unfortunate student tried all means to reverse William's decision, but he failed. Our Hitler's decision was final, and we accepted the fact that no person was able to reverse the Fuhrer's order.

From the start, William's confidence seemed clouded by insecurity and frustration. Our first test was based on the objective procedure and graded so that a right and a wrong answer would cancel each other. Well, the performance of the class was so low that the highest score was sixty-five points out of the 100 points possible. My score was 45, but I blamed this on myself for not studying carefully.

I was determined to do well on the next test. It never occurred to me to look for a scapegoat, especially not my instructor, as I did not feel any kind of hatred toward him.

The reaction of the students as a whole was total silence, as if we were mourning the death of a friend. Most students felt discouraged, and it was, by then, too late to drop the course.

As the second test approached, I devoted all my time to studying for it. And I believe now that hardly anyone could have mastered the assignments better. I was such an optimist when I took the examination. I was sure my grade would be high.

Afterward, to shock the entire class, the instructor announced that the highest grade was seventy. My score was 55. I reacted with dismay and frustration, despite the congratulations of many students who received worse grades than I did.

One said, "Faisal, 55 with William equals more than 100, even with Keynes."

I laughed and told my classmate, "Remember, when Keynes took the British Civil Service Exam, he received his lowest grade in economics."

Students began to go one by one to reason with the instructor about their grades. William the Great stuck to his guns and refused every student's petition.

But it was fate who forced me to be the target of William's bombardment that day. I was not planning to attempt to reason with him at all. However, I felt happy when my answers were compared with the student beside me. He noticed one question where my answer was exactly like his. But he received 20 points for it, while I received zero. My classmate congratulated me immediately, saying that my grade would be the highest in the class.

We felt so sure that William had made some mistake, I went straight to him and showed him my answer to that specific question. While he was trying to find some excuse, I told him that he had given 20 points to a student whose answer was like mine. I said I believed it was just an oversight that I had not received credit for that question.

William asked to see the other student's paper. He was puzzled for a while but was too stubborn to admit to even a minor mistake. Finding no valid explanation, he accused me of copying the other student's answer. I countered, in front of the class, that if I was cheating, he should have kicked me out at the time of the exam. Furthermore, if it was just a suspicion, how could he prove that I had copied that student rather than the other way around?

The instructor lost his temper, because he couldn't find a logical excuse to meet my counterargument. The class atmosphere grew tense, especially since most students realized I was right. At that stage, I wanted to be diplomatic with William, so he might break the impasse without embarrassing himself further. So, I said, "Mr. William, I don't accuse you of anything. What I think is that you were in a hurry to grade the paper and that you simply missed giving credit for that answer. Furthermore, let me assure you that I have not cheated in any exam, in all my educational experiences."

I really thought that he would become more level-headed and assign a certain time in his office for a private discussion—but he proved once more that he considered himself above human mistakes. When I reached my seat, he shouted that I must leave the class immediately or he would kick me out of the university.

That was the beginning of my battle with that arrogant and self-centered instructor, who had written on my test paper a request for me to write more clearly in the next test. Later, that statement proved to be crucial.

I left the class boiling with anger but determined to fight William until the end.

When I entered Mr. Wilson's office (the office of the foreign student advisor), he knew something was wrong. He asked what it was.

I lost my restraint and simply exploded, forcing Mr. Wilson to shut his door and to call Mrs. Green, his secretary, and Mr. Hawkins, his deputy. My first statement was, "Damn it! I never felt like I was in a military establishment, until today. Howard University has reached the stage where no student can even open his mouth to correct a simple mistake by an arrogant instructor."

As I told them the story, Mr. Wilson became truly angry. He checked my file and said, "Faisal, your previous work is proof that you are a good student. I will fight this case with you to the end, if you have witnesses."

I told him I was sure many students would support me. I made it clear I was determined to take the case even to the president of the university, if I did not receive the verdict of an impartial hearing. Through my determination, Mr. Wilson saw where the truth lay.

He became enthusiastic to fight for me and for Howard University's reputation.

ψ ψ ψ

The first step Mr. Wilson and I took in that long battle was to go and see the dean of students. The dean checked William's record at once and was amazed to find he had been on the honors list at Howard. At first the dean was suspicious of me, but upon Mr. Wilson's insistence, he became more interested in the case. Finally, he called the dean of the liberal arts school, who fixed 2:30 p.m. on that same day as a time to receive Mr. Wilson and me.

At lunch, Mr. Wilson tried to persuade me to drop the course to avoid the whole mess. I refused, on the grounds that the course was required for my degree, and I had already put so much effort into it. About 1:30 p.m., Mr. Wilson called me to his office, and when I entered, I could see he was really disturbed by the way the case was escalating. He realized that my battle would be the most challenging one he had ever handled. Nevertheless, he was now determined to prove to everyone in that school that an instructor did not have the right to deny a student his right to learn.

I am sure Mr. Wilson became such a strong supporter of the cause only after he had contacted some other students in my class and realized that he was backed by solid facts. Toward the end of our meeting, Mr. Wilson told me not to worry, because he was with me all the way.

At the appointed hour, we entered the office of the dean of the school of liberal arts. The dean tried very hard to find a compromise, by convincing me to drop the course. I refused, and so the next meeting was set at 2:30 p.m. the following day, with the head of the economics department, William, the dean, the foreign student advisor, and me.

That meeting in the dean's office was extremely tense. It was clear from the beginning that the head of the department and the instructor were on one side, and that Mr. Wilson and I were on the other. The dean was not yet sure which side he would take.

The head of the department was completely unobjective from the start. He repeated over and over that the case involved a clear-cut offense by Faisal, and that the disciplinary committee should act immediately. William, according to the department head, had only performed his duty. Furthermore, he said I was so arrogant they could not reason with me.

Mr. Wilson rejected the department head's accusation, on the grounds that the instructor had failed to explain to me his decision for not giving me credit for a specific answer. The two opposing stands were then clear. The department head believed blindly that the instructor was right, while Mr. Wilson did not. They continued arguing until the department head exploded, saying, "Mr. Wilson, this is clear-cut cheating, and you'd better leave any action to the disciplinary committee."

When the dean heard the word "cheating," he thought the whole matter would be solved on the spot. He probably assumed that the department head had proof to substantiate his accusation. While the dean attempted to capitalize on the cheating angle, I defended myself by stating that the instructor did not mention cheating except when he was not able to answer my question. I said that I believed his accusation was no more than a cover-up and an attempt to scare me. Furthermore, I added, why had he not asked me to leave the class if he had realized I was cheating? Why had he not written something on my paper if he wanted to avoid embarrassing me in public?

The dean examined the paper and realized my point. He began to cross-examine William, who lied and could not convincingly defend his accusations.

The meeting adjourned and the dean again fixed 2:30 p.m. the following day as the time for another meeting. The department head's next actions proved beyond a doubt that he had begun to lose his rationalism. First, he called Mrs. Becker, the director of the International Student House, and told her about the whole affair. Mrs. Becker, who had been a college instructor, was outraged. She reasoned that the matter was so personal it should be kept as private as possible, especially while the matter was still ongoing. Second, to my surprise, the department head called me. I was asked to meet him in his office at 8:00 a.m. the next day.

I went. He tried very hard to persuade me to drop the course. I wish I had done so, but I rejected his suggestion and went to tell Mr. Wilson what had taken place. Mr. Wilson was elated, because he realized that the department head had begun to lose ground, since the accusation of cheating had been proven false.

When we all met in the dean's office, it seemed strange that the department head did not begin to show any moderation. Rather, he switched his emphasis and stressed over and over again that if Faisal was not going to be punished the whole position of the department head would be undermined. Mr. Wilson countered that the case had nothing to do with the department head's position. The question was whether an individual student at Howard University was entitled to an open discussion with his instructor. Should the instructor be allowed to use weak excuses and attempts to intimidate his students while performing his main responsibility?

It was clear from the discussion that the issue of cheating had vanished. At that time, I realized that the dean's position had begun to tilt toward Mr. Wilson's and mine.

I was sure the next meeting would be decisive. I went to the International Student House, feeling much happier than on previous days, and got another call that night from the head of the economics department. Once more he asked me to see him in his office at 8:00. a.m.

When I met him, he was arrogant and quickly lost any objectivity he had ever possessed. First, he claimed that to be an economist, one had to be a flexible person. He said I should realize that in US universities, the instructor was the master, not unlike the British system. To that I answered that I had not attended a British university to compare the two education systems, but from what I had heard and read I believed that just the reverse was true.

He changed the subject by saying that he had nothing against foreign students—and to prove his point, he told me he was married to a Japanese woman.

I thanked him for that feeling but refused to go further. After all that sidetracking, he came to the point, which he thought would scare me.

"Look, Faisal, I am the head of this department. If you want to have a bachelor's degree in economics, then agree with my suggestion and drop the course. Neither Mr. Wilson nor the dean will help you on this account."

Thus, the Great Head concluded his presentation. I was really angry then and told him without the least respect that I was planning to get a bachelor's degree in economics and to keep the course no matter what. When I finished, I conceded to myself that Howard University would not be the place from which to graduate, no matter the outcome of my case.

Before I left the department head's office, he again accused me of being stubborn and inflexible. What made me laugh was when he said, "Go even to President Kennedy, but no one will help you."

The next meeting in the dean's office was the hardest. I took the offensive from the start by insisting I would not accept any compromise. Second, I made it clear that I would not drop the course. Third, I declared that I had little faith left in the honesty of the instructor or even that of the head of the economics department. After that, I revealed all the threats the department head had uttered that morning. Everyone but Mr. Wilson was astonished.

The instructor countered by insisting that my unrealistic demands were proof that I was nothing more than a troublemaker. For the first time since the encounter began, I found myself obliged to answer William directly.

I said, "Instructor William, I want you to realize that I came from Saudi Arabia, at least 7,000 miles away from the United States, not to cause trouble but rather to get educated. That education remains my final goal. My dedication is evident in the fact that I came at my own expense, without the help of even my family." I was quiet and self-possessed when I spoke, and I was sure the dean was impressed with my diplomatic way of addressing my antagonist.

When he answered me, he threw the committee into confusion. He said, imprudently, "If you come from as far as 7,000 miles away, I come from seven blocks south of Howard University."

The dean and Mr. Wilson, I learned later, understood the instructor's use of "seven blocks" to mean that he was an American, while I was a foreigner.

The department head tried to convince the committee that what the instructor meant to show was no more than his background in an inner-city area, and his pride, that he too had made it on his own. No matter what the intention was, William's answer was enough to show the dean the instructor's inability to state his ideas clearly and convincingly.

The dean became so irritated that he demanded to know, immediately, what right the department head had to threaten me. The two gentlemen's voices rose so sharply that I was asked to leave the room for a while.

As I waited outside, their shouting continued. When I reentered the room, the dean asked me to name a professor I trusted. I mentioned the name of Professor Annagnos. The dean said, "Faisal will sit in William's class. He will, however, have no right to ask the instructor for any explanations. Professor Annagnos will be responsible for answering Faisal's questions, as well as for grading his papers."

When the dean finished, the head of the department announced that he would not accept such a humiliating verdict for an instructor in his department.

I do not know the exact events following that meeting, but after two weeks of continued conflict between the dean and the department head, the verdict remained as first outlined by the dean.

Finally, the right triumphed, and not the wrong. Howard University's dean of liberal arts, and its foreign student advisor, restored to that institution of learning all the respect in my heart. Both of them defended the right of a student in an open and free institution to say "no" to an arrogant and unfair instructor. They defended student Faisal S. Bashir, who happened to be an Arab of Muslim faith, against two American citizens, one White and the other African American. They humiliated that arrogant instructor, despite their both being African American, as he was.

Nevertheless, I eventually paid dearly for my triumph over instructor William. I did not get the final grade Professor Annagnos thought I was entitled to, due to nothing except the circumstances and William's hatred. What happened was that no one asked William to hand over my class grade card to Professor Annagnos. And so, at the end of the term, William sent in the card with a "D" grade. I protested, but by that time I had lost interest in renewing the fight. That "D" grade was the first and last one I ever got in any economics course.

⚘ ⚘ ⚘

It appeared to me, by December 1964, that I had to leave college when the semester ended. And so, I saw before me the inevitable defeat of my goal for an education and no way to try avoiding that disaster. I was helpless and realized that a college education was a luxury beyond my position, as I was surviving only by the postponement of what I owed the International Student House.

But one day a new hope injected some kind of strength in me, and I began to plan for one last try. My final attempt was to write an article for *Al-Qassim* newspaper in Riyadh, Saudi Arabia. That newspaper was the one that had published my second article, earlier, when I had my writing streak in Dharan, Saudi Arabia.

What I wrote was no more than a desperate cry for everyone to read and hear. I offered myself for sale, exactly like a bottle of Pepsi-Cola, the "Drink of Hospitality", or like a Saudi barrel of oil in the international market. I titled the article "A College Student for Sale." Although the editor changed the title, he kept nearly all the rest, with only some diplomatic touches here and there. I awaited the issue of the paper that contained my article, and upon seeing it I felt good. I resigned myself to the fact that I had done all that I could. I did not expect anything material to come from that article. I just felt it was a way to pour out my frustration for everyone to see.

Surprisingly, my final and most desperate attempt proved to be the most effective one. First, dear Mohammad Ali Al-Shwaihi called to summon me to the embassy as soon as possible. He insisted that I should bring my certified college record with me.

My first interpretation of Mohammad's request was that he wanted me to send another application to the Educational Mission. Really, I did not feel optimistic, but I went ahead to get my certified record and to pay a visit at the embassy. Mohammad was smiling all over, as he asked whether I had written to a newspaper back home. I said yes. He congratulated me, saying he thought I was right, and that it was the best way to shake up some big, inefficient officials. While we were laughing about the title of the article, Mohammad handed me a check and the *Al-Qassim* newspaper, which followed the one that contained my article. Before examining the check, I saw on the first page one of the King's sons, pictured under a big heading, "A Prince's Contribution." As I read the article, I realized that the prince was the first to respond to my call.

The check was from him, and it was worth $491.00. I really felt elated and moved by the prince's fast response.

While I was contemplating my new situation, Mohammad saw that I had indeed brought my record—and so, he informed me that at last His Excellency, the ambassador, would see me.

He received me and wrote a good and strong letter to the minister of education, supporting my demand for a scholarship. That article really did a lot. When I left the ambassador's office, Mohammad was smiling again. The cultural attaché had just called him from New York. Within 24 hours, I would receive the $500 I had been entitled to have as a non-scholarship student in need of aid.

I thanked Mohammad and left the embassy. Within two days, Faisal progressed from a penniless person to a happy individual, having paid all his debts to the house.

ψ ψ ψ

When I received my grades at the end of the semester, I felt dejected. Mr. Wilson tried hard to minimize the impact of being on the probation list. He emphasized over and over again that probation could be cleared with hard work, and that after that there would be no harm. However, I told Mr. Wilson, to clear the probation I had to register for the spring term, and this I was not able to do. I lacked enough money to cover all my expenses—but this too changed.

Before spring registration started, I received the most beautiful telephone call of all my life. Dear Mohammad Ali Al-Shwaihi called me at 5:00 p.m. and told me I had been granted a full scholarship from my government. At last, financial security was a fact.

What a relief! Now, Faisal, there will be no excuses except your own irresponsibility for future failures. There will be no more scapegoats to blame if you get kicked out of the university for scholastic reasons. You are secure financially. Ibtisam left for Iraq, and she left you behind on the probation list, fighting for your future and the fulfillment of that goal that forced you away from your father, your mother, and all of your lovely tribe.

Ibtisam left you, Faisal, without even telling you that she loved you. Even so, she wrote you a card every day, from the day she left the United States until she reached Baghdad in Iraq. In Rome, the rain you liked so much reminded her of you. The classical music she heard in Madrid forced her to shed tears, because that was the music you loved so much. And when she got sick in Seville, she only wished that you were beside her, rather than her mother or other relatives.

All this she said, but she refused to say that she was in love. So, Faisal, run for your life while you are free. Fulfill your goal before it is too late!

My grades at the end of the spring term of 1964 were more than enough to clear my probation mess. I ended up with a three-point average out of four possible. And when the summer sessions of George Washington and American Universities started, I registered for four courses, totaling 12 semester credits. My average at the end of the summer sessions was 3.5 out of four points. I was especially proud that one course in which I received an "A" was a high-level course in money and banking.

13

CUPID AND HOMECOMING

In August 1964, I said farewell to Howard University and transferred to the University of Oregon in Eugene. But before I moved, that same month, I met Stephanie Ann Wegner, who had just graduated from Douglass College, the women's college of Rutgers University in New Jersey. She had recently been appointed the Editorial Assistant of the *Journal of Home Economics* in Washington, D.C.

My acquaintance with Stephanie was sudden and accidental. One Sunday morning, I was reading the newspapers at the International House, when I saw four young women at another table. One, a blonde, I'd never seen before—so I introduced myself. She said her name was Stephanie, and she and her friends left.

I saw her again, and again. She was staying at the house that week. I asked her to dinner and a movie.

She agreed to go, but what confounded me on that outing was that she insisted on paying for her food. I was insulted. This in no way agreed with the way I was raised. I insisted on paying and was rather forceful about it.

On the way from dinner to the movie, Stephanie said to me, in response to something I'd said, "Faisal, you really put your foot in your mouth."

I had no idea what she was talking about. I'd put my foot in my mouth?

"It's an expression," she explained. And once I understood, we laughed hysterically together.

Stephanie was beautiful. She had a fine sense of humor. She entered my heart immediately.

I left D.C. soon after that, but once I was in Oregon we kept writing to each other. With the passage of time, I realized that my relationship with Stephanie was much different from all previous adventures with girls. And so, Faisal fell truly in love for the first time in his life.

That love was honest and pure. It was not aimed to prove anything except the true meaning of love and respect.

๛ ๛ ๛

In June 1965, I realized that I was required to take only six hours in art appreciation before I would graduate with a bachelor's degree in economics. However, when I looked at the summer session courses, it was clear that there was no single course to fulfill the required hours. The requirements imposed on me by Howard University did not agree with what was offered in Oregon.

Consequently, my next long-term aim came into view earlier than expected. The graduate school accepted my proposal to begin graduate courses for my master's degree, provided that I graduate officially with my bachelor's degree no later than March 1966. I agreed, and a new fight began.

In March 1966, I received the bachelor's degree in economics, but in addition I had already accumulated 30 term hours towards my master's degree in the same field. I had the university certify all my work and I sent a record of it with the bachelor's degree receipt to the Educational Mission in New York.

About two weeks later, the great counselor from the mission sent me a letter in which he gave me one month to pack for the return journey to Saudi Arabia. I tried to deal with him diplomatically, emphasizing that so far, my government had paid for only two years of my college education. I asked if it wasn't reasonable to allow me to stay until the end of August 1966. By that date, I promised him that I would be able to get my master's degree.

But the counselor gave a harsh response.

First, he voiced his suspicion that I was cooking up some fishy tricks. Second, he simply did not believe that I had accumulated 30 graduate hours. The man seemed convinced that even if I stayed until August 1966, I would not be able to finish my degree.

Since some Saudi Arabian students who came with me still needed more than two years to finish their bachelor's degrees, I did not blame him for having some doubts. I knew that someone who graduated among the first ten students in high school in Saudi Arabia needed at least up to the end of 1968 to finish his bachelor's degree.

Nevertheless, I argued with the counselor that my previous hard work and the sacrifice of my summer vacations were proof that I would be able to finish. Also, I reminded him that he was aware of my being the first Saudi student to make the honors list twice at the University of Oregon. But the final letter from the counselor was definite; if I did not go home, he would cut off my scholarship.

I ignored him completely and went straight to work. By the end of the spring term, around June 1966, the counselor suspended my scholarship and stopped my monthly payments. That did not scare me, but I prayed to God that everything would be all right and that the master's degree would be a fact by the end of August. More than anything, I was afraid to fail, especially when many students around me expressed their doubts.

I continued to work hard and pushed all doubts out of my mind. At that point, I was really in a race against time and had no chance to wait and think. During that difficult trial, I was happy to be able to see Stephanie once in a while.

And then, my second year in Oregon, Stephanie was granted an assistantship to study for her master's degree in home economics at Oregon State University, about 60 miles from the University of

Oregon. Our relationship grew closer as time went on. I went to see her often; she came to see me in return. I was not committed to her at this time, in an official way, as I was too aware of how I would eventually return to Saudi Arabia—and when I did, where would that leave us? But my feelings for her were strong. I was in love with her.

One day, before the end of the summer session, but after I had passed my master's general examination, I decided to demand all my suspended monthly payments from the counselor. About that time, King Faisal was coming to the United States on a state visit, so I timed my letter to coincide with his arrival. I sent it to the newly appointed ambassador, telling him the whole story, and asking him either to reason with the counselor or to discuss my case with the King. I don't know which step the ambassador took, but after about two weeks I received two of the four payments to which I was entitled. At least, and at last, that counselor had to come up with something.

By September 12, 1966, Faisal S. Bashir had earned his master's degree with a grade point average of 3.33. I felt like I was the happiest person on earth. First, I had accomplished more than I had planned to do when I came to the United States. And second, I proved to the counselor and all other doubters that I was able to fulfill my promises.

ψ ψ ψ

After four years and six months of hard work, Faisal the Bedouin began preparations to go back to Saudi Arabia. Before I left the United States, there was Stephanie, whom I loved. There was Stephanie to face and to tell honestly what I felt about the future of our relationship.

I had already told her many times that, before I met her, I had not even entertained the idea of marrying an American girl. Not because I disliked them, but rather due to the differences in living, between Saudi Arabia and the United States. I told Stephanie over and over that there was no place in this world which offers so much abundance and variety in life as the United States. I said that it would be very difficult for an American girl to live in a place like Saudi Arabia. I was basing my judgment on what I knew of Saudi Arabia when I left in 1962.

I made it clear to Stephanie that I had duties to perform toward my country, my tribe, and my family, and that I would not deviate from fulfilling them to the best of my ability. But I would forever keep in mind the respect I felt toward the United States and its people, and I would always keep in my heart respect for that country.

My thoughts and feelings were not based on Hollywood life or sky-scrapers. Rather, they were based on the notion that the strength of the country stemmed mainly from its citizens' beliefs in an open society and the freedom of its individuals. I still believe that as long as the United States preserves those qualities, it can find acceptable solutions to all of its problems. I felt that failure to achieve a better society would come only if its leadership lacked commitment to those ideals.

I departed, praying to God that everything would be all right, and that despite what I'd had to do, somehow Stephanie would some-day be my wife and help create a family much different from the one that raised me.

卉 卉 卉

When I reached Riyadh in October 1966, I had two tasks to per-form: first, to find a job and, second, to locate the place where my family and tribe were camping.

The first task was fulfilled when I was accepted to become an eco-nomic advisor in the Central Planning Organization of the gov-ernment of Saudi Arabia in Riyadh. The second task proved to be more difficult. It took me 11 days to find that the tribe and my fam-ily were camping in Turaif, a small town in the northern part of Saudi Arabia.

My reunion with them is beyond my power to describe. I never felt so happy and speechless as I did on that day. When the DC 3 aircraft of Saudi Arabian Airlines landed, the small airport of Turaif was crowded with people. It looked as if a big official personality, not Faisal, the new college graduate, who had just found a job a week prior, was coming to Turaif. But to the tribe, I was the biggest personality they ever dreamed to see or wanted to receive with honor and dignity. To the tribe, the "almost lost Faisal" was home at last.

I greeted everyone. Some I remembered very well. Others I had never met. Some were not even born in 1959, when I left to work on the east coast of Saudi Arabia. Others had grown too much to be recognizable to me. The brother I had left at age 11 was already married and had a daughter. Another brother, whom I had left at the age of five, was 12 and already grown into a young man. And the boy who jumped into my lap, in the car, happened to be my youngest brother Naif, whom I had not seen in my life. A very shy girl, standing nearby, was shedding tears of happiness. She was my youngest sister, whom I had left at age two. And lastly, there was a boy who seemed fascinated by the whole scene. He was my youngest cousin, another relative who had never seen me.

Not one of the old men volunteered to tell me the names of all who greeted me. To them, they were all my relatives, whether the relationship was based on a blood link or not. I was absolutely speechless, uttering only a few words here and there. Some people told me later that the words I spoke were mixed with words of the people I came from (meaning English words).

When we reached my father's tent, I recognized the parent who cared so much about me and who loved me so dearly. He was also the father who had contributed nothing to my college education. As usual, he was quiet and reserved on the surface, but he failed to cover his emotions, as usual, and began to smile when I walked toward him.

He smiled and pronounced one sentence before he hugged me, "Welcome home, Faisal the Stubborn, who has made everyone proud of him."

"Oh! Father, I missed you. Oh! Dad, it is good to see you healthy and happy. Oh! Beloved, hard-working father, I am at last home and secure again."

My father told me that my mother had left about a month before to see her relatives in Iraq. I felt so sorry for not seeing her at that moment, but I immediately sent one of the tribesmen to bring her. She did not come until much later.

The tribe I had left poor was prosperous. Those who had few horses when I left were driving trucks and pickups. The tribe I had left united was dispersed all over the desert, and most of the young had left to work in the cities. But all in all, it was a happy reunion for Faisal and the Al-Sba'a Tribe. That night, many dignitaries of other tribes came to see me and to congratulate the proud father and tribe on my return.

I was so silent, throughout the hours of our reunion, that a sense of unease came over most of the old tribesmen. They thought that I was not able to understand their language, and that I now knew only English. One of my dearest friends came and told me this, and I began to laugh to myself. I decided to reassure the old men that I was still the Faisal they remembered.

I began by asking each one about his sheep and his family. I was careful to use the dialect with which they spoke. Everyone laughed when I told them that at last, it seemed that I had freed myself from the thief—referring to my description of education as like a thief. All felt reassured and happy that I had not forgotten the traditions of the tribe.

And so, life went on for about 28 days, before I went back to Riyadh to start my job. In all, more than 60 lambs were killed to honor Faisal, who had returned.

ψ ψ ψ

The tribe was disappointed in only one aspect. Everyone thought I must marry one of my cousins—but I refused. The one they had chosen for me was illiterate, and I thought marriage with her would be impossible, because neither she nor I would be happy.

Instead, I continued corresponding with Stephanie. And that went on for a year, as I settled into my work in Riyadh, and all the while my parents searched for a bride I would consider more suitable than their first choice had been.

By the time my first year back in Saudi Arabia was ending, I found that I was still in love with Stephanie. I didn't want to be with anyone else.

But there were only more problems with that. People dated in Saudi Arabia, but it was nothing like in the United States, and I couldn't go back there again. I was a Bedouin, and I was supposed to marry a Bedouin. Even marrying an Arab woman from the city would have been frowned upon.

I spoke to an official, who devised a way to try to make this situation work. He wrote to the consulate in the United States, telling them that Stephanie was my fiancé. If our relationship was, in that way, official, Stephanie could come to Saudi Arabia—against the will of her mother, who disapproved—and without my having to tell my parents.

Later in the history of Saudi Arabia, something like this would be unthinkable—but things at that time were still relatively open.

And so Stephanie came to Riyadh, and we knew we had to try to make our relationship official. We were both very much in love.

Sometime after she arrived, we went to see a judge I was friends with, to ask if it was possible for us to marry. He said no, we couldn't, because Stephanie was a Christian and I was a Muslim—but then, he added, it had been done before. I had to go to the mufti and get permission.

I traveled to see the Grand Mufti, and learned from his son, who acted as his secretary, that it would be simple, that all I needed was to write a letter to the Mufti requesting that an exception be made, that I be allowed to marry a Christian woman. This son of the Mufti was worldly, and rather advanced compared to those around him.

We were talking about this in the vicinity of a group of other officials, judges who presided in the region. One of them approached and asked me who I was. I told him. He asked where I was from, and I answered. More questions ensued, and when he finally asked why I was there, what my business was, he blew up. He insisted I could not marry a Christian.

He went to speak to the Grand Mufti, who was there in the hall where I stood and continued talking with his son. A blind man, he nodded while the judge who was so angry with me seethed and explained the situation.

The Grand Mufti was unmoved. He approached me amiably, ignoring the judge who had voiced his objections, and listened as I explained the situation.

"Where," the Grand Mufti asked, "do you intend to live?"

"Riyadh," I replied to him.

Like the judge before him, the Grand Mufti blew up. He insisted that Christians could not, did not, live in Riyadh.

Still, despite my failure there, I was determined to marry Stephanie. We would later travel to Beirut to get married, circumventing the restrictions we faced in Saudi Arabia.

However, I had to tell my parents about it, so I traveled to Jordan, where my mother was at that time.

I entered the tent where she was staying, and in the men's side of the tent my hands and knees shook. I was so afraid of what she might say, and how this news might affect her.

Then, abruptly, I told her, "Mom, I'm going to marry an American girl."

I thought she would scream, or worse. But instead, she said, "So what, son? It's okay."

I couldn't believe it. I still can't believe it.

But it turned out that there was a precedent for this sort of thing. Someone in another tribe my mother knew had married a woman from Germany. It was not unheard of.

Still, I had to tell my father. I was too afraid to tell him myself, and so I conscripted a man from the tribe, a lieutenant general in the army, to go and tell my father for me.

My father, I later learned, was shocked at the news. My uncle was shocked when he learned of it as well. The whole tribe was shocked. But I ignored them, and I went to Beirut. I secured permission from the ambassador there, to marry a non-Saudi. The ambassador was very forward-thinking, and more courageous than other Saudi ambassadors. Other officials tried to overrule his decision, but the ambassador overcame those objections, and on the 18th of September 1967, at the embassy in Beirut, Stephanie and I married. We returned to Riyadh.

And so, Faisal the Bedouin and his new wife lived in the most exclusive, upper-class area of Riyadh called Al-Malez, rather than in a tent with his tribe. He drove the latest Ford Mustang instead of riding camels and horses. His work was as an economic advisor, rather than being the chief of a tribe or a shepherd. Hot dogs, shish-kabob, and steak replaced a diet of camel milk and dates. Beethoven, Tchaikovsky, and Bernstein provided music in place of the Al-Rababa, the musical instrument used in Bedouin life, or the singing of tribesmen as they pulled water from wells for their sheep. The qualities of being illiterate or barely able to read and write were replaced by holding B.S. and M.A. degrees, and by definite plans for obtaining the Ph.D. Yes, dear reader, this is what happened to Faisal S. Bashir, the young Bedouin.

As it happens, many years later, I encountered once again that lieutenant general who had delivered the news of my upcoming wedding to my father. I told him how afraid I'd been, how convinced I was then that my father would want to kill me.

"Ah, Faisal," he said. "He did. In fact, we all wanted to kill you."

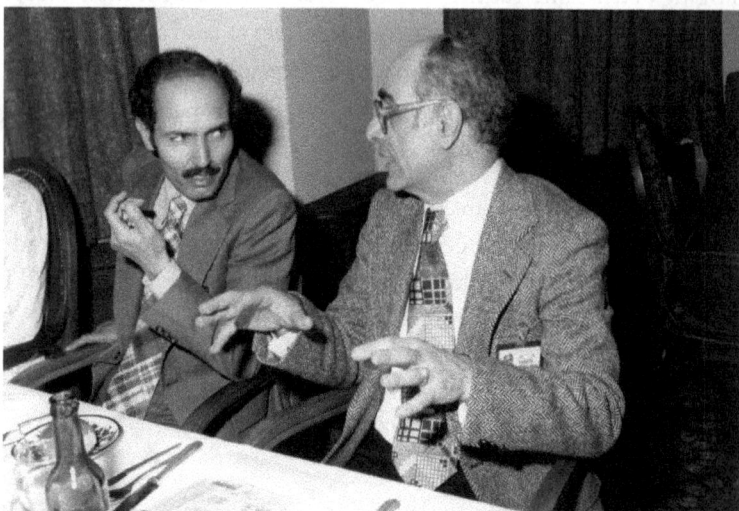

At the World Economic Forum in Davos, Switzerland (1979)

Interacting with President Ferdinand Marcos of the Philippines (1981)

Cutting the ribbon commemorating Kemya's first shipment of polyethylene

On the Mobil oil tanker Monrovia in the industrial port of Yanbu (1981)

Standing next to Indira Ghandi, Prime Minister of India (1982)

Meeting of the Board Members of Kemya in Houston, USA (1982)

*Visiting Kemya's marketing company as Chairman
in Munich Germany (1985)*

*Speaking at a joint Saudi-American trade
conference in Atlanta, Georgia (1986)*

Meeting Former USA President Jimmy Carter in Atlanta, Georgia (1986)

*With King Fahad at the ceremony commemorating
the Petromin and Shell joint venture (1986)*

My dear friend and my right arm the CEO of Saudi Hotel &
Resorts Company (SHERACO) Eng. Abdulaziz AlAnbar

PART THREE

14

Nice Degree ... Why are you poor?

I entered government service in October 1966, after obtaining the approval of the Council of Ministers, chaired by King Faisal. At that time, someone with a master's degree had to be appointed by the King. And so, I began my government service in the Central Planning Organization (CPO).

It did not take long for me to realize that there was not much to do. Saudi Arabia was not in such a good financial position, and I began to try to think of things to do to keep me busy. I submitted some topics for research, which were rejected.

I went to the King's advisor, who was acting as president of the CPO, and submitted my resignation. He tried to reason with me to stay in my position, but of course I refused politely. By the time I reached my office, my immediate boss was unhappy with what I had done, and he agreed to one of my topics of research to keep me busy.

I went all over the country for almost six months, in search of the industrial sector, which was primitive. That research kept me busy and introduced me to many Saudi businessmen and people and convinced me that Saudi Arabia at that time had a long way to go, if it was to develop an industrial sector for something other than oil. I submitted my research results and waited.

And then, in June 1967, the Six-Day War was fought between multiple Arab countries, including Saudi Arabia, and Israel. Israel won, and the whole Arab world was shocked. Gloom and despair prevailed all over.

I married Stephanie in September 1967, and in late 1969 I went to the United States to study for my doctorate, this time secured financially by a government scholarship.

ψ ψ ψ

I returned to Saudi Arabia with a Ph.D. in economics in October 1973. The Bedouin boy who dreamt about being able to read and write as his ultimate goal in life came home with the highest degree a university could offer. Neither I nor my family, not even the people in the tribe, or anyone else, could have thought of such an accomplishment, because of my nomadic background and its morals.

I returned home with Stephanie and our children, Sami and Ramsey, armed with a degree. I arrived with hope and determination to make the most of my investment in education and the long struggle, and to produce a rewarding outcome for me and all those I loved. By October 1973, one could feel that Saudi Arabia was waiting for something to happen, and that there was something one could almost touch in the air. This was the beginning of the first financial boom, due to the rise in oil prices, and for me there was a bit of a culture shock.

Looking for a house to rent, I was faced with the first shock because of the high cost of houses, compared to 1969, when I departed for my studies. With the help of some friends, I found a small villa for which the rent was almost half my yearly income. Inflation was high, and the price of goods and services increased daily. By the time we settled in Jareer Street in Riyadh, I was in debt to the tune of two years' pay. Suddenly, the enjoyment of being first in this or that achievement subsided, and the struggle for material survival began.

I spent a lot of time, at the end of 1973, trying to figure out a way out of the financial difficulties I faced with my family. By the end of that year, my confidence was so low, I began to doubt the value of my struggle for education and became pessimistic about my future. What added to my pessimism, during those days, was that I was surrounded by the signs of comfort and financial wealth of people who were mostly illiterate or had very low levels of education. I began to think they were almost laughing at us, the educated ones.

A Saudi with a master's degree in mining engineering summed up our situation when he said what a waste of time and effort it had been to pursue an education. He quit his government job and began to work for his brother, who was a multimillionaire through land speculation. I never thought that education was the means to great financial wealth, but I thought a higher college degree must give one a comfortable life, materially as well as non-materially, in a government job. However, pay was low, and I was frustrated.

Gloom and despair were my prevalent feelings in 1974. What a way to end a long struggle, and at this stage of life. I had tried to deviate from my nomadic life and had become the first Ph.D.-holder from the tribe, but I was in a very bad situation.

Those were my thoughts in those days. I have to admit, I was unfair in my assessment of my situation, charged with emotions, far from cool-headed analysis and patience. Every time I took stock of my situation, I found hopeless results. Frankly, I became almost certain there was no light at the end of the tunnel, no matter how many grades in government service I was promoted. Did I set unrealistic goals for myself after obtaining my degree? I certainly did not. But what induced me to be so afraid was the cost of living, due to the high level of inflation, which prevented me and others from having decent and comfortable standards of living. During 1973-74, any returning Saudi student who didn't own a house, or come from a wealthy family, was in an uncomfortable situation. Neither government pay nor an income from the private sector was enough to meet the cost of comfortable standards of living, especially due to the high rent in those days.

And so, as a nomad at heart, I began to think seriously of finding an additional job, hopefully with the government, to supplement my basic salary. What added to my agony was that my father and part of the tribe were scattered all over the desert in Northern Saudi Arabia, Jordan, Syria, and Iraq, and the news coming from them was not good. And so, the return of the native son with a Ph.D. felt like an empty and hollow occasion.

During those days, I began to remember those, including my father, who had advised me that education was not that rewarding. Oh, I knew they were wrong, but when one is down and almost beaten the unthinkable becomes almost true. Sometime, in the fall of 1974, while I was at a low cycle of my life, writing economic papers to keep myself busy, I met in my office an American journalist, Georgie Ann Geyer, from one of the major Chicago newspapers. The meeting, or interview, developed into some kind of research about my background and whether it was true that I grew up in the desert as a nomadic person. To me, it was not a big deal to be originally a nomad, and to now be settled and urbanized. It was, I reasoned, happening all over the Arab countries of the Middle East, and especially in Saudi Arabia.

That interview was the first time I met a foreign journalist, which developed into some kind of continuous request for interviews. This taxed my time, especially from 1976 to 1982. Geyer wrote two flattering articles, which I am still grateful for. What fascinated her were the odds against me pursuing an education, given my nomadic background, and how in the end I had made it. She noticed I was reserved, and I sincerely said, "What is the big deal about a Ph.D, and what is it used for?" She was shocked to hear what I said. As I've mentioned, I was at a low level of confidence, due to the real and imaginary hardships I faced. All my life, until then, and throughout that long struggle to free myself, once and for all, from the traditional life of the nomad, which had continued for centuries, I had hoped that there would be better days through better education.

Now that I had ended my quest for education (degree-wise, at least), after taking all relevant factors, present as well as future, into consideration, I came to the conclusion that a better day might not be achievable after all.

When the journalist asked me where my father's tent and the rest of the tribe were, my answer was simple and honest: "I really don't know. They could be anywhere from Saudi Arabia to Syria, Iraq or Jordan. I wish I could be with them at this moment, because I really do not see that much value in the work I am doing."

A few months later, a friend sent me the article that the journalist wrote about her meeting with me. It was favorable, but what moved me most was the human observation that I looked like I was haunted. It was a perfect description of my situation, especially the mental one. I was at a crossroads, for the first time in my life, not knowing what to do. I was almost caged, stripped of all energy. And that definitely produced that haunted look that the journalist correctly noticed.

My haunted look was a product of my perceived situation, especially my mental one. I was living in a society where traditional nomadic life was still common—where, to some extent, human achievements were measured by physical things. What was the value of an economic working paper? What impact did it have on my father or my tribesmen?

I was trying to prove to all those I love, and especially my tribe and my smaller family, Al-Mershed, that my struggle for education and the path I took, to abandon the nomadic way of living, was the right one and the way to a better future.

Here and there, I began to hear and see how my loved ones began to look at me negatively and almost began to believe that they thought I wasted a lot of time, to reap almost nothing at the end, and that I would have been better off if I had stayed with them. They wanted instant success, materially and nonmaterially.

I reached a stage where I wanted to tell many of them to leave me alone, and to say that those who did not help in my education had no right to voice any judgement about my achievements. Relationships between me, my family, and most of the tribesmen became frosty, to say the least.

Faisal Al-Mershed's story was discussed by all those who knew me or my family, which were many people, and I was judged either a big success or failure, mostly by those of the older generation, including my uncle and father. They saw me as a failure—but younger people saw some positive results. At least I could read and write!

Oh! What a life. Certainly, I was comforted by my urban friends, Saudis as well as non-Saudis, where in those days Ph.D.-holders were few.

That is not the case anymore, I am happy to say. Saudi Arabia did not shy away from investing in human capital development.

In addition to those friends, Stephanie was a solid base to lean on. Almost all the time, and no matter how bad my mood was, when I came home from the office, a welcoming smile was on her face.

Stevie, I am grateful forever for the support you gave and your patience with living in Saudi Arabia in those days.

And while I cannot speak for her here in much detail, I can say that Stephanie loved living in Saudi Arabia at that time. When we first moved there, she wore western clothes for a couple of months but soon began to dress like a Saudi woman. We almost never fought. Until our divorce, many years later, we never had a problem. She had a full life in Riyadh, and the smile she greeted me with when I came home to her each day was a genuine one.

ﷺ ﷺ ﷺ

Having resigned myself to the fact that there was very little I could do to change my situation, I began to work on the second five-year development plan, like all other employees of the Central Planning Organization (CPO). (The agency changed its name to the Ministry of Planning in 1976.) I grew involved with my work, which became an escape from the bleak future I imagined myself hooked into without an escape.

In 1974, few Saudi nationals were experienced in development planning. There were few of us degree-holders, mostly from western universities and in particular from the United States, but we had little experience. We worked side by side with experts from all over the world. I counted, once, people of 16 different nationalities working in the CPO, which became almost a training agency for us Saudis. And despite personal anxiety and discomfort, little by little, with the passage of time, I began to enjoy my work, and with that my confidence increased, which led me to assess my future prospects.

My future began to take different hues and shape in my imagination, most of it not as bleak as I visualized before the end of 1973 because almost overnight, Saudi Arabia would turn out to be one of the most financially wealthy countries in the world.

The country had plenty of oil, and the price per barrel for crude oil went from $3.80 to $5.00 to $11.20 in almost a year and a half. Correspondingly, government oil revenues jumped from $4.3 billion in 1973 to $ 22.5 billion in 1974.

These figures along with the figures of oil production symbolize to every planner that, from the financial side, the sky was the limit. Any constraints on Saudi Arabia's development would not be of a financial nature. And so, with that financial intoxication, I and many Saudis began to feel that a new, happy, and promising dawn was coming to Saudi Arabia.

Certainly, all hoped that it would be smooth sailing, so to speak. Every time we almost finalized a list of projects to be included in the plan, an additional one was added. Why not give the Saudi people what they wanted and were deprived of throughout their history, now that finances were not a constraint? Give the people of Saudi Arabia the schools to educate them, the hospitals to take care of their health problems, and the roads the country needed to ease travel and connect each region with another.

In a nutshell, why not transform Saudi Arabia, as soon as possible, from a poverty-stricken country to one that was wealthier? This was why we planners had a hard time finalizing a programs list, which became like a wish list. It was hard to convince people that money couldn't buy time needed to implement projects, especially when the country lacked companies to build things while needing to import almost all goods and services that were essential to the Kingdom's development.

By the time the Second Five-Year Development Plan was published, its total appropriation (projects only) reached $150 billion. Mind-boggling, yes; unthinkable, no. No one can accuse Saudi Arabia of trying hard to distance itself from its poverty-stricken past as soon as possible, despite most of us planners voicing caution. Most foreign advisors and visitors, including those who became our partners in the petrochemical industry, doubted we would accomplish half of what we envisaged. Even the mass media did not give us the benefit of the doubt. On the contrary, some even emphasized that our heads must be examined to see whether we were sane, especially with regard to the petroleum chemical industry, which was huge, and included many basic industry projects. That led to the creation of SABIC, Saudi Basic Industry Company, which became one of the largest chemical companies in the world, and certainly a shining star in the crown of Saudi development to this day.

As I saw it, I was lucky to be at the center stage of that development, no matter how small my part was, although no one can deny that Faisal the nomad boy was at the center of the creation of modern Saudi Arabia. I am still grateful to my country and its leadership, who gave me the chance to be a part of that.

Huge government expenditures, plus that of the private sector chasing limited available goods and services, increased the cost of everything. Therefore, by the mid-seventies, the country faced one of the highest rates of inflation in the world. And so, I and many planners began to hope for a slowdown in order to cool the economy and not miss the opportunity to develop the country.

That led the leadership to send me to the Iran of the Shah in 1976. He was declaring to the world how he was able to develop the country with a low level of inflation.

My trip did not lead me to believe what his majesty was proclaiming, and so I reported my finding to my government's Inflation Committee, and Saudi Arabia's development continued at the same pace with little hesitation.

ꙮ ꙮ ꙮ

Back to my personal life. On 21 June 1974, Stephanie gave birth to Lisa, the only daughter I had at that time, in the National Hospital in Riyadh—and what a beautiful and happy occasion it was. In the summer of that year, most financially able Saudis left the heat of the country to take their vacation in Europe, the United States, or nearby Arab countries.

I and other mortal souls took our vacation in Saudi Arabia, in my case in Riyadh, the capital, where temperatures averaged no less than 40 degrees Celsius during the day. But it was dry, which made it bearable. And while I was still not happy with my situation, some signs of hope appeared here and there.

I began to enjoy my work, because we educated Saudis began to feel excited after our leadership pushed us to be real decision makers. By the end of 1974, I was promoted from the junior grade of ten to a senior grade of twelve; the civil service cadre has fifteen grades. With that promotion, the government increased the total pay of all grades, almost doubling our salaries. And so, I and others became more relaxed and more confident, notwithstanding the fact that our government pay was about one-third of that of the private sector. I reasoned that confidence and happiness were not only derived from material gains. No higher pay in the private sector or anywhere would equal the happiness and pride I derived from my job in the government at that time. I decided that I would not leave that laboratory of nation-building, as long as I derived satisfaction from it.

Working on the Second Development Plan (1975–1980) increased my horizon and scope and shifted my interest from a narrow personal one about my own self and my immediate family, and sometimes, here and there, the pull of tribal interests, to that of my country as a whole. I, and others like me, were determined to work hard for better and shining tomorrows.

Gone, as far as I was concerned, were the limited, narrow tribal nomadic interests in my background. They were replaced by the broader and more rewarding interests of Saudi Arabia as a whole.

In reality, though, I was participating in the destruction of my roots through development, by pushing for the settlement of nomadic tribes, and the loss of most of their traditions. In other words, the lives of my father and ancestors, which I fought very hard to escape from.

15

Building the New Saudi Arabia

While the country was boiling with excitement and looking with hope and confidence to a promising future, we were shocked by the assassination of King Faisal in March 1975, at the hands of the son of his half-brother. This heinous act was done at a majlis, at which the King opened his residence to citizens who sought an audience with him. After being shot twice, he was taken to the hospital and pronounced dead. His assassin was convicted of regicide and executed, as Saudi law dictated.

The transfer of power to King Khalid and Crown Prince Fahd was swift and orderly. Many journalists wrote later that they expected to see soldiers and tanks in the streets of Riyadh. Instead, they saw the spontaneous and moving sorrow from the people of Saudi Arabia at the passing of King Faisal. The Saudi royal family, led by King Khalid and Crown Prince Fahd, exhibited sorrow with dignity and grace. The Hall of Riyadh government headquarters, inside as well as outside, was absolutely jammed with thousands of people who came from all over the country, as well as from outside of Saudi Arabia, to pay their respects and condolences.

I remember it took me about one hour and a half to reach the royal receiving line inside the hall. No barriers were erected, nor special rooms created; high and low, rich and poor, were massed together, and the scene was absolutely moving. Although precautions in such a situation were required, security cannot be maintained by force alone. On that day, while I was sandwiched, in the open air, among thousands of people, I certainly had no doubt that the country's leadership had the respect of the people.

A moving scene took place while I was standing in the street. Here came Prince Saud Al-Faisal from inside, moving among the waiting people, holding his arm in a cast after a skiing accident.

That scene was to me one of the saddest. A son had just lost his father, yet he was moving among people in a very dignified manner. Prince Saud repeated that graceful performance the next day, when I and many others went to pay respect to King Faisal's children in the King's palace. When I entered, the children of King Faisal were alone, and only the eldest prince, Abdullah, was absent. As usual, they were standing in the receiving line in order of age and seniority, and when I greeted the last one and noticed the sadness on the faces of those young men who had just lost their father, I felt almost suffocated and just wanted to get out of there.

When I did leave, I heard someone call my name. I turned and saw Prince Saud, who said I should not leave without having the customary cup of coffee, a sign of hospitality and welcome. To me, that gesture, and their calling my name, which happened to be the name of their deceased father, symbolized courage, grace, and a human touch.

I drank my coffee as fast as I could, and fled, because I was unable to stay in that room with all that sadness which one could feel and almost touch. Saudi Arabia and I continued our journey on the road of development with optimism and determination.

ψ ψ ψ

The Kingdom, at that time, was the place most of the famous and powerful people, from all over the world, wished to visit. Kings, presidents, heads of governments, tycoons of commerce and industry, journalists, legislators, all came or wanted to come. The minister of information at that time claimed that Saudi Arabia received, in one year, about 700 journalists from all over the world. With that flood of visitors, Saudi Arabia became a household name everywhere. All this sudden fame and financial power took place when the country was not prepared to receive so many people, especially not with its inadequate infrastructure, such as roads, airports, seaports, etc.

To summarize, Saudi Arabia lacked almost everything except money. While those of us in planning worked on our tasks, I was reading about us in the international mass media. Any Saudi who claimed knowledge of this or that about Saudi Arabia was courted to give speeches or comments, which led to some of us almost becoming stars, like in Hollywood. Most of us were aware that information seekers who followed us were interested in the country's economic power as well as the impact of development on Saudi society rather than super-personal powers—but some missed the real aims of the seekers when they saw their names in print or on TV. And with a severe shortage of almost everything, and an abundance of money, I could not help but observe that the most frustrated Saudis were the rich ones.

The reason for such frustration was the old saying: "money can't buy peace, comfort, and tranquility all the time." There was no dependable electrical supply, no running water, telephones, or paved roads. Just imagine leaving your house for work and returning to find that you can't enter your own house because of the digging of water, electrical, or telephone lines—and facing this discomfort for a long time.

Things were physically not available to be bought on the market. Once, we planners were called to brief the Crown Prince and other officials in the palace about the Kingdom's progress of development, and while we were waiting for our presentation, the electricity was cut. We were in the dark for a while, before kerosene lanterns were spread all over the place. Most of the time we economists preach the value of a fair and just mechanism of distribution in the economy, but in those days there was only a mechanism for distributing discomfort and misery all over Saudi Arabia. No one, weak or mighty, was immune to shortages.

There were many reasons for those shortages, such as the availability of financial resources in the government, as well as consumers' sudden increased demand for everything, while the country was being built almost from scratch. There was not enough supply of needed goods, services, and patience, and so inflation skyrocketed.

Human nature is the same all over the world. When a consumer has the means, and the purchasing power, to get what he or she wants, they usually want it fast, or frustrations and complaints will follow. Those characteristics were abundant in Saudi Arabia in those days. And no matter how much the government spent, to expedite the implementation of projects to meet rising demand, there were physical barriers. There was not enough manpower to build needed projects as soon as they were demanded. The Kingdom was lucky this frustration did not lead to dislocation in the structure of the society, which might have led to instability.

There were many reasons for that, such as the influx of millions of workers from all over the world, and the obstacles that delayed building projects as fast as possible. I counted at that time that there were 132 different nationalities working in Saudi Arabia.

I believe what saved the country from that instability, which many people, especially journalists from all over the world, predicted, was that citizens of the country were busy earning a lot of money, whether they were professional or not. Government expenditures trickled down. Also, most citizens were aware that the government was doing its utmost to develop the country, and to raise their standards of living, which they were entitled to and had been deprived of for a long time. The country's development was done openly, for all to see, and was international in nature.

There were no hidden agendas nor secrecy about why Saudi Arabia was going through that much trouble. The aims were clear for every fair-minded observer to see—and that, in my opinion, saved Saudi society from the dislocations many countries faced when they went through their development.

And so, we pressed forward, and with the passage of time our efficiency at doing things increased, and the speed of our development in all its facets quickened.

By the end of the seventies, even prophets of dooms and gloom could not help but admire the country's achievements, despite how mistakes were made here and there, which were expected in such a fast development. The country and especially its leadership deserved respect for a job well done.

ψ ψ ψ

In the summer of 1975, after the schools recessed, I decided to take a vacation with my family. It was our first vacation since I graduated from college in September 1973. I went to see my boss, Mr. Hisham Nazer, who was in Jeddah, with the government. To my misfortune, he told me it was okay to go, but first I had to stay for a few days to head the Saudi delegation in negotiating with the visiting delegation of a far eastern country.

After he described the situation in detail and gave me advice, I panicked and said, "Why me?" There were people senior to me in our agency, and I was junior in comparison to the head of the foreign delegation. Mr. Nazer refused all my arguments, and I stayed, of course, and received the foreign delegation, headed by the vice minister of foreign affairs of that country.

I noticed, when I met the Saudi delegates, that most of them were senior to me, especially the one who represented our Ministry of Foreign Affairs. This minister almost took over as head of the Saudi side, until I took him aside, in the presence of most of the Saudi delegates, and told him who was to be the lead. Until this day, I have not understood the logic of making the CPO a counterpart to the delegation from the foreign ministry of another country, but that was what happened. The protocol was that I, as head of the Saudi side, must accompany the foreign delegation head on his individual visits to Saudi ministers in their offices.

In the visit to the governor of the Saudi central bank, I learned clearly the aim of the foreign delegation's visit. The aim was to solicit a $500 million loan from Saudi Arabia. The governor was diplomatically evasive, but it was clear that he was not in favor of granting it.

As a matter of fact, he told me to do my best not to have the head of our guests see King Khalid, who was in Taif, about a two-hour drive up the mountain from Jeddah. My counterpart made it clear that he would be honored to see the King, and he was determined not to go back to his country without doing so. I promised him I would do my best, but deep in my heart I was working against fulfilling his request—diplomatically, of course, like all those ministers who had, in my youth, prevented me from seeing the King and his ministers as I looked to secure a scholarship to study in the United States. The tables had turned.

In one of our meetings, late at night, the head, my counterpart, stood and thanked me for arranging to meet the King the next morning in Taif. I was caught off-balance, because I had no idea about it, and as I mentioned before it was not my intention for them to meet, as I had been advised. I answered him with a smile, diplomatically of course, and told him I would be happy to fulfill his request; he should be ready at 6:00 a.m. the next day.

I was shocked at that development, but I had no choice, and so in the morning we were on our way to meet the King. Upon our arrival at the Royal Court in Taif, I saw the head of protocol, whom I did not know, and told him who I was, and that maybe I should brief the King. He told me that the visit was a courtesy call, and the King did not need any briefing. He said this in a not so nice way and pointed to a chair and told me to sit there and keep quiet.

When we met the King, I introduced the foreign delegation, and I said, "I am Dr. Faisal Al-Bashir, the head of the Saudi side in the negotiation." The King had his translator beside him, and after a few greetings, to my surprise, my counterpart requested the loan from the King.

King Khalid was puzzled by his request. I shook my head, and His

Majesty understood that it meant no. He answered politely that the loan should be discussed with the relevant Saudi agencies, and then he would see. When the guests took their leave, I was the last one to leave, and the King asked me, "What did you say your name was?" I told him, and wanted to leave fast, because our guest had already left the King's office. I was afraid they were already in the cars, waiting. As a matter of fact, the head of protocol was standing by the door and urging me to leave—but how could I leave the King?

The King asked me from what part of the country I came from, and when I told him from the North, he was not sure he recognized my last name, Al-Bashir. Then I told him my family name, Al-Mershed.

He smiled, and asked me about my uncle Rakan, and whether his eye operation had gone okay. I was really amazed that the King still remembered the operation my uncle had the year before, when the King was in the area of Aljouf in the North of Saudi Arabia. He asked me about the family and told me to carry his greetings to my uncle and my family.

All this time, people were listening, and our guests were waiting for me, instead of the other way around.

Then, when I reached the door of the King's office in a hurry, the King called me back and asked what I had specialized in for my doctorate.

I told him economics.

Again, he said a few kind words and let me go.

When I came out, it felt so good to see the head of protocol in particular, because of the way he had treated me. He was almost running, to tell the waiting guests in the cars that I was held by the King because he was inquiring about my family.

My prestige skyrocketed, in the eyes of all Saudis who were present, as well as non-Saudis. Certainly, I was elated, and to this day I feel gratitude to King Khalid, for how nice and decent he was to me every time I saw him from that day forward.

On our way back to Jeddah, our guests were impressed by his majesty's humane gesture toward me, and I was of course happy to show how the leadership is so close to its citizens. Thus, a trip I did not enjoy, on the whole, ended up being a very pleasant one.

ψ ψ ψ

I was a part of the nation's development, involved in it daily and enjoying it with all its ups and downs. In 1975, I was promoted from grade twelve to fourteen. It was a big jump, to say the least, and a welcome one for Faisal the Nomad.

That year, after King Faisal's death, the CPO hosted a special meeting that started at 8.00 p.m. and ended very late, after midnight. Attendees were H.R.H. the Crown Prince, the first deputy prime minister (Prince Fahad), the second deputy prime minister (Prince Abdullah), the head of the national guard (Prince Turki), the vice minister of defense, the governor of Riyadh region (Prince Salman), the president of the CPO (Mr. Hisham Nazer), the vice president of CPO (Dr. Fayez Badr), and me.

The subject of the meeting was the presentation of the Second Five-Year Development Plan (1975–1980), sector by sector. The format was that each sector's experts entered the conference room, presented their work, and left, to be followed by the next section. We stopped the presentation for dinner around 10:00 p.m., when the municipal sector was onboard. I was impressed by the seriousness of the discussion and comments of the present leadership of the country, to meet the challenges of development for the sake of the country's welfare. A light comment followed, before we recessed for dinner, and during the girls' education presentation, the Crown Prince caught me by surprise.

He looked at me and said, "Faisal, no more excuses for young Saudis not to marry Saudi girls, because the country has educated Saudi girls."

I was really surprised, because I had no idea he knew I married an American woman. Come to think of it, I wish I had told the Prince that my second wife would be Saudi, as I was permitted to have four wives. But even knowing my traditions, there were some limits to comradeship. I felt that imaginary lines should not be crossed between the crown prince and a Saudi citizen. I refrained from saying anything.

Certainly, I was lucky and happy to be present that night, and to observe from such close range the behavior of the leadership toward the development of Saudi Arabia. I was delighted by the openness of the princes and how friendly they were. Although I had met some of them before, I never had the chance to be a participant with them in a discussion of this magnitude. At that time, I thanked the Almighty that I never left my government job to work in the private sector, because no matter how much I earned, my rewards in that sector would have been dwarfed by my reward of being present at the creation of the new Saudi Arabia.

During the dinner break, food was served in the big hall of the building. The princes and staff of the CPO were side by side, sitting on the marble floor of the hall. The atmosphere was festive, and the Crown Prince and his brothers were friendly with everyone. When I stood to get my dessert, the Crown Prince urged me to eat a lot of sweets, because I was slim enough, not like most of the people around the main table. At that moment Prince Abdullah said that he didn't see any municipality projects for Hail, a city in the North of the country.

Being the coordinator of the presentation, I told him that after dinner we would be going back to the conference room, because the presentation was not finished, and he would see Hail projects, as with all other cities.

I should have stopped there, but I continued by saying, "Don't worry, our uncles came from the same tribe, Shammar."

I was alluding to the fact that his mother and mine came from the same tribe, which was located in and around Hail. But the Prince didn't know me, and it was an unnecessary addition to my answer. I regret it to this day, despite the fact that many people saw nothing wrong with it.

What bothered me about that comment, although it was the truth, was that it could be interpreted that one of the seniors from the country's leadership was only concerned about the welfare of his nearest relatives, rather than the people as a whole. I might be wrong, but that has been a source of my discomfort until now; however, we all live to learn from our mistakes.

Prince Abdullah and his brother Salman went up to wash, after which he came directly to me, standing with colleagues, and asked, "What does your Uncle Rakan think of you?" I realized then that Prince Salman had told him I come from Al-Mershed family.

After that incident, I became friends with Prince Abdullah, later our King, until he passed away and Prince Salman took over as our King in January 2015. All my life, and especially in our Majles in the tent, when I was growing up, I observed and was taught to be careful and think before speaking. In that instance, I certainly did not follow what I was taught. I crossed that imaginary line, and got carried away with Prince Abdullah, who was one of the senior members of the leadership of the country, specifically, the second deputy prime minister, the third man in line to be the King which he became). That incident with Prince Abdullah, in the presence of his brothers, including Crown Prince Fahd, showed how a real leader will not be bothered by an uncalled-for comment by a thoughtless bureaucrat like me.

After dinner, we went back to the conference room to continue the presentation, at the end of which the Crown Prince asked me a macroeconomic question. It concerned how high the country's national income would be at the end of the plan.

I am glad that before I answered His Royal Highness, I remembered the advice of professor D. Wells, a member of my oral exam committee for my degree in September 1973, when he asked me, "Now, Faisal, you are a holder of a doctorate of economics, do you think that you can answer any question your King asked you?"

With the intoxication of hearing my name prefixed with "Doctor" for the first time, my answer was, "Of course, and on the spot."

The professor was kind and gave me the advice that saved me from shooting from the hip and making a fool of myself in answering the Crown Prince's question. He said, "We teach here theoretically to learn how to analyze, to be critical and careful from jumping to conclusions with your King or whom you are advising. I bet you in two years of actual work you will learn how reality is different from theoretical university teaching."

I certainly did, and my answer to the Prince was simple. Give me more time to analyze and go through impacts of each sector of the national income, and maybe then I can give you a more rational answer.

It was a night to remember, in the history of the development of Saudi Arabia, which continued its march to transform its economy from a primitive one to a modern, diversified one. In a way, Saudi Arabia was trying hard to catch up with economies of the late twentieth century, when its economic base belonged to a backward and primitive past. I personally struggled and developed, too, through participating and charting projects beyond the magnitude of those I read about in the economic history books of most countries.

ψ ψ ψ

Speed of construction was a must, in order to meet the country's demands, and so we paid dearly for that requirement in financial resources as well as in discomfort. Cities were built all over empty lands, as fast as possible, and so all other needed infrastructure projects began to change the face of Saudi Arabia's topography in a short period of time. Those of us who were directly involved with planning, through construction or follow-up of projects, began to doubt the country's ability to finish what we'd planned in the Second Development Plan.

It was a very bad feeling, but I never stopped to think, because there was no time to think, and the pressure at work was high. Also, it is human nature to push away the unwanted as far as possible, and not to think about it. Sounds of development in the country were almost like music for everyone to hear. With cranes reaching high, and roads being laid, the sounds of machinery were heard day and night. Dust produced by roads being paved, in some places, was like fog all over the cities. Environmentalists had a hard time in those days in Saudi Arabia.

Little by little we began to relax, with every positive result, no matter how small, whether it was a thank-you from a consumer who had electricity connected to his house, or an article in a newspaper that reflected the happiness of people at how the newly paved roads reduced dust.

Before the end of 1975, there was a major government restructuring. Some new ministries were established, and the CPO was renamed the Ministry of Planning (MOP). My title changed from Director General to Assistant Deputy Minister for National Planning.

In that period, I borrowed heavily, to buy land to build a home in Riyadh. For the first time, the nomad Faisal was going to have a concrete modern villa to call his own, and not a tent as a home—with a permanent address, financed mainly through a real estate fund the government created to help citizens build their houses. It was a loan of about $80,000.00 ($=3.75 Saudi Riyal-S.A.), interest-free for 25 years, and 20 percent of it was from a grant. It was of course an easy loan, and I believe that that real estate fund, which was like a mortgage bank, was the most successful fund the government established in those days—despite how many loans went unpaid. Government development aims were to help people, not to stuff its coffers with gold, so to speak.

While I was working hard and trying to build my villa, which took three years to finish, my financial worries were put to rest forever in 1976. The source of that financial security was a generous land gift from the government, which I sold at an astronomical price during that high-inflation period. I was not the only citizen who received a land grant; it was, and still is, the tradition of the government to grant free lands to its people.

1976 was the most difficult and uncomfortable year of Saudi development that I participated in. Although some progress was made, shortages of almost everything persisted and even increased, mainly because of congestion at the seaports, which was the biggest obstacle to importing goods to supply the market and reduce inflation. Waiting periods for ships to unload averaged three months, which shipping companies took advantage of by charging for waiting that long. They began to use the oldest ships in their fleets. Some were barely seaworthy. The government even used helicopters to unload ships on the high seas before they reached the congested seaports. It was estimated that we were losing almost one-fourth of cement bags in the sea by unloading that way. People began to complain, and newspapers printed critical articles, most of which were directed at the Ministry of Planning, when in reality that ministry was not the cause of delayed construction. The Ministry participated with other ministries, to set their plans and follow them, as well as to see how construction projects were going. We shared some of the blame, but certainly not all of it. However, we were in the news most of the time, because the MOP had a very organized public relations campaign, so we took most of the blame.

That year, we discovered how the cost of projects was changing monthly. Companies argued that they must hedge against inflation, which was legitimate, but we found that the cost of things imported by Saudi Arabia were higher than those in neighboring countries. That was clear-cut price discrimination, which led me to write a simple linear equation asking why we should not use the price of oil to retaliate by the same percentage against those countries who overcharged Saudi Arabia. I really wrote it out of frustration, and I was aware of its shortcomings and difficulties, but not our ability to harm those who harmed us. That was the period of the shortage of availability of crude oil all over the world, which Saudi Arabia had in abundance.

In reality, Saudi Arabia was in a position to charge whatever price it wanted. My paper was received with a lot of support, and some criticism, which was expected. It went from one committee to another until it faded and died, but not before it cost one of the biggest international companies in its field a contract worth almost a billion Saudi Riyals, when I discovered they were overcharging us by double the price.

ψ ψ ψ

As I have mentioned, one of the most obvious obstacles to development at that time was congestion in seaports. The appointment of Dr. Fayez Bader, after about a year and a half, solved it. He succeeded in his job. The supply of goods to the market accelerated, and that lowered the level of inflation. The country began to relax.

16

NOMAD TO DEPUTY MINISTER

Although 1976 was a difficult year for the development of Saudi Arabia, on personal grounds it was a good one. I was financially secure, building my villa slowly but surely. My family was happy, and my name began to be recognized in government circles. And from a professional point of view, I was excited and proud when the publisher, John Wiley and Sons Inc., agreed to publish my book, based on my Ph.D. thesis, under the title *A Structural Econometric Model of the Saudi Arabian Economy: 1960–1970*. It was released in 1977. The agreement was for that book to be the first of two volumes.

Despite my personal so-called success and happiness, my confidence was down because of the huge obstacles in the way of the country's development. All of us in the country saw that development as a once-in-a-lifetime opportunity. It was implemented openly, for all the world to see, and so observers who visited the country, whether journalists or others, were doubtful of our ability to accomplish what we planned.

That doubt was not very helpful in building confidence. I and many in planning and other fields began to question whether it was worth it to push so fast when inflation was so high, which might be a problem for the economy for a long time. And so, an almost open campaign in the local newspapers began to advocate slowing down; some went as far as to say that it was better for Saudi Arabia to stop the programs of development altogether. Again, we in the Ministry of Planning were blamed for all that misfortune. We tried to reason with those doubters, as well as loud advocates, that development requires sacrifices, whether material or non-material.

Availability of financial resources helped, of course, but not enough.

There were few listeners, and still fewer people were convinced.

Simply put, the people of Saudi Arabia were fed up and were tired of all the shortages of things, and the discomfort that entailed. Many began to hope to go back to simpler days.

The atmosphere for us planners and most government officials was depressing, notwithstanding all the support we received from the leadership of the country, and especially Crown Prince Fahd.

During that period of difficulties, I received a summons from the Council of Ministers' Secretariat, to meet a newly established committee on such and such day in the Institute of Public Administration (IPA) in Riyadh. On arrival, I found two Saudi economists whom I respected. Both were either directly or indirectly employed by the Ministry of Finance and National Economy. Upon entering the meeting room, there were ministers of finance, commerce, transport, civil service, and planning (its deputy minister, instead of the minister, who was outside the country). When the discussion started, I realized that the ministerial committee was entrusted to look into the Second Development Plan's projects, to see which ones could be eliminated completely, frozen for a while, or have their implementation extended. The immediate purpose was to control the high level of inflation through reducing government expenditures on the Plan. To my dismay and disbelief, most suggestions were to recommend ceasing implementation of the Second Development Plan as the most effective remedy to deal with inflation.

My argument was simple: granted that the level of inflation was unacceptable, but it would be harmful, especially in the long run, to stop the plan, and it could be more harmful to deprive the country of projects needed to create an economically productive base for the first time in the country's history. I urged the committee to go through a thorough analysis, to see which projects could be eliminated, like office buildings—but I urged them to please leave productive projects untouched, no matter how much short-term discomfort prevailed.

My suggestion was twisted to mean the opposite, and they took what I'd said to mean that I agreed mostly to scrap the plan. I was shocked to hear that from my minister upon his return, and that was the beginning of what almost amounted to a campaign to discredit me by misquoting me or lying, which reached the level of treason.

A few days after that committee meeting, on the front page in bold letters, the famous *Herald Tribune* newspaper announced that the government of Saudi Arabia had scrapped the Second Development Plan. The title was a shock, and the details of the article did not support the title. Still, the damage was done, from an information point of view.

But the plan was saved, and those who believed in its merits continued to fight for its survival and the development of Saudi Arabia.

That famous committee meeting was followed by the establishment of another committee to look into the financial position of the government of Saudi Arabia. It was headed by Prince Saud Al-Faisal, the foreign minister, ministers of finance and petroleum, and the governor of SAMA (the central bank) and planning. I was present, with my counterpart from the Ministry of Finance. We later drafted the committee paper that showed a very healthy financial position, to be submitted to the leadership of the country.

Somehow, the establishment of two committees, one after the other, gave me an uneasy feeling, like something was being looked into. I was unable to put my finger on it, but I knew it had to do with the Second Development Plan.

ψ ψ ψ

At this juncture of my story, I should state the following with regards to the development of Saudi Arabia and the thinking of its people.

Like all countries in this world, in Saudi Arabia people have different opinions about things, especially about programs for trans-formation of the country. Within the government of Saudi Arabia, there were high officials—and, I might add, some in the leader-ship—who did not look favorably on certain details of the plan, on philosophical grounds. And that group would, every now and then, put some new ideas in, which conflicted with what the plan said.

An example was, why not have general, broad guidelines of eco-nomic growth, instead of this plan? I and many others did not un-derstand what they meant by this *growth* thing, except that they were against detailed planning.

One day, my minister asked me to meet an ex-finance minister from West Germany, who was well-known as a financial expert. I was really excited to meet him, though by that time I had met many famous people, so I was immune to star fever.

I was expecting an economic discussion but was disappointed when our meeting degenerated into what amounted to threats if I refused to hand him the financial position papers of the govern-ment of Saudi Arabia. Those were top secret. I tried to reason with him and asked him who sent him to the Ministry of Planning to ask for this specific document. He answered that someone in the Ministry of Finance had sent him. Then I told him that person had a copy, and I couldn't understand why he'd sent him to me. There must be some kind of misunderstanding somewhere, I said.

He left my office after telling me that he came to Saudi Arabia at the request of Crown Prince Fahd through Chancellor Helmet Schmidt of West Germany, and that I should hand him a copy of what he requested. I told him I was still puzzled as to why the Min-istry of Finance did not give him the document. I said if he brought me the direct order from Prince Fahd, I would oblige.

A few days later, he visited me, this time accompanied by another person. Again, he insisted that I should give him the document, which again I refused, and he left.

It seemed to me that the other person was there to be a witness to my refusal. Needless to say, I lost respect for him, and I had no doubt he reciprocated the same feeling for me, which culminated in me criticizing his final report severely—in a very objective way, I believe. The proof of this was that his report died in the corridors of power in the government of Saudi Arabia. His recommendations, as I understood them, were typical of bankers who are more interested in money accumulation than a development planner, who sees money as no more than a tool to enhance the welfare of society, and who felt that money should be spent for that purpose before inflation depreciated its purchasing power.

🌿 🌿 🌿

In November 1976, Dr. Fayez Badr, the deputy minister of planning, was promoted to head a newly established independent agency called Ports Presidency. The vacancy of his previous position created some kind of competition, because senior positions in the government were rarely vacant, and the number of ministers and deputy ministers was limited, unlike today. I made the decision then that if I didn't get the position, I would resign my government position.

There was tremendous psychological pressure on me. Every now and then an acquaintance dropped by to tell me that so-and-so had already been submitted to the King to fill the position. In one meeting, at the Ministry of Petroleum and Mineral Resources, I was representing the Ministry of Planning as acting deputy minister. One of the members of that meeting, who had a ministerial rank, took me to his house and told me to stay in the Ministry of Planning until the vacant position was filled.

At that moment I realized how the position was generating friction among some government ministers.

In another meeting, in the Higher Committee for the Development of Riyadh, headed by the Governor of Riyadh, Prince Salman, the

Prince referred to me as the deputy minister of planning, and I corrected him by saying I was acting deputy minister. He paused and indicated that he was under the impression that I was appointed and in the position.

About a week later, in January 1977, Faisal the Nomad was appointed Deputy Minister of Planning. It happened when my name was mentioned on the 9:00 p.m. news. One of my tribesmen was in my house, and when he heard my name, he said, "Is that you?" When I said yes, he asked, "Why didn't you tell me?" I laughed and told him it was because I did not know about it until then.

He was so happy—it was like I was his son. He began to recite a story of how he spent about two days in the desert, searching for a gazelle, after he heard that I had lost mine, when I was about eight years old. I asked my mother about the story, and she remembered it.

What he meant was that I did not disappoint him and those who believed in me, and that I had made them proud. I missed him when he died in 1980.

ψ ψ ψ

The first congratulation I received, the morning after my appointment as deputy minister, was from Prince Salman, Governor of the Riyadh region. I was really moved by his sincere happiness and his wish for future success. He never failed to amaze me and all those who knew him. He was always one of the busiest princes in the Kingdom and yet was able to remember even the small touches of human kindness. As an administrator, he rarely told people to come tomorrow. If he could solve the matter on the spot, he did. I and many others are grateful to him for keeping his door open to all kinds of people, who are in contact with him daily.

A few days after my promotion, the Minister of Planning, Mr. Nazer, held a general meeting to start thinking about the Third Development Plan 1980–1985. He made it clear to all listeners that the deputy minister was in charge, and no one should come to him unless the deputy minister was unable to deal with the matter.

This kind of directive closed all loopholes in the minds of those who were senior to me and competing for the job before my promotion. In running the ministry, I did my best to be a team leader and trust and support all subordinates. I even alleviated the anxiety of those who had been my seniors, by giving each one of them the authority to run his department the way he wanted, provided the job was done. I delegated as much as possible, and I believe that in that way I created an atmosphere of respect and friendship. I could concentrate on the things I thought were my direct responsibility, in economic matters and membership in government committees and boards. I never believed that a team leader should derive respect from being a secretive and centralized decision maker.

ψ ψ ψ

1977 continued to be a good year. My house construction was going slowly but surely, and no surprises disturbed my peace or my family. The country was busy, and one could feel it gaining more confidence. Discomfort was getting less severe with the passage of time. And more goods were entering the market, which people hoped would tame inflation.

My landlord started to signal his unhappiness with the amount of rent I was paying him, though I had another year to go on my rental contract. I tried to reason with him, without success. One day, after entering my house, coming from my office, a man I did not know introduced himself as the new owner of the house, and asked me to vacate it, the sooner the better. I told him that by law I was entitled to stay for another year, according to my contract, but I was willing to increase the rent. We economists always talk about fair prices and wages, and I was aware that my rent was probably no more than 20 percent of the going rate in the market.

The new landlord left me, without agreeing on anything. I solicited the help of my original landlord, and raised the rent by about 150 percent, but my offer was rejected.

A week later, I received a summons to be in court on such and such a day at 8:00 a.m.—what a convenient hour. My minister and other staff advised me to either ignore the summons or send someone else. I had never been in court in my country, and honestly, I was curious to see what a court looked like and how business was conducted, so I went on the specified date and hour to find my landlord waiting there.

I reasoned with him, to accept my raised rent, but he refused. When we were called, we entered a simple office, where a judge, who was blind, and his clerk were sitting. The judge asked me to present my case, and I told him that the government had established rent control to save renters from unfair landlord practices, and I still had one year to go in my contract. I had offered to increase the rent but was rejected.

My landlord presented his case, claiming that he bought the villa to move his family from a less comfortable house south of Riyadh to a nicer place in the Almalaz area. To my surprise, the judge addressed my adversary by saying, "And you say you do not have another house?" When he said yes, the judge turned to his cleric and dictated the verdict that I stay until the end of my contract at the same rental cost.

Of course, my landlord objected, but the judge put him down by telling him that he knew that he had other houses.

We left the office, and my landlord tried to convince me to give him the raised rent I'd suggested. This time I refused him.

Back in my office, the deputy minister of planning was a happy person, thanks to winning the case. He had satisfied his curiosity about Saudi courthouses, which I never entered again.

That case with the judge, the simple office, and the swift verdict reminded me of my tribe's way of solving problems. It was simple, direct, and final; in my tribe, it was much the same, except that the judge was usually a well-known tribesman, accompanied by two witnesses.

ψ ψ ψ

While I was living it up and content with my lot, here came Salhoub, who was born and raised around our tent, and had settled in Arar in the North of Saudi Arabia, driving a taxi. He came to tell me there were many opportunities in the country to make money. I told him I was happy with what I had, and he exploded, saying, "You can get more and help people like me in the process." He explained how, and I realized it did not conflict with my job.

It was during the start of building King Khalid Military City in Hafr Al-Batin, near the border with Kuwait, that the government ordered the contractor to hire any needed equipment from Saudi citizens, like dump trucks. I told Salhoub, my informant, to give me some time to investigate, and in the end, I was convinced what he told me was correct, so I borrowed about three million Saudi Riyals from the National Commercial Bank (today the Saudi National Bank) and bought 11 dump trucks.

Salhoub was shocked by the number but relaxed when I told him he was in charge and would be compensated handsomely. The next day, he hired drivers and took the trucks to the contractor in King Khalid City, and they were leased for almost four years. It was a rewarding contract for all of us, especially dear Salhoub, who quit his taxi business. For a while he physically collected thousands of riyals every month, until I opened a bank account in the city, when a bank was established there.

Salhoub built a new house in Arar and retired on an income I gave him as a reward for his advice. He passed away in 1982. I felt then, and still feel now, a lot of happiness from what I did for Salhoub. In his house, once, he saw me suffering from a severe sore throat, and he cried when he saw how uncomfortable I was.

☙ ☙ ☙

Life continued to be pleasant. I was enjoying my work. We moved to our villa at last. My father and mother visited us in our new home. Also, Stephanie's father, Dr. Wegner, and her mother, who was working with the joint commission between Saudi Arabia and the United States, in charge of establishing an agriculture laboratory, came to live in Riyadh, and were so happy to see us in our home. Being in Riyadh, we saw them often, not like my father, who barely enjoyed the city for a week before he went back to his sheep and some of his tribesmen.

Development and its programs continued unabated. As an economist of quantitative specialties, I regret that we were unable to analyze the economic viability of each project, including the interdependency between projects. We were unable to do it because the pressure of the country's needs was mounting, and the leadership was trying to speed up implementation of projects.

We certainly wasted a lot of financial resources, because when the choice was between the speed of implementation and slowing down to save money, the preference was obvious. Money was available, so we should go on as fast as possible with development. That speed in particular was the main source of the waste, plus the effect of inflation, which remained a problem. I hope that my emphasis on the desire to speed development, at almost any cost, will not be interpreted as that we were working without a frame of reference. As a matter of fact, we had a yearly budget and the plan to refer to.

The pressure I was under was tremendous, but it was bearable because I was getting positive signals that I was doing a fine job. Alone in my office, sometimes, I began to remember those college days when as students we thought making decisions and explaining them to listeners were simple matters.

I remembered the take-home exam in regional economics, where Professor Allen of the University of Oregon, during my master's degree study, asked: "Students, consider yourself as an advisor to a head of government who is not an economist. Explain to him how input, output, and linear programming economics tools help him in sharpening his arguments, to convince people to support his government's economic programs."

In my position, which was the real world, not the classroom, I found myself unable to apply those tools to Saudi development without reducing its speed of implementation, which was almost taboo. For the first time in my life, I faced inner anxiety without being able to share my thoughts with a friend or loved one.

The source of that anxiety was the trust the country's leadership placed in us, to build a nation anew. Maybe I was one of those Saudis who took the matter as a personal challenge, when, in reality, I was part of a group facing the same task.

That group was really small, relatively speaking. There were about 20 ministers and about 40 deputy ministers, who were involved in running the government under the leadership of the King and the Crown Prince. To my fortune or misfortune, I was the only deputy minister in my ministry, and that ministry almost had to be in every committee or board to do with development. The ministers and I were with others, and were involved almost weekly, if not daily, sometimes making decisions or recommending decisions to higher-ups. And the Crown Prince, especially, was not of the opinion that we should slow down. He felt that all effort, individually or collectively, must be made to enhance the country's development.

Through the follow-up report of implementing projects every year by the Ministry of Planning, the Crown Prince noticed that one ministry was lagging in spending its budget. He reprimanded that ministry, by saying, "The government is not interested in accumulating money, but rather appropriating money to be spent on development projects, to uplift standards of living for the Saudi people."

That was a direct and a clear order for us to hurry up executing projects.

In my case, in addition to my portfolio as deputy minister, I was a member of the committee or board of directors of: Saudi Basic Industry (SABIC), chairman of one of its subsidiaries called Kemya, the Petroleum and Mineral Organization (Petromin), the Ports Presidency, the Water Desalination (SWCC), the Saudi National Airlines (Saudia), the Saudi Industrial Development Fund (SIDF), the Tech Committee for Petroleum, the Petromin-shell Refinery in Jubail, and still others. Plus, I was occupied at least a month every year for the yearly budget preparation at the Ministry of Finance and National Economy.

While I was doing my job, it seems I became popular with journalists visiting the country, which became another load to carry. I enjoyed this popularity at the beginning, but with the passage of time I became tired of it.

Realizing that I was being stretched almost to my limit, I suggested the establishment of a position called Deputy Minister for Technical Affairs, to run the ministry and free myself from administration of the Ministry of Planning. Mr. Nazer, the minister who would have to send the suggestion to the Crown Prince for approval, refused. He gave me advice, that the Ministry of Planning and Administration leadership structure was the best structure he could think of. He based his opinion on his experience as the deputy minister of the Ministry of Petroleum and Mineral Resources before he became the minister of planning.

At this point, I must warn my readers not to think I was the only government official under tremendous pressure to perform. There were many like me, whether ministers or deputy ministers, who were doing their utmost for the development of the country.

That situation reminded me about an observation I heard from a British World Bank official, who supposedly said he feared for many of us, as unhealthy consequences could come from the hours of work we were subjected to. I knew a few government officials who went to hospitals because they were unable to take it.

ψ ψ ψ

During those days, and especially in 1977, although I was completely absorbed by my work and enjoying it, every time I saw my father in Riyadh, or when I visited him now and then, I urged him to settle. I pointed out to him that no matter how much he loved the nomadic life, and no matter how difficult emotionally it would be to abandon it, he must settle, and that nomadic life was gone forever. I reasoned with him many times that he was fighting a lost battle, and that it was the natural process of societies to move gradually from nomadic life to a settled one.

He rarely disagreed with my analysis, and promised often to settle, but continued to live in his big tent, and sometimes abandoned the big tent for a small one, making it easier to follow his sheep from one place to another, where grass was available all over the desert of northern Saudi Arabia, Jordan, or Iraq. I was told once that he was rescued by helicopter in the Jordan desert during a heavy snowstorm and still refused to abandon what he considered a beautiful way of living.

There was no doubt in my mind that he was struggling to reach the right decision and was afraid of the unknown. I did not blame him. I pointed out to him often that financial resources were available, and I took him in my car to show him lands I owned in Riyadh, where we could build him a house around some of the tribe's houses in the city.

He always liked the idea but vanished the next day after promising he would be back. I became so frustrated with my father that I began to rationalize with myself. I sang the praises of nomadic life with other tribesmen, and now I couldn't accept or even sympathize with my father as he was trying to live that life.

239

In a way, I became alien to the roots I came from, all because of my pursuit of education, which was, and still is, a means by which a human being changes his situation to a better one, by harnessing his or her potential as fully as possible, for the welfare of that individual, and ultimately society as a whole.

Each of us contributes to the world we live in, in proportion to our abilities, which we mainly derive from education and experience. That was my assessment of education and how important it was for the development of human ability. Short of that assessment, I reasoned, education is useless.

17

THE END OF INNOCENCE

In the summer of 1977, and in many following summers, my family joined the Saudi exodus for vacations in cooler places. Those were the days when Saudis were armed with a lot of money and the desire to explore the world. Some were well-behaved, made their country proud and were good ambassadors; others were not so. True and made-up stories were published all over the world, describing how Saudis behaved as if we were different human beings from the Texans, for example, when they discovered oil. Or, for that matter, Californians after the Gold Rush, or the Japanese in the 1980s.

Traveling all over this world and seeing and tasting the good and the bad in it, the Saudis got educated fast. In reaction to some incidents of bad behavior, printed all over the world, there were some people in Saudi Arabia who advocated for not allowing such poorly behaved people to travel abroad, by confiscating their passports. The government rejected such suggestions, and I am glad, because I believe positive consequences of international travel outweigh the negative ones. Many prophets of doom and gloom urged the government to restrict free international travel, to save Saudi society from its bad influence, but the government stood fast and refused. Needless to say, Saudi society came out of that travel boom as normal as any society in this world.

The year 1978 saw many development projects completed, and citizens became less vocal in their criticism. And no doubt the Saudi people began to reap the fruits of that development, by having more schools, roads, hospitals, factories, etc. Gone were the days of sleepy Saudi Arabia, where its people supposedly accepted their lot in this life with low standards of living. Experts who reached such conclusions about the Saudi people learned their lesson—human beings, when given the chance, will always strive to better their standard of living materially as well as non-materially.

The story of Saudi Arabia's development and successes needed to be told. And so, many Saudis, including myself, were given the chance to tell the world about the transformation of the country in that short period of time. With the passage of time, my name became known to the mass media, inside Saudi Arabia and internationally. I became more willing to give interviews in praise of Saudi Arabia's achievements. I was happy to give those interviews, despite the headaches I faced every now and then, and my personal feelings of less and less enjoyment, the more I delivered those interviews. The famous law of diminishing returns in economics applied.

But it was difficult to stop suddenly when moving at high speed. I continued cruising, singing the positive consequences of Saudi development in raising the standards of living, and protecting human dignity from poverty, illiteracy, and other ills.

In order to avoid misunderstandings about my worth and importance, I must mention here, for the last time in my story, that I never forgot or overlooked who had the ultimate power to approve or disapprove projects of development in Saudi Arabia. I was working within a frame of parameters set and approved by the leadership of Saudi Arabia, represented by the King and the Crown Prince. And no matter how much positive reaction I got to my speeches or interviews, I knew my limit and tried hard to never cross that imaginary line of the limits placed on me. Every person, no matter how high and powerful he becomes, is a small factor in the development of a country.

I have to mention this personal belief because I felt very sad for some of my colleagues, who were intoxicated with their worth and power, and crossed that imaginary line of correct behavior. Their so-called importance vanished as fast as the mirage in the desert, when it went to their heads. The leadership rejected them, and so did Saudi society.

The socioeconomic system of the country was, and still is, dynamic. Government officials, whether ministers, deputy ministers, or someone else, were not passive actors but initiators who performed, in my opinion, very well under tremendous pressure and enormous challenges during the most exciting period of Saudi development of the last century.

The year 1978 saw the preparation for the Third Development Plan, 1980–1985. The government selected 14 Saudi professionals from ministries and agencies to draft the plan's strategy. All meetings, for almost four months, took place in the Ministry of Planning, after which it was submitted to the Council of Ministers and received the King's approval. Then it was the responsibility of each ministry and independent agency to draft its specific plan, coordinating with the Ministry of Planning. The plan's preparation ended at the close of 1979 and got its approval at that time from the Council of Ministers and the King.

The period of the preparation of the Third Development Plan was a relaxed one. All factors were favorable for Saudi Arabia to embark on another cycle of development. I and others who were directly involved in planning looked with optimism to the future of Saudi development, to fulfill many dreams not yet accomplished.

ψ ψ ψ

On personal grounds, I was satisfied by my situation, living in my own home at last. What added more happiness to me was that my father at last decided to settle down and rent a house in the city of Hafr Al-Batin. He started, with two of my brothers, to build their own villas. My father selected that city, about four hours' drive from Riyadh, so he could be near his sheep, which he kept.

His plan was simple and appealed to him greatly: every time he got tired of urban life, he would follow his sheep and be with them no matter where they were in the desert, looking for grazing areas. Usually, he took two or three smaller tents, and little by little moved with the sheep and a few tribesmen with tents like his to find better grazing areas.

In a way, the movements of my father and his tribesmen were dictated by the welfare of their sheep, and certainly they were trying to relive their past nomadic life. In fact, however, my father's life retained far from any semblance of his old nomadic life, but he was happy, and we (my brothers and I) let him live the way he desired.

Once, I was chatting with him, and he opened up about how one week with his sheep and some of his tribesmen was more relaxing than staying in an air-conditioned concrete villa in a city.

Oh! Father, I give up. I was lucky that you did not follow my advice at the beginning of the 1970s, when I insisted that you should settle in a city.

And so "live and let live" became my strategy with my father, as long as he was happy and comfortable by his own standards. We were very close, and he began to enjoy his trips to Riyadh to see his grandchildren, Sami, Ramsey, and Lisa. The fast development of the country created a phenomenon in the structure of most families, where different generations lived in the same house. The illiterate and literate lived side by side. To me, this phenomenon of different generations living in the same house contributed to the stability of the society and saved Saudi Arabia from most negative results of fast development, socially speaking. On the individual level, this phenomenon was like a raised flag. It always reminded those of us who became intoxicated with our worth to be humble and never forget the background we came from. So, the cohesion of families held.

☙ ☙ ☙

By 1979, the success of Saudi Arabia's development was clear to all unbiased observers. Those who had questioned our ability to build what we dreamt of, especially in the petrochemical industry, tried very hard to join us, to be partners with new projects. Articles of praise in the mass media began to appear more often, and so we planners felt more comfortable and believed beyond a doubt that success cures most ills and shortcomings on the individual as well as group level.

Saudi Arabia was stable, optimistic, and almost at the stage of take-off, as development experts call it when a group of insane people, to say the least, on 20 November 1979, shocked us and the world at large by seizing Al-Haram Al-Makki (the Great Mosque in Mecca). Hundreds of radicals, under the influence of a charismatic leader, had invaded the mosque and trapped tens of thousands of worshippers there. They were driven out only after two weeks of fighting that left hundreds dead. In addition to that, at the end of 1979 came the revolution that overthrew the Shah of Iran, and the Soviet Union's invasion of Afghanistan. This collection of events impacted the environment in the Kingdom in the years ahead and directly impacted personal decisions, which I discuss in due course.

The day Al-Haram was seized I was in a meeting in my office with a congressman from the United States when my office manager entered and told me about that horrible occupation of the Great Mosque. My guest cut his stay short when he noticed how emotional I was, and gracefully expressed his sorrow and wished Saudi Arabia the power and luck to end this insane act as soon as possible.

The next day, I received a call from a friend, urging me to meet Mr. Ed Bradley of CBS, a well-known US network, for an interview. I turned the request down, because I was not prepared to meet anyone to talk about Saudi economic matters while the Great Mosque (Al-Haram) was occupied by insane, misguided extremists. It also happened that day that the ministry had two important guests; one was the Brazilian minister of planning, and the other was the United States's Treasury Secretary.

While I was going around the ministry, accompanied by the Director of Administration and Finance, I saw two men I didn't know. When I asked my companion who they were he said they were from the Internal Intelligence Service looking for an employee of the ministry who was working in the ministry library. When the men of the service saw me walking, one of them recognized me and took me aside to tell me they were looking for the employee. I told my companion that the Director of Administration could help them and walked away.

I felt, after walking a few meters, that the servicemen were not satisfied by my instruction to my companion, so I went back and put my hand on the shoulder of the senior officer and told him not to worry, as we were part of the government. I asked the Director of Administration, who was still keeping me company, if he knew the employee's home address, which he should tell the officers. His answer was that he told them two days prior, when the officers were in and out of the ministry.

I left and passed my minister, and while talking about our foreign guests I told him in passing that the Internal Intelligence Service was looking for an employee of the ministry whom I did not know.

During the day, we received our guests, and around 3:00 p.m. I left my office and went home. At around 4:30, while I was resting in my house, I received a call from my minister, who was agitated and asked me repeatedly what I did that day, because Prince Salman, the governor of Riyadh Region, had just called him, asking him and me to meet him in his office urgently.

We met the governor, who was unhappy, needless to say. He told us that the intelligence officer quoted me as saying that the Ministry of Planning was not an executive agency with the power to arrest people, and that it was their responsibility to do that job.

I cleared up the misunderstanding, and certainly Prince Salman was relieved, and so were all of us. However, I was very angry at the misrepresentation of what I had said. I remembered past incidents of people twisting what I said about restructuring the Second Development Plan, when high inflation almost caused the government to stop its implementation.

And so, I became accustomed to the phenomenon of others twisting what I said, whether it was done innocently or intentionally. After clearing up the matter with the governor, the minister and I went to meet the King, accompanied by our guest, the Brazilian minister of planning. The King was very sad and angry, of course, about what was happening in Makkah in Al-Haram.

࿇ ࿇ ࿇

A few days later, the Ministry of Information convinced me to meet CBS, which I was happy to do, despite the agony I and others who respect me faced later on. Misrepresenting what I said became like a habit for some sources, and I became accustomed to it. This one incident, however, beat all of them in ugliness and aimed to destroy me once and for all.

During Al-Hajj holiday in 1980, I was in Davos, Switzerland, sharing information about Saudi development to about 63 chief executives of major European corporations, arranged by the European Management Forum (now the World Economic Forum), urging them to consider investing in Saudi Arabia.

Upon my return to my office in Riyadh, I found on my desk my mail and articles from some U.S. newspapers. As I recall, without reading my mail, I went to say hello to my minister in his office. I found him criticizing one employee of the Royal Commission for Jubail and Yanbu. It happened that my minister was vice chairman of that commission, independent of the Ministry of Planning. He addressed that employee by saying, "What I was told about you was true, not like what I hear about Faisal."

I asked the minister, "What are you talking about?"

He then opened up about what he called an agonizing night for him and the minister of information, about the interview I gave to CBS, and referred me to the minister of information, who had the details. Back in my office, I read news articles in the *Christian*

Science Monitor, the *NY Times, the Washington Post,* and, if I'm not mistaken, the *L.A. Times.* They stated that my interview with CBS was broadcast on Tuesday, 21 October 1980, under the heading, "The Saudis" at 10:00 p.m. EDT in the United States.

I honestly had a hard time remembering that interview because it was done during the occupation of Al-Haram in November 1979, almost a year earlier.

By the way, I was not the only person interviewed at that time. There were princes, ministers, judges, and Saudi girls interviewed in their schools. It was a very good representation of Saudi society. To my fortune or misfortune, it seemed I had left a positive impression on viewers, and especially newspapers, which some of the articles on my desk detailed in a flattering way. I was of course happy to read about this, but I was perplexed by what my minister had told me.

I went and met the minister of information, in the presence of his deputy, my dear friend Dr. Abdulaziz Khojah. As they explained it, my saga was as follows: while King Khalid was having dinner in his palace in Jeddah, in the presence of Prince Nayef (Minister of Interior), Dr. Abdo Yamani (Minister of Information), Ismael abo Dawood (Chairman of the Saudi Chambers of Commerce), and a few others, he received a telex informing him that the Deputy Minister of Planning, Dr. Faisal, was on CBS criticizing Saudi Arabia and in particular its government, and that he declared that he would not go back and was happy he had left it behind.

When the King informed his dinner guests the content of the telex, the three gentlemen I mentioned defended me and doubted the truth of the accusation. One of the guests present, I was told, went further to say that he guaranteed that I had not said what the telex indicated, unless I had gone crazy.

The King refused all his guests' defenses of me. He was known to sleep early at night, but at 11:00 p.m. the minister of information received a call from the King confirming what was in the telex.

While I was listening to the details of my story, I was so angry. Certainly, such a story amounted, in my opinion, to treason against my King, country, family, name, and tribe. And whoever framed it was hoping to end me once and for all—but who was the sender of the telex?

After the King's call, the minister told me he went to bed still hoping against hope that some miracle would happen to convince the King otherwise. He was awakened at 1:30 a.m. by the King, to tell him I was innocent of the accusation.

What caused that change was that the King's daughter was in the United States and watched the broadcast and was excited to see it. She called the palace in Riyadh, to tell her family that she was coming home soon and bringing with her the videotape as a present for her father. When she was asked, "Is this the one with Dr. Faisal, the deputy minister?" and she answered yes, she was told the King was still awake, looking for Faisal. Surely, she was amazed that the King was still awake at that hour, and so she talked to him and told him the truth, which was completely opposite of what that horrible telex contained.

After hearing my saga, which forced my King to stay up almost all night looking for me to discover the truth, I left to attend the inauguration of the headquarters of the National Guard in Riyadh, to which I had been invited. On my arrival, Prince Abdullah, who was second deputy prime minister and President of the National Guard at the time, was greeting the guests. When he saw me, he inquired about my so-called story on CBS. I was tense and angry, and I told him I really did not care, as long as the truth was known. Then, when I entered the hall, many dignitaries greeted me. It was like the safe return of a lost friend, which proved that the story was all over the place and I was the last to know about it, due to my absence in Switzerland.

On my way to my office, I passed by our neighbor, the president of Youth Welfare (now the Ministry of Sport) to see its head, who was King Fahd's eldest son, Prince Faisal. I visited him in his office, to discuss some matters relating to the Saudi Swimming Federation, of which I was the head. During our discussion, the Prince mentioned how much he enjoyed seeing the video of CBS's "The Saudis" and how effective he thought I was. I told him I had not seen it yet, but I added, regardless of what he said, what was the use?

He was astonished and realized there must be something wrong. When I told him about what had occurred between the minister of information and the King, he immediately urged me to go and see the King, who would tell me what had happened.

The Prince was definitely angry, and so he called his uncle, the Minister of Interior, Prince Nayef, who was present at that dinner with the King when the story in that telex spread, and arranged an appointment for me the next day to hear the story directly from Prince Nayef. I went the next day and met Prince Nayef in his office, who told me that he tried to convince the King that the story in the telex could not be true.

When the King refused to believe it, he left and called two people in the United States, who saw the CBS broadcast and was satisfied that I did not say what the telex to the King had indicated. I thanked him for explaining, and for his trust, and left his office.

I was still tense and upset, and thought, what was the purpose of such disinformation, and who had done it? The only reason I could think of was to destroy the reputation of the human being called Faisal, the Deputy Minister of Planning of Saudi Arabia.

When I finally watched the show, I saw that what I'd said was straight from my heart and very sincere. When the interviewer, Mr. Bradley, realized I came from a nomadic background, he asked how I had done it.

As I recall, my answer was along the lines of: "I really don't know. You might say I did it my way. I was like a particle in the sea, at the mercy of the waves and winds."

Nomadic life is so beautiful when rain is abundant. Everyone is a relative, one feels secure, and you can touch everyone around you. Not like this impersonal, urban life. But when there is a drought, nomadic life is one of the harshest lives one can imagine. The survival of the fittest does exist in the desert. I am glad I left it behind. I derive comfort now when I see children of nomadic tribes following the same path I took.

I realized immediately that whoever sent the telex to the King either did not understand English very well, was naïve, or was a professional twister of phrases to suit his ultimate aim to hurt me.

Simple observations will raise suspicions. First, I was not in a TV studio; the interview was done in the living room of my house in Riyadh, where I wore my national dress. Second, I said in the interview: "I am glad I left it behind," referring to the nomadic life, *not* Saudi Arabia. That phrase, I think, was the basis upon which the informer built his accusation in the telex. They added a few extra sweeteners, such as being interviewed the next day by newspapers, as I was told by whoever read or informed me about what was in the telex.

As far as I am concerned, the episode could be entitled, "When the King Did Not Sleep: Looking for Faisal, the Deputy Minister."

I have alluded to being sought out by journalists. I, for one, never sought anyone out directly. It happened that some people who knew me, whether government officials or others, found some value in my giving interviews and talks. I reasoned that it was fine, in the service of my country, and if in the process I got some satisfaction. Why not? As for my nomadic background, I never looked at it as more than a natural and logical process in my life cycle, and especially in the late 1970s when there were many people who made it in Saudi Arabia with similar backgrounds.

To be blunt, I never had a label on my chest announcing that I was a Bedouin. At that time, I was really not a Bedouin, I was an urban government official. I say this not because I was ashamed of my nomadic background but rather to state facts.

Fortunately, it ended in my favor, as had a few similar incidents in the past, because of the decency and generosity of King Khalid, who kept searching for the truth and listened to all sources. To me, that was the logical way to do it, before reaching a final decision.

18

—

Farewell Dear Uncle

In late 1979 my Uncle Rakan came to Riyadh, accompanied by his eldest son, Trad, who had already made a doctor's appointment for him at the King Faisal Hospital, because of his swollen feet. After an examination of his feet, the doctor insisted he should see a throat specialist in the hospital, because his voice had changed a lot. Uncle insisted that there was no cause for alarm and tried to convince us that he had a cold.

Few of my cousins were around, but because I knew English, my uncle insisted I should be with him. Up to that date, my uncle never accepted my marriage to an American girl, and while we were in the examination room, and a nurse was doing what was needed before the doctor arrived, he asked me what nationality the nurse was. When I asked her, she said she was American, from the state of Tennessee. I told my uncle, and he said, a country that is the most powerful and influential all over the world—it was nice to be friends with, and no harm to marry from.

Thus, my uncle at last approved my marriage to Stephanie. I felt happy, though it had taken since 1967 to get that approval. But it was approval nevertheless, and a nice gesture.

When the doctor entered, accompanied by an interpreter, and after examining my uncle's throat, he said my uncle should stay in the hospital for a thorough examination. Directing his instructions to the interpreter, not knowing that I knew English, he said he suspected that my uncle had a tumor.

To me, the word meant "cancer," and my uncle noticed my shock. I tried to recover and told him that the doctor insisted he must stay for a few days in the hospital, under observation, and then he could go back to his sheep and enjoy his life as before.

I will never forget the impact of my uncle's statement. He said, "Son Faisal, sheep are not worth that much, and not a source of comfort in reality. I want you to be beside me in the hospital all the time."

He noticed something major was wrong, from the look on my face, and I almost disintegrated and fled the room. After I recovered my balance, I went back and assured him that I would stay beside him and went to tell my cousins the news.

While I was talking with my cousins, here came the doctor, to apologize for his not being careful in talking with the interpreter, because he had no idea I knew English.

Dr. Peter McArthur, from Canada, became a friend until he retired from the hospital many years later.

My uncle left the hospital to go to a hotel about two weeks later, and Doctor McArthur assured me that he saw no signs of cancer in my uncle's throat. He made an appointment to see him six months later. Uncle Rakan was suspicious that something was wrong, and one day he was so depressed that he refused to take his medicine. It happened that some of the tribesmen in his living room in the hotel did not see me and were asking my cousins where the doctor was.

My uncle told them that the doctor was here a few moments ago, and why were they asking? Clever cousin Trad seized on the chance and told his father that the tribesmen were referring to me, because I was more of a medical doctor than most of those he saw in the hospital. When they called me and told me about my uncle's refusal to take his medicines, I came immediately, and when I offered him his medicine, he took it fast and asked me, why didn't I tell him that I was a medical doctor? I laughed and realized why my uncle was obeying my advice by taking his medicine when I offered it to him.

Oh, dear Uncle Rakan, how little did you know the great difference between a Ph.D. in economics and a Doctor of Medicine—but at that moment, who cared? I was willing to claim anything falsely, to introduce even a few moments of happiness to you in your old age, and especially when you were not feeling well.

I told some of the tribesmen to accompany him in his car and take him to the desert around Riyadh, to enjoy an evening out of the hotel. When I met him in the morning, my uncle was counting the time by the hour, ready to head north, to enjoy a life he was raised in and grew up with, with all its beauty, ugliness, and hardships.

彝 彝 彝

The Third Development Plan, 1980–1985, was approved by the King, and I and others who worked very hard to prepare it felt relieved and happy. One main feature of that plan was a major strategic shift in development emphasis. Instead of concentrating most development expenditures and projects on the axes of Jeddah (on the West Coast) to Dammam (East Coast) via the capital Riyadh (Central Region) in an almost straight line, the emphasis shifted to the north and south of the previous imaginary line. It was determined that development must concentrate in places away from big cities, in order to reduce the flow of internal migration to those urban centers.

I have to admit, now (writing in 2020), that we did not do a good job executing that strategy, because urbanization through big cities took over.

By July of 1980, my family and I were on our way to the United States, for vacation, via Japan. I was to lecture about economic matters in Saudi Arabia and, especially, the Third Development Plan, as a guest of the Japanese government, in association with an organization interested in improving the relationship between the two countries.

I had never visited Japan before, and I was looking forward to seeing that great country. Before I left Riyadh, a friend of mine from the Ministry of Petroleum and Mineral Resources gave me advice: do not be frustrated when you receive many questions about the same topic. It is the Japanese way of collecting more statistics and information about the same subject, like the income of Saudi Arabia. Mind you, the questions usually, in appearance, do not seem similar, but in reality, they are.

On arriving in Japan, we were treated royally by our host and stayed at the New Otani Hotel in Tokyo. The next day, I met the minister of MITI (Ministry of International Trade and Industry), which I was told was one of the most important ministries in Japan. It was very hot and humid in the minister's office, and I noticed the minister was not wearing his jacket, while I was very formal in my suit and feeling uncomfortable. The minister smiled and told me that I was at liberty to take off my jacket, because he could not turn on the air conditioning in his office.

And so, when in Rome, do what the Romans do. I took off my jacket.

In the afternoon, in the big hall of the Otani Hotel, my lecture started and was followed by a press conference. Both took almost four and a half hours. I noticed that most of my listeners brought secretaries with them and were writing during my lecture. And of course, I remembered my Saudi friend's advice when many questions were asked about the same topic in different formats.

Usually, my host took me in the morning and returned me in the evening. I was really working and did not see Tokyo. I am glad to say my host took care of my family admirably.

After three days, I was asked what I would like to see. I had heard about Kyoto, the former imperial capital of Japan, and what a wonderful, beautiful city it is. To me, Tokyo did not look different from any other modern city, like New York or Chicago. However, Kyoto certainly was a unique city, in a class of its own, and I am glad my family and I saw it and enjoyed staying in it for one day. We left Japan for Hawaii, taking with us fond memories of that beautiful country and its hospitality.

One week in Hawaii was a logical stop to unwind before reaching our house in Santa Barbara, California.

By the end of August 1980, I went back to Saudi Arabia, and left my family behind to follow me later, when schools reopened in Riyadh at the beginning of October that year.

ψ ψ ψ

On the 10th of December 1980, Stephanie gave birth to our son Bendar in King Faisal Hospital. Two months after that, the whole family was enjoying living in a real Bedouin tent, with some die-hard tribesmen and their sheep, which my children enjoyed seeing and playing with.

I learned that my uncle's tent and other tribal tents were not far from our location, about 40 km from Hafr Al-Batin. I had not seen my uncle since his medical checkups in Riyadh, so I went to visit him with two men from the tribe and my children, Sami, Ramsey, and Lisa. Upon arrival in my uncle's tent, and after greeting all the men in Almajles, one of the men who came with me noticed my uncle wanted to reach out to the children but was hesitant.

Aljaib, the tribesman, called on my son Sami to recite his ancestor's names. When he did, my uncle was so happy that he asked Sami to sit on the pillow he rested his arm on and insisted that we must have our lunch. I convinced my uncle to let us skip. I wish I had not suggested that, because he forced me to take the sheep we were to eat for our lunch in our second car, the children riding inside it. The children loved it, and it went with us to our house in Riyadh, about 400km away, where Ramsey acted out his ancestor's nomadic life by being the shepherd and feeding the sheep every now and then.

Uncle Rakan, I wish I had accepted lunch in the tent that day, because the sheep became a menace in the house in Riyadh, where the children refused to let it go, every time I suggested we get rid of it. It took me until June of that year, when schools closed and we went for vacation, to tell the driver to take it, and upon our return his excuse should be that the sheep got sick and died. White lies can sometimes solve a problem.

ﯦ ﯦ ﯦ

One day in June 1981, while I was preparing to receive a Swedish delegation led by that country's minister of industry, I received a call from my cousin, Thamer, who told me that his father, my uncle Rakan, was rushed to a hospital in Kuwait, which is not that far from Hafr Al-Batin, where his tent was located.

Thamer urged me to come soon from Riyadh, because my uncle was in critical condition. When the Swedish delegation left the Ministry of Planning in the evening, I was lucky to have the Saudi Ministry of Petroleum and Mineral Resources' plane ready to take me to Kuwait.

Upon my arrival at the airport in Kuwait, Thamer took me directly to the hospital to see my uncle. I was left alone in his hospital room for about 15 minutes and left. With my cousins, brothers, and some tribesmen, we spent the night talking to each other, but none of us had the courage to talk about what would happen if Uncle Rakan died—until Thamer mentioned it himself.

The next morning, Rakan Al- Mershed passed away, and all of us followed the ambulance that carried his body from Kuwait to Hafr Al-Batin in Saudi Arabia, to be buried, as he wished. My father was informed by one of the cousins ahead of us and he was waiting in the cemetery when the body arrived. As usual, Sfouq Al-Mershed, my father, who had just lost his older brother, did not show a lot of emotion. He encouraged everyone by keeping busy supervising the grave preparation. I noticed one of the tribesmen, who was my uncle's age, sitting on the ground, hitting it with his stick, so I went and sat beside him. Hiji was weeping and looked up at me and broke my heart when he said, "He (Uncle Rakan) loved you so much." And then I too wept with him (I am also crying as I write this at 11:00 a.m. on Tuesday December 1ˢᵗ, 2020, 39 years after my uncle's death).

I called my office in Riyadh, to send me my driver in my car. People from all walks of life paid their respects and condolences to us in my uncle's tent for about one week. During that time my father refused to leave his brother's tent, even to go to sleep in his villa. He almost stayed continuously reminiscing for three days about the past until we fled from him, to force him to sleep.

Rakan and Sfouq Al-Mershed, as brothers, were examples of love, respect, and loyalty to each other, and their brotherhood was taken as a noble example by all tribes who knew them. A week later, I went back to my office in Riyadh, sad but accepting the inevitable reality of losing my dear uncle, and worried about my father, who kept his sadness and agony inside in order not to worry us.

19

—

THINGS CHANGE

During 1981, Saudi Arabia was developing with ease and confidence, and most observers could not help but admire the achievements that had taken place since 1973. The supply of goods and services were adequate and at reasonable costs. Inflation was tame and at acceptable levels, relatively speaking. That led to a more adequate estimate of the cost of projects' construction, which was definitely less than before when inflation was high. As a matter of fact, some of us who were directly involved in planning began to warn about the appearance of extra capacity in some of the infrastructure sectors, which in the long run might lead to a lot of waste.

Being successful did not bring love to the country from the developed international community, which most of the time urged developing countries to work hard to uplift standards of living for their people. That is exactly what Saudi Arabia did, but developed industrial countries wanted us to do it without getting a fair price for our only source of income—oil. They were getting more income per barrel of oil through taxation than the price per barrel a producing country like Saudi Arabia was getting, and still those rich and developed countries were unhappy and never stopped criticizing Saudi Arabia. Almost any increase in the price of crude oil meant to them that Saudi Arabia was not producing enough oil to meet international demand, as if we were the only producing country responsible for meeting that demand. And if we produced more, some countries accused us of dumping and flooding the market to control the price of oil.

Saudi Arabia was almost always criticized either way, and that reminded me of Chancellor Adenauer of West Germany's comments, when in the sixties his country became wealthy after the destruction of the Second World War.

He was criticized by others for not helping the world enough. His comment, as I recall, was, "We are noticed now because we are wealthy."

Wealth usually brings with it power, envy, and jealousy, and during that time Saudi Arabia was noticed, and received almost all of those. The so-called armchair experts never stopped telling us what we should do.

I will never forget the lecture of a minister of a very wealthy industrial country, in my office, who told me that Saudi Arabia should do its utmost to reduce the price of crude oil. I explained to him that we had been the source of moderation of oil prices since 1973, because we produced more oil than we needed, to finance our development, with the belief that we did not want to hurt the world economy which we are a part of. I turned to my guest, the minister, in an undiplomatic way, and said, "Your country has more wealth in the real sense and is a producer of oil. Why not set a good example and reduce your oil price?" He smiled and said his country was a small oil producer, compared to Saudi Arabia.

Again, he didn't answer my question, and for the record, when that minister's country became a major oil producer, his country charged as much as the market could bear.

It seems that most of the time it is much easier to advise and suggest to others a very noble course of action and yet avoid it when it is a burden. This is life, full of contradictions that make it an interesting and exciting short stay on this planet for all of us human beings.

☙ ☙ ☙

Since the beginning of 1980, and especially after the approval of the Third Development Plan, I began to entertain the idea that maybe it was an appropriate time to make some changes in my life. Feelings of emptiness began to appear often, and I began to question why I started to feel that way. Do luxury, the abundance of material things, and relative success contribute that much to human emptiness? Did I realize that my future, if I stayed in my job, offered no more challenges?

All in all, I was tormented alone for almost six months. At the end of this, I reasoned that all my life I was going at full speed to free myself from perpetuating the kind of life my father and his ancestors lived, and I had succeeded in charting a way of life that was appropriate for the present as well as future days. I was living a new life, one that had never been led by any member of my family, Al-Mershed, nor for that matter my largest family, the Al-Sba'a Tribe. I had choices and did not need to prove my worth to anyone, including myself. It was time to enjoy different opportunities and a slower pace.

And so, at about the time schools recessed in 1981, before leaving with my family for vacation, I submitted my resignation to my minister to take it up to Crown Prince Fahd. During the summer of that year, and on my vacation, I lectured about economic matters and in particular the Third Development Plan of Saudi Arabia in New York, Chicago, and San Francisco.

While I was doing all that lecturing, I was almost testing myself about my resignation. I realized, sincerely, that I did not have that emotional charge or satisfaction I usually derived when I discussed and analyzed Saudi economic matters. More and more, with the passage of time, I became convinced that I made the right decision at the right time. Why resign a senior post, and a promising one? First, I didn't get any more satisfaction from what I was doing. And that's what I told the Crown Prince, when he asked me why I did so.

Second, the Al-Mershed relatives, and especially my brothers and immediate cousins, began to move to Riyadh. And most of them, in particular my cousins, needed help materially as well as non-materially. I was determined to help them and not live in comfort while seeing my relatives in need. Although my government was very generous with me, and my total pay, monthly salary, plus bonuses at that time, were relatively high, it was not enough for me to be able to extend help, no matter how small, to my relatives or anyone else, especially from my tribe.

A reader might question, was I obliged to help? My answer is yes, not because of established law but because of my inner feelings and my traditions. I happen to derive a lot of happiness from helping others as much as I can. I grew up with it, and it was written in my conscience.

While I was waiting for a decision about my resignation, Mr. Nazer, my minister, tried to convince me to reconsider my decision and stay. I refused, and told him my resignation was not sudden, but rather that it took me almost a year to reach this decision, so it was final. I had to make that clear because when it became known, some people thought I'd had some major disagreement with Mr. Nazer, and that I was forced to resign, which was not true.

As a matter of fact, Crown Prince Fahd, I was told, indicated that if I wanted to move to a different position in the government, I could. However, I was really tired and only wanted to get out. The Crown Prince proved his respect for me when he left his door open for me despite all the rumors that I had left my country forever, generated by those who specialized in manufacturing negative and unfavorable news about me, as they did in the few incidents mentioned before. I was and still am in debt and grateful to my King Fahd, peace be upon him, who gave me a few consulting jobs, and in a few instances suggested taking other jobs, which I turned down politely, of course with thanks, after I left my position as the deputy minister of planning.

In May 1982, I was informed that my resignation was accepted, which became known to some acquaintances around King Khalid's death, peace be upon him. Again, some people, sincerely or insincerely, interpreted my resignation as a bad move for my future in the government, not knowing that I had submitted my resignation a year prior, so I went around to explain why I did it. Some very powerful people were so angry that they gave me a dressing down, so to speak. I tried to explain that there were no hidden reasons for my decision, except that, honestly, I was tired and believed that I had no more to contribute. One of them was very upset with me and said, "I am tired now. Does this mean I should resign?" I almost answered by saying, Your Royal Highness, do not compare yourself to a mortal soul like me who knows his limits and is not that important in the structure of the government of Saudi Arabia. I was and still am grateful for all those reactions and the advice I received from those people who kept their doors open, whenever I needed help.

That resignation from my post as deputy minister of planning also meant I left every board of directors I was a member of because of my title. What about other boards I was the Chairman or Member of by my name? I went around to the ministers, to submit my resignation. All of them advised me to stay cool and rejected my requests. I have to admit that they were right, though I was, to some extent, emotionally driven to sever my relationship with all my posts. Their advice was that if I left every post I occupied, it might be interpreted as me leaving my country. Again, I am indebted to all those who expressed coolheaded, logical analysis from which I really learned to never act under the pressure of emotions. "Sleep on it" is a very useful saying indeed.

I have stated all the above, about my resignation, not to glorify a person called Faisal S. Al-Bashir Al-Mershed, but rather to show how personally and humanely the system in my country treated me. It made my exit from a very senior and rewarding job, to some extent, a peaceful one. I left in a friendly way, which was important to me, because of my love for my country, which was and still is very generous in spending and helping its people achieve higher standards of living through its human development.

♉ ♉ ♉

I drifted most of 1982/83, although I was still involved in some of the government corporations, like the refinery of oil and the petrochemical company, both located in Jubail on the east coast of the Kingdom—but my pace was much slower than before. I began to travel frequently between Riyadh and London, where my family was located at the time. And so, the nomad of yesteryear became the nomad of modern times, when modes of travel were more comfortable.

At that time, I thought I was forgotten, until I went to pay my respects to Crown Prince Abdullah in his office in Jeddah. After he mentioned a few nice words about my late uncle and family, in the presence of a few ministers, he surprised me by asking where I had been. I told him I had become a traveler, like Ibn Batotah (a famous past Arab traveler). He then continued by saying, "Faisal, you are a Bedouin, who like the falcon flies all over the place," symbolizing the flying by circling his hand over his head, "but at the end always comes back to his original place, called Alwakr in Arabic."

I got the message, and I was naive to think that some people would ever stop spreading unfavorable news about me or anyone else. As far as I am concerned, those kinds of people were addicted to such behavior, because they were empty and lacked anything of value to keep them busy.

After seeing some friends, I learned that rumor had it that I had emigrated to the West and would not come back to Saudi Arabia. The way the gossip was spread hurt me a lot, because to me it connoted ingratitude to my country, my family, and my friends. I have nothing against immigration as a means to better human life. My tribe and other tribes did it when the Arabian Peninsula was not a good source of living. In my case, I had no reason to turn my back on my country, which gave me one of the happiest and most productive intervals of my life.

Now that I had left my main government job, which was a senior post, I must state a few beliefs and personal observations. I left with the conviction that the time was right to leave that job, as I mentioned before. Nevertheless, I almost lost my composure in a few encounters with people who showered me with so much love and respect.

Friends, I am grateful and indebted. I left never having hurt a human being, directly or indirectly, during my service. And during that service I met and noticed many high-achievers—some considered me to be one of them. True and noble achievements are those that benefit the society one lives in. And achievers, in my opinion, were divided mainly into two categories. One achieves but is always at war with himself and the people around him. He is in a perpetual struggle to go somewhere to achieve higher goals without noticing, or being careless about how much damage is inflicted in the process. This kind of a person is dangerous on the personal as well as the societal level, and eventually his way of doing things will lead to many mistakes. He is driven mainly by personal ambition, no matter how much he or she denies it.

The other kind of achiever is always aware of how much his actions benefit people around him and the country at large. He is the kind I like and respect, who derives his satisfaction and happiness from helping others to be happy and satisfied and knows that such a result must be beneficial to society as a whole. I subscribe to this approach because it embodies sharing.

One of the best characteristics of tribalism was sharing. Materially sometimes, and non-materially most of the time.

In addition to such feelings and beliefs, I was lucky not to lose sight of how small I was in the equation of Saudi development and who had the ultimate power. I say this to all people, because some colleagues were intoxicated by their positions, and that led to mistakes, which harmed them as well as others. Equally true, I always tried to give my honest opinion in a polite and firm way, despite some people who thought otherwise. To some individuals, firmness meant aggressiveness. I behaved that way from the absolute belief that those who trusted us expected the best advice from us.

We were appointed not to be decorative items in councils but rather active contributors to the subject under discussion.

Again, I stress this truism because I saw many high government officials who attended meetings without contributing, although they were capable of it. And I was advised to keep quiet, indirectly and politely, because such behavior would be good for my future. But how can one do that, when those who appointed a person urge him to give his best advice, which will not be delivered by being quiet? A balancing act is required in this life, but not at the expense of being honest with oneself and to those who trust him.

ψ ψ ψ

I believe it is appropriate, now, to describe the Saudi environment in the early eighties and its impact on my decision to live with my family abroad. As I mentioned before, all of the events of 1979 (the Soviet invasion of Afghanistan, the Iranian revolution, and the seizure of the Great Mosque (Al-Haram in Makkah)), had direct and indirect effects on Saudi Arabia, most of which were negative, and particularly on the social side. From a simple, open, forward-looking, and optimistic society, enjoying, for the first time in its history, fast development, extremism began to appear. This turned the society, and the country at large, almost, into a closed environment. Gone, even, was the cheerfulness of the people, which had been prevalent in recent times.

Never did I see Saudi Arabia so sad and really pessimistic as I did in that period. Even during the financial shortages, the country was more a place to try to live in, rather than to flee from. All those ugly characteristics were products of extremist actions in the name of Islam.

I never thought to live permanently abroad, but when I saw many Saudi families leave the country, I began to seriously entertain the idea, because what those extremists did turned our lives into something almost equal to hell.

267

These developments in Saudi Arabia were tied to events that took place both in the country and elsewhere in the region. Iranians overthrew the Shah in 1979, leaving it to Khomeini to take over.

Then, in 1980, the first Islamic conference in Saudi Arabia took place, with representatives from Iraq and Iran present. The Crown Prince of Saudi Arabia implored Saddam Hussein not to go to war with Iran—but it was to no avail. The war started and dragged on for eight years. Our country stood with Iraq throughout, and as the years passed things changed in the country.

A man and a woman might be walking in the street, in the middle of a city. It could be anyone, whether they were wealthy or poor. Whoever it was, they were likely to be approached by an official, who would confront them, asking how they were related, and if they were married. If they were married, and said so, the official would demand proof.

These men were representatives of a body called The Committee for the Promotion of Virtue and Prevention of Vice, a government agency focused on morality in Saudi Arabia. They were determined to impose morality on everyone. At first, they were merely annoying, but after some time they were sanctioned by the police, who often accompanied them as their harassment campaign continued.

They began imposing rules that seemed utterly arbitrary. They would tell a man his robe was too long, that it was not to reach his foot. Men were all but required to have beards.

These men stopped and confronted me more than once. They stopped a friend of mine, and he was so rattled, so intimidated, he stopped leaving his house.

It came about that no matter what time of day you left the house you would find someone standing outside, waiting to stop and interrogate you, to ask where you were going and why.

The extremists had all but taken over the country, and it made the place inhospitable. I heard that around 5,000 Saudi families moved to the United States at this time, to escape the atmosphere of suspicion and the constant disrespect.

The government sought to appease both the men from this committee and those who protested this treatment, which left citizens essentially at their mercy. They had reason to appease them, as the committee threatened a revolution if anyone moved to stop them from carrying out this long campaign.

All the things they did were supposedly in the name of erasing all ills in Saudi Arabia, when in truth their aim was to take over the country and do what the Mullahs did and are still doing in Iran.

ψ ψ ψ

While I was in my government job, every now and then, Saudi businessmen as well as non-Saudis offered rewards, at least financially, and jobs if I ever left my government service. And so in 1983, while I was free as a bird, so as to speak, enjoying my solitude and still not knowing what to do, an offer was presented from a non-Saudi businessman, to move to London so we could work together. He was rich, and had businesses in energy, real estate, and shipping all over the world. I accepted his offer, believing every promise and the conditions he said without even a piece of paper as a contract.

Eventually, that rosy and promising future ended in nothing, and showed how naïve I had been to trust him. So, Faisal, welcome to the private sector business world, where human worth, most of the time, is measured by a material yardstick, and promises are not always fulfilled. I failed in my first attempt to be a businessman, but I learned a lot from that failure. I learned to be less trusting, and to be careful and cynical toward extended offers, no matter how famous or rich the one was who made the offer.

I considered one positive outcome of that failure to be when I moved the family from Santa Barbara, California to London, to be nearer to Saudi Arabia.

20

Public to Private

While I was in a position of doing nothing, and not knowing what to do, despite some offers, a call came from Mr. Mohammad Aba Al-Khail, Minister of Finance and National Economy, urging me to accept the nomination to be Chairman of the Saudi Hotels and Resort Areas Company (SHERACO, now called Dur).

I was hesitant, but Mohammad was a dear friend, and I knew he would not let me down, so I was elected to be the chairman of the largest public company in its field in the country.

In SHERACO, I found a company who was a sole owner of all its assets, no partners at all, which studied and designed many hotel and resort areas, but implemented few and never distributed dividends to its shareholders. It was also run as a government agency, as if it were not a profit-oriented company.

Future tourism, then, was bleak, because the country did not permit international tourism. And so with the help of the board of directors, some of whom were major shareholders, I led the devising of a new structure for the company: first, to accept partners up to 50 percent; second, to try to train Saudi manpower to run present facilities and future ones, instead of outsourcing to international companies; third, to run the company as a profit-making company, as it should be; fourth, and urgently, to sell two hotels, one in Riyadh and the other in Dhahran, on the East Coast, to the government, which would convert them to hospitals. I say urgently because signals of the financial rationalization of expenditures by the government appeared, although it was very minor in scope in 1983, compared to what happened later on.

I went to the minister of finance, to procure the company money, and Mohammad Aba Al-Khail, who had convinced me to take the job, did not disappoint me. He tried to pay by installments, as agreed at the time of the sale of the two hotels. I argued that the company needed cash to expand in implementing already designed projects. Dear Mohammad paid the full amount, as I requested, which amounted to about 300 million Saudi Riyals. That was a great financial shot in the arm for the company, to say the least. Mohammad was a dear friend then, and still was, after he left his position.

I reported my first success to the board of directors of the company, like a student who had passed his first major exam with high marks. I learned many things from some of the board members, who were senior to me age-wise, and had a lot of experience in the private sector. I told many of them how inefficient the company was and told some of them that I was determined to relieve the manager (the CEO) of his position.

Some members were guided by their sympathies and friendship and were less enthusiastic about my idea of relieving the manager. In the end, it was my decision to submit my proposal to the board, which backed me up. One of the directors suggested he carry the burden of telling the manager the decision, because he was the one who brought him to the company. I thanked him and informed all that it was the chairman's responsibility to do that, and so I did, face to face with the manager in my office. I learned from that action how tough it was to face a person who was losing his job. It was ugly, no matter how right and necessary it was.

ψ ψ ψ

Later in my tenure the board of SHERACO decided to build a residential compound, a gated development, for Saudi families only, on land it owned on the east coast of the country in a place called the Half Moon. It was one of the most beautiful pieces of land that one could dream of, not far from Al-Khobar. To the company's misfortune, because they did not show any interest in developing the land for a long time, the Ministry of Defense claimed it, and incorporated it into adjacent land which they held.

The Ministry offered to pay us what we paid to purchase the land from the government. I refused, for two reasons. First, the company was serious about building the residential compound, and second, the purchase price compared to the market price at that time was not that much. It took me a lot of lobbying, with the help of the minister of municipalities and rural affairs, to get the land back and get permission to start preparing the location for buildings on the compound.

I have to tell the story of this project in detail, because it was big, using a new system of building (cement pre-casting), and because it was the first development project the company started under my leadership.

We planned for the development to be around 260 townhouses and about 60 big, detached villas. It took the company about six months to prepare the site, after which I signed a contract with a Saudi company that had the most modern cement pre-casting factory, owned by three wealthy Saudis. The system of pre-casting was new to Saudi Arabia, and the company decided to get the best specialized contractor available, which we did.

By the end of 1989, the contractor had almost finished building the shells of most buildings, despite all the obstacles the project encountered, such as doubts about its economic viability from some big shareholders. At that time, we noticed the contractor slowing down in performance. When I inquired why this was the case, I was told that some kind of negotiation was taking place between the partners, to inject about 10 million Saudi Riyals ($2.66 million) into the company. Knowing how wealthy the partners were, I was not that worried about the slowdown in our project's progress. So, I was shocked when the contracting company declared bankruptcy. I was sure there were other reasons, other than the issue of the 10 million Riyals injection, that contributed to the decision to declare bankruptcy. Consequently, our project, which was called

Gulf Village Compound, came to a halt. That led to many who doubted the economic viability of the project to believe that bankruptcy was the final kiss of death.

While we were trying to find solutions to our predicament and complete the project, I noticed reluctance to go ahead from some members of the board. I panicked and threatened—diplomatically, of course, because some of them were shareholders—those members: either they support completion, or I would go back to the government, as a shareholder, and tell of our inability to proceed with the project. Furthermore, I assured the less enthusiastic members that the Ministry of Defense was more than willing to take over, and then all that we spent on the project would be written off as a loss.

The threat worked, and I went back to find out what had forced our contractor to declare bankruptcy. What I found, mostly, was an ego problem of a few rich partners, each accustomed to getting his way, who refused to compromise. I was sure some would deny my assessment and say that all of them acted based on rational business analysis. Realizing that, I called on the financial guarantors of the contractor, National Commercial Bank (NCB) and Riyad Bank, and cashed in their financial guarantee, which amounted, as I recall, to about 19 million Saudi Riyals (18 million of which was from NCB).

The contracting company's bankruptcy was big news because the partners were well known, and the project was big. Some criticism of how I handled the matter reached me, and people said I was an uncompromising person, and so on. Until now, I never believed that bankruptcy was a rational business decision, but rather no more than the desire of each partner to strip the contracting company of its most modern cement pre-casting factory. It is a belief, rather than a fact, that may or may not stand in a court of law.

Later the contracting company was asked by the government to pay the unpaid wage bill for the workers. The invoice was sent to us to pay, on the grounds that some work on the project was completed, so far without compensation. While that was true, I told the governor of Riyadh's office, who interfered in the matter, that I would not pay because we had a case against the contracting company for the cost of the delay of the project. The case amounted to 80 million Saudi Riyals and was raised to the Grievance Board, the highest authority, we thought, which arbitrates such cases. Jumping ahead of time in my story, it took the Grievance Board nine years to tell us it had no jurisdiction in such a matter. (I used that useless Board decision as an argument to support judicial reform, to attract investors, when I was involved in reform discussions years later in the Higher Economic Council, headed by Crown Prince, later King, Abdullah.)

My struggles on behalf of SHERACO were of limited success as far as I was concerned, because the Gulf Village project was still dormant. And while we in SHERACO were trying to mobilize to continue building the compound, the real kiss of death happened when Iraq invaded Kuwait on the second of August 1990.

Everything stopped in the region except the military mobilization to liberate Kuwait. I really began to think, after that horrible invasion, that my first project working in the private sector as chairman of SHERACO would never be completed and would be a reminder of my failure as long as I lived. I began to believe that some kind of curse was ready to create obstacles every time we tried to proceed. All I could do was wait, and hope for the liberation of Kuwait to come as soon as possible.

Fortunately, Kuwait was liberated, and SHERACO completed building the Gulf Village compound and quickly sold its units to Saudi families in cash. The village ended up being the address to live in, when visiting the east coast of Saudi Arabia. We did it, and the shareholders of the company were happy beyond their expectations, while the doubting prophets of doom had bitten the dust, so to speak.

ψ ψ ψ

SHERACO began expanding into the management of entities owned by other investors, in addition to its core business of building hotels and resort areas. In addition, the company continued to pay dividends to shareholders annually, which kept them happy. SHERACO was on the right course to be ready to take off and expand, and I was enjoying that environment immensely, helped by Engineer Abdulaziz Al-Anbar, the Managing Director (CEO) of the company. He was and remains one of my dearest friends to this day. He was the CEO every chairman dreams of, and I, as well as the board of directors, were grateful to him for his excellent work for SHERACO.

The company expanded by building a luxurious, smaller compound in Jeddah, on the west coast of the country, in partnership with a landowner in that city. Also, we built a hotel in the Tabouk region in the northwest of KSA. The region is now the talk of inhabitants of the country, if not the world, being the location of the future city called Neom. Also, we built many very nice villas in the Diplomatic Quarter in Riyadh, and we continued distributing dividends to shareholders. I was commuting between Riyadh and London, where my family was located and where my children were in school. Things were going nicely, and I was content with my life.

One day I was told that the Minister of Petroleum and Mineral Resources was looking for me as I had been nominated to be the Secretary General of OPEC based in Vienna, Austria. It took me a while to know who had nominated me. I did not like that nomination. I did not want to be in that position, because I was happy with my situation personally as well as from the business side. But when I was told by the chief of the royal court that King Fahd was the one who had nominated me, I had no choice but to accept the nomination.

And so, I went with the Saudi delegation to OPEC meetings twice. I was so happy that members of the organization failed to agree even to hold a vote, because one member said the time was not right. When that member, who happened to be the Minister of Energy from an Arab country, asked if he was refusing the Saudi nomination, he resorted to saying that the time was not appropriate. The position was ultimately filled by Professor Subroto, the Minister of Energy of Indonesia. I was very happy with the outcome, and that so-called Arab brotherly love was not used.

ψ ψ ψ

In addition to my job at SHERACO, and my business in my consultancy center, I was vice chairman of the Saudi British Society and member of a cultural committee between Great Britain and Saudi Arabia.

One day, through that committee, I received an invitation to attend a conference on the 50-year anniversary of something related to Great Britain (I am sorry for forgetting the official name) at which the main speakers were Prince Charles, the Prince of Wales (now King Charles), and Dr. Henry Kissinger. I knew Prince Charles as our Honorary Chairman of the Saudi British Society from the British side, with Prince Faisal, King Fahd's eldest son, from the Saudi side. I was familiar with Prince Charles' thinking as it related to building a bridge of understanding between the Western world and Islam. He was one of the early leaders in the West who was so far-sighted about understanding Islam. In that conference, the theme was the necessity to understand Islam in the West. Sorry to say, some listeners at my table were taking the Prince's comments lightly, by joking that maybe the Prince of Wales had converted to Islam.

The second speaker, Dr. Kissinger shocked the audience, and especially the British, I believe, by emphasizing that the special relationship between the United States and Britain was not as it had been, because leadership in the United States had shifted from New England and the East Coast of the United States to the Southwest and West, which had less attachment to Great Britain historically and the so-called special relationship.

It was a nice sunny day in London, so after the conference I walked to our embassy on Curzon Street, to see my friend, Dr. Ghazi Al-Gosaibi, the Saudi Ambassador, whom I had not seen for a while. Ghazi was a giant man, physically and intellectually. A poet, author of many books, he did very well in the posts he occupied in the government, such as at the Ministry of Industry and Electricity during the first financial boom of the mid-seventies. We were friends and greeted each other as such, when we met at that time in the embassy.

Ghazi was one of the people who was almost sure he knew who had spread false information about me, every time I gave interviews or appeared on TV. We chatted mostly about our families and especially our children. Then he told me I looked official in my suit, so I told him I had come from such and such a conference and mentioned the main speakers. He was amazed that he was not invited, to which I said: "See, Ghazi, we mortal souls are sometimes given the chance to feel important by being recognized. And to me as a welfare economist that is what I call a just a distribution of fame." We laughed, and I took my leave, this time by taxi, to my house in St. John's Wood in North London.

Dear Ghazi, all your friends, and I consider myself one of them, missed you when you passed away in 2010 after a long battle with illness. Rest in peace, abo Sohail (abo means father, and Sohail is Ghazi's eldest son).

21

A Father's Advice

From the years 1983 to 1990, I was commuting between Riyadh and London all the time, except during British school holidays, when my family joined me at our home in Riyadh. And so modern nomadic life continued. And while I was enjoying my work, with the passage of time, I grew tired of commuting and began to think of moving the family nearer to Saudi Arabia.

Sad to say, my desired place, Riyadh, was not an option, due to its suffocating environment. Extremists were still making life unlivable in Saudi Arabia as a whole. My wife and I visited Bahrain, which is across the King Fahd Causeway from the east coast of Saudi Arabia. We knew some friends who worked in eastern Saudi Arabia but lived in Bahrain; the distance was not far. It was the second-best option at that time, and it was certainly more comfortable to travel between Riyadh and Bahrain, which takes no more than 40 minutes by plane.

We decided to move to Bahrain, and on that visit, I paid a deposit to rent a house. Around mid-1990, we shipped our household belongings, including a car, to Bahrain from London.

It was when our belongings arrived at the seaport in Bahrain that Iraq invaded Kuwait, and the whole region's picture became unclear. We waited about three months for the situation to resolve, while our things were still in the container at Bahrain's seaport. Eventually, our container came back to London. I lost an opportunity to live nearer to Riyadh, and lost financially as well, which was insignificant compared to what Kuwait and Saudi Arabia suffered as a consequence of that dishonorable, senseless, and horrible invasion.

ڜ ڜ ڜ

During mobilizations in 1990/1, to liberate Kuwait from Iraqi occupation, many media correspondents came to Saudi Arabia. One
day I received a call from the British ambassador, whose name I
believe was Sir Alan Munro, asking me to meet the crew of BBC
2's *Panorama* program. I declined, due to being busy and not in the
mood. While we were talking, I mentioned I was going to visit my
father in Hafr Al-Batin on the border with Kuwait. The ambassador
surprised me by saying, "Will you be willing to meet the crew in
your father's house?"

At that moment I had no excuse, and so two days later the BBC
crew had dinner with me in my father's home. The next day, we had
lunch in the tent of one of the tribesmen in the desert about thirty
kilometers from the city, where the TV interview took place. Most
people present were from my tribe, Al-Sba'a.

During the interview's recording and photography, my father was
tense. He had never done such a thing in his lifetime.

I was beside him as a translator. He was asked about Kuwait's situation, and whether he supported women driving in Saudi Arabia.

His answer was immediately no, but he said he supported women's
education. At that time, my two youngest sisters were studying at
King Saud University in Riyadh.

His answer took me back to those past days when he was against
women's education, and when he tried to stop me from going further than studying past the third grade. I took a deep breath, out of
respect for my father, and said: "As a footnote, the gentleman on
my left, who happens to be my father, was a few years back against
women's education, so give him some time." I was implying that
with the passage of time he might change his opinion about wom-
en driving in the country, as he had about education.

That footnote became controversial after the episode was broadcast. Those Saudis, who were of an older generation, did not understand the aim of my comment, the footnote. They accused me of being impolite to my father, which was the most insulting thing to me. Others who understood the aim considered the comment appropriate and informative about social changes in Saudi Arabia.

Oh! Father, forgive me if I annoyed you. I was really praising you, and through your changes was proud of telling the world about the beautiful human development that took place in Saudi Arabia.

By the way, I told my father, and he just smiled and never showed me that he did not like what I had said. Also, that tape ended up being the most precious one I still have, because it was the first time my father and I were filmed for TV—so thank you, British ambassador, for insisting on the interview.

☙ ☙ ☙

While I was settling into my private sector job and other activities, such as my consultancy center, mainly focused on economics research and surveying, jointly with a foreign group from Cyprus, my relatives, Uncle Rakan's children (first cousins), began to settle in Riyadh. All of them were at different levels of needing help. Some needed guidance, while others needed guidance and material help.

To help or not to help was not the question—the decision was how to help. The task was a big one, because the number of family members in need grew with the passage of time. My father noticed my dilemma, and I discussed the matter with him often. Those cousins were mostly married to my sisters.

I have ten sisters, all born in tents in the desert, and happily all still live in Riyadh, except one who is in Hafr Al-Batin. The help had to be given. As far as my brothers were concerned, three of them, Abdul Mehsen, Sami, and Nayef, were graduates from U.S. colleges, working in the oil, government, and banking sectors respectively. The others were around my father in Hafr Al-Batin, keeping busy by looking after my father's sheep or doing some small contracting here and there. So, from this side, my relatives' demands for help were not that much.

With regard to my cousins, my father was very clear to say, help your cousins as much as you can but never partner with anyone, because business, most of the time, spoils relationships between relatives. I followed my father's advice, and with the help of my brothers we decided that the best plan was education. And so, from each cousin's house, I pushed the eldest, with the help of their parents, to pursue studies. Some, male and female, went all the way and graduated from colleges, mostly in Saudi Arabia, others from colleges in Britain and the United States. Thus, starting with a single house, the Al-Bashir (Rakan and Sfouq's children and grandchildren) branch of the Al-Mershed family now has about 45 houses, as of the end of 2020. Most of their residents live comfortably, relatively speaking. I am proud of my family's performance, and the ability to adjust to changes required by modern human social development, and I certainly can say the same about my larger family, the Al-Sba'a Tribe.

ψ ψ ψ

In 1992, after Kuwait's liberation and the BBC2 *Panorama* program Desert Shield, my father began to visit the King Faisal Hospital in Riyadh. After about three months in and out of the hospital, my father passed away. For almost ten days my home was swamped by those beautiful and decent people, day and night, who came to pay their respects and deliver their condolences. From all walks of life, princes, high government officials, and friends, sent messages by phone or telex. They conveyed a lot of feelings of those noble human beings who were unable to come in person. I told myself not to cry, until I almost broke down in front of all present, when a minister referred to an interview I gave: "Faisal, now you cannot refer to your father, one who never ate canned food."

To those people who came from the Arabs of the Middle East, and especially from the Kingdom of Saudi Arabia, I say I love you all and am grateful for your sympathy, on behalf of my immediate family, Al-Mershed, and my tribe Al-Sba'a of Greater Aneza. Your presence during that period of mourning was the most honorable and sincere signal of respect to the memory of my father to which I am, again, indebted forever.

After a while, I fled Riyadh for London, and a month later I began to remember those days of agreement and disagreement between my father and me. And so, I published something like an obituary in *Asharq Al-Awsat,* one of the major Arabic newspapers, entitled: "The Struggles between Generations, a Mirror of Human Development in Saudi Arabia."

In that article, I described how many times I disagreed with my father's ideas until I almost reached a stage where I convinced myself that there would not be a common ground of understanding between us. All the disagreements were done with respect and love, of course. My father was of the opinion, during my development, that no matter where I went or how high I reached, eventually I would come back to his way of life.

That opinion created a huge gulf between us, physically and mentally, especially during the struggle for my education.

Oh! Father, how arrogant and naïve I was when with the passage of time I began to realize that you were the source of wisdom, and I began to learn and believe in your sayings. With the passage of time, both of us began to converge toward each other and enjoyed our meetings and discussions, despite the huge gulf in education between us. Never did I forget your advice, when you were teaching Ramsey, my second son, a game, and he was late to go to bed. and I pushed him to hurry up to go to bed. After he left, you said, "Faisal, what is the hardest punishment a father can inflict on his son?" When I did not answer, you said, "To beat him, and if you start this kind of punishment at an early age, it will lose its effectiveness and with the passage of time a father will lose his son's respect."

In reality, I never physically punished my children before or after your advice, dear Father. I followed the way you raised me, by not punishing me physically, but sometimes I wished you had instead of that verbal criticism when I annoyed you or behaved in a way that was not up to our tribal traditions. I know you did not like to express your affections openly, though I knew you were the source of all love, as far as I was concerned. Loneliness and sometimes sadness reminds a person things he forgets when he is happy,[2] and I am at this point, even on 11 December 2020, lonely and sad because I lost you.

---

2   These words are paraphrased from a Dionne Warwick song, "Loneliness Re-members What Happiness Forgot."

22

New Beginnings and Old Callings

In 1999, life continued, with me traveling between Saudi Arabia, Britain, and the United States, for business as well as to be with my family. My children were grown up. Sami, the eldest, graduated from Vanderbilt University in engineering, later to earn an MBA from Georgetown University. Ramsey graduated from the University of San Diego in business, Lisa from the University of California, San Diego, later earning a law degree from Georgetown University. And last, Bendar, the youngest, graduated from the Tisch School of Fine Arts of New York University in photography.

Stephanie and I were under tremendous pressure, at that time, with regards to our marriage. We discussed separation a few times, as grown-up and mature human beings, and in the year 2000 we divorced. I gave Stephanie what she asked for, the least I should have done for a good lady, the mother of my children, who was my first love in my life.

Seven months later, I married my cousin, Amal Al-Mershed. Amal was much younger than me. I had seen her from afar, once, and had never talked to her before. Our marriage was an arranged one, back to the old tradition. I had asked my brother Sami to look for a wife for me, with the help of my sister Aljoharah. They did so and recommended Amal to me, and I accepted her, after which I asked Amal's parents to marry her. I am glad they accepted my proposal.

Amal proved to be a good wife in managing and organizing a big house in Riyadh. With the passage of time, we got to know each other better and developed love, and I am happy that I married her. She proved to be more mature than her age indicated. She noticed that I derived, and still do, a lot of happiness from helping others materially as well as non-materially, and so she never objected but

rather encouraged me, and still does. She has proved to be generous in spirit and otherwise. I certainly love her.

After one and a half years of our marriage, she gave birth to our
first son, Rakan, who is (in 2021) in the second year of his business
studies in Al-Faisal University in Riyadh. He is followed by his sister Haya, who is interested in studying marketing and fashion. She
is also looking forward to applying to a university, most likely the
same Al-Faisal University that her brother is attending. AlBandary
is my youngest daughter, and she is studying in the eleventh grade.
She never forgets to remind me that, as the youngest daughter, she
is entitled to be spoiled, and yet determined to study medicine,
despite my advice that it is too early for her to choose. Nawaf is
our last child; he is now (in 2021) studying in the eighth grade at
the King Faisal School. Certainly, at this age, he is more definite in
choosing Riyadh's Al-Hilal football team rather than choosing any
academic subject.[3]

I am very happy to have them, and needless to say I will do my utmost to help them to succeed in this life, no less than what I did for
their brothers and sister (Sami, Ramsey, Lisa, and Bendar), whom
I have from my first wife.

꽃 꽃 꽃

On 17 April 1999, the Supreme Economic Council was established
and chaired by the Crown Prince, and later King, Abdullah. I was
appointed with others to be in the consultative part of that council,
mainly as advisor to the chairman, although we attended almost all
meetings of the council and participated in all its discussions freely.
In that council, I realized how decent and farsighted the chairman,
Prince Abdullah, was, whom I really did not know that well before.
He was open and straightforward, to the detriment of some members of the Permanent Committee, all ministers of the council.

---

3   In 2024 Rakan graduated from university, Haya is in her last year of university,
    AlBandary is in her second year of law school, and Nawaf is in his second year
    of high school.

He encouraged us to be frank and give the best of what we had in our profession, which included economics, engineering, business administration, etc. Many of us took advantage of that openness, including me, and became vocal in criticism of the government bureaucracy and how such administration was hindering Saudi development. As one example of how the council discussions were open and frank, an incident I will never forget involved a minister and myself, in the presence of Prince Abdullah.

The topic was how most college students were not very diligent, as they extended their time to graduate and crowded the universities, hindering the more serious new students. Also, from the financial side, the so-called failed students were paid monthly allowances from the government to attend colleges of higher education. Thus, the council agreed to give those slackers one extra year to graduate or be kicked out of college, for the sake of incoming new students.

During the discussion, a minister who was a former professor at King Saud University in Riyadh, got carried away with his argument. He said students at universities in Saudi Arabia were very spoiled. I was shocked by his generalization, as I understood it to be about all students, and said: "I cannot see how students are spoiled when they have no living accommodations in their universities. Aren't we appointed by the leadership to tell the truth as best as we know it, and carry the true picture of what's happening in society?" The minister directed his next comment to the Prince, saying that he was more aware of what was happening at the university, meaning King Saud University, than Dr. Faisal—which should have been true. However, I refused to back down, and it was a very tense few minutes. On the third try, a courageous minister said to the Crown Prince and the whole silent council: "Your Royal Highness, what Faisal is saying is true. Some students who own cars are living in them in the streets."

I believe that I did my duty, by sharing what I knew to the leader, and it was and still is his responsibility to act. He did, and housing for students was restored to the universities, especially at King Saud University, which had closed and deprived students of housing for some reason or another.

About a week after my appointment to the council, I was asked to meet Prince Saud Al-Faisal, the Foreign Minister, who told me to prepare to be the Ambassador of Saudi Arabia to China. I tried to get out of it, but Prince Saud was dear to me, and I respected him, since I had been a member of the Petroleum Committee, which he headed when he was the Deputy Minister for Petroleum in the Ministry of Petroleum and Minerals, in the early seventies.

In the end, I gave up and agreed to go to China as ambassador. When I stood to leave, I mentioned to Prince Saud that it was up to him to relieve me of my appointment to the Supreme Economic Council. He paused and said that, in that case, I should stay on the council, because to him I would be more useful to the country than as ambassador. Did the prince forget my appointment with others, by royal decree, announced all over the mass media? Did his aides forget to tell him about it, or did he reconsider his suggestion, and find that my reminding him was a very diplomatic way to withdraw sending me to China? It was not my concern, because I was happy to get out of being ambassador to China—with due respect, needless to say.

ॐ ॐ ॐ

In passing, at this stage of my story, I have to mention that the appointment I was very happy to have, although I was not consulted, was as a member of the higher council of Aramco, chaired by King Fahd. Maybe my happiness was derived from some kind of revenge towards Aramco, which declined to employ me after my high school graduation about 60 years prior.

To those who have accompanied me throughout my story, I must sincerely say, I was honored by all those nominations, which I considered as signs and proof that I was liked and had many friends in my country. This is regardless of that ugly clique who never tired of spreading lies and twisting what I said. Also, I must emphasize that all those relative personal achievements, which were very small compared to the beauty and size of the humane development of Saudi Arabia, never went to my head. I, of course, was, and still am, happy to have them, but thanks to the Almighty, who kept me steady and balanced.

☙ ☙ ☙

I believe it is time to end the story of my long journey by saying: to my beloved Saudi Arabia, I hope and pray that you continue to prosper and stay holding your head high, not out of arrogance and disrespect to others, but rather as a sign of thanks to Almighty God, who led you and hopefully will lead you to an environment of more peace, happiness, and prosperity. On personal grounds, I say to my Saudi Arabia, I am honored and sincerely grateful to have had the chance to be a small actor on your stage of development.

To my tribe of Al-Sba'a of greater Aneza, I hope I was a good example and model to some of your members to follow toward a modern way of life, based on knowledge derived, mainly, from pursuing education.

And finally, to my family Al-Mershed, I hope I did not let you down and gave all the help I could with love and respect.

Epilogue

In previous pages in my story, I touched here and there on economic matters, and most importantly and especially on Saudi society and the environment in which that society lived, especially between the beginning of 1985 until 2015. We mostly lived in an interval of gloom during this time, an interval I might call the prohibition era for Saudi Arabia—prohibition from being happy to enjoy life.

When Saudi Arabia became financially comfortable and began to harness all its visible, as well as hidden means of strength, to develop and uplift standards of living and enhance the welfare of the society, something happened to detour the Kingdom from those noble goals. And so, during that period, 1980 to 2015 Saudi Arabia was limping, unable to utilize all its strength economically, socially, and otherwise in a coherent strategy to move forward. While national plans were written and adopted to be implemented, the results were unsatisfactory, and so Saudi Arabia continued to limp. While each regime was able to contribute to the welfare of the Kingdom, it was in a patchy way, here and there, all over Saudi Arabia. We were frustrated by our inability to use all the strength of the Kingdom to do better, and it was as if an invisible force was ready to stop us every time we wanted to take off. We wasted almost 40 years of our lives, either going in circles or doing very little in most facets of the country.

And we continued to move slowly, doing things the same way we learned a long time ago, with very few changes, relatively speaking, while the world was passing us at a very high speed. Saudi Arabia became an unhappy environment to live or do business in. Most of us in planning were expecting something major to happen, to move Saudi Arabia to higher rates of achievement, and seize the opportunities of financial abundance offered us. Others and I began to write articles in national newspapers, to emphasize the need for new thinking and ways of doing things, and the need to eliminate once and for all, those invisible forces that hindered our development for almost forty years.

These forces stemmed from two main sources. One was a group of high government officials who always cautioned the country from moving fast by emphasizing that the time was not right and were too inept to tell us when it was the right time. I wrote an article to that effect, out of frustration, saying it was time to get rid of the group who said the time was not right. The second source of our obstacle was certainly the misguided and extreme group that came into being starting in 1979 and wanted to turn Saudi Arabia to the time of past centuries by not accepting any new ideas of living, or not doing things or accepting the natural way of human beings, by allowing our culture to be influenced by other cultures. This group, as I mentioned before, turned our Saudi environment into an unpleasant one. And so, we waited for that so-called force to free us from those two obstacles, in particular to move to a happier and more productive and comprehensive environment.

The force we hoped for arrived when King Salman came to power in 2015, with his dynamic Crown Prince, Mohammed. So many times, we were faced with false starts, to move drastically forward. And I have to admit I was not sure personally how to judge our new regime.

We know King Salman, not only as the longest serving governor of Riyadh province, but as a leader of action who wants things to be implemented yesterday instead of today. We know King Salman, with respect to his titles, as the one who initiated the establishment of charitable organizations to build houses for the poor, led and helped in establishing private higher education institutions, and planned Riyadh to be a nice urban center as the capital of Saudi Arabia, to house organizations such as embassies. We know him as the governor who brought desalination water from Al-Jubail on the east coast of Saudi Arabia over a 400 km distance, and insisted, for security, to have two huge, parallel pipes so that one serves as a spare in case of an emergency.

Governor Salman was known to respect time by being in his office daily no later than 8:00 a.m. In addition, he met people in the great hall of the palace daily, to listen to them and solve matters of interest. He certainly is not a bureaucratic leader; in addition to all the mentioned qualities of King Salman, in my opinion, his most respectable ability is that of sharing with people their sadness and happiness personally, or by communicating his feelings.

All this and many other attributes we know about King Salman, but unknown to me and other people was the young Crown Prince Mohammed, whom I never met, though I have known his father and many of his uncles for over half a century. I had to wait and see how this dynamic and young leader would do, hoping for the best.

I did not need to wait long to realize a star was born in Saudi Arabia. From his first full television interview to his comments here and there, there was no doubt a new fresh breeze, and a powerful one, was spreading all over the Kingdom. He immediately eliminated the two obstacles mentioned above. Gone is the "time is not right" group, and those extremists who made life in the country unlivable. He has empowered women to participate and help in the development of Saudi Arabia, one of the first steps of which was allowing women to drive legally for the first time in our history. He opened the country to tourism and initiated a visa system and never hesitated to advise the King to change course if the applied regulations proved to be not right.

Two examples stand out: as a means of helping the government financially during recession, it was suggested that government employees' yearly allowances be frozen for the time being. That was an economically wrong step during a recession. He didn't hesitate to scrap it. The second example was when VAT was increased from 5 percent to 15 percent, and it was found that the real estate sector was hit hard. It was then reduced back to 5 percent, when the negative economic impacts were proven. We were accustomed in the previous time to wait a long time to correct such inefficient government decrees, mainly because of the "time is not right" group and their way of doing things.

The social environment changed in a short time, welcoming happiness and the enjoyments of life with arts of all kinds flourishing from cinemas to concerts, etc. And the oddity of Saudi Arabia of being the only country in the world prohibiting women from driving, or arts activities of all kinds in the open, vanished.

Saudi Arabia became a normal, smiling, and happy country after a long period of gloominess. In the economic field, the young and dynamic Crown Prince published Vision of 2030, which is a very detailed program of development, with its follow-up and implementation steps of major projects in the Red Sea for tourism to Neom, the city of the future in the northwest of the country in the Tabouk region, to major energy and technology centers in the east coast of the country.

Adding to all these projects and others not mentioned is Citizen's Account, which is a monthly payment to subsidize the cost of living and alleviate the financial hardships of low-income people, totaling almost 12 million citizens out of a total of about 22 million Saudi nationals. Projects continued to be announced and implemented all over the country, the last of which was 11 billion Saudi riyals ($=3.75 riyals) for Asir province in the southwest of the country.

To me and others at this stage, we need no more convincing or proof that our young and dynamic Crown Prince Mohammad is a real leader, who with real deeds is moving the country into the twenty-first century, to be the new Saudi Arabia, known as an open society, welcoming interaction with all cultures in this world, with a productive and diversified economy. We were convinced by real, major deeds, announced and implemented quickly. And what beautiful deeds they were, which we had waited a long time to see. They were in all parts of the Kingdom and touched every facet of Saudi Arabia; in a very short period, Saudi Arabia went from a closed society to an open and happy society, with a very precise and comprehensive strategy and its plan of implementation.

And when the King announced women could drive cars in KSA, which was a very major decision, I wrote my last article in *Al-Jazeerah* newspaper, in celebration (17/5/2017), entitled: "The mark erased forever," in which I visualized all Saudis, whether for or against women driving cars, marked to be citizens of the only country that does not allow it, and were recognized by everyone in the world by that mark.

I am now, in 2024, a very satisfied and happy senior citizen of Saudi Arabia, thanks to our King Salman and his forceful and dynamic Crown Prince Mohammad, who certainly did not hesitate to erase any obstacle in the face of our proud and honorable human development.

Addendum

The following is an essay I wrote in the late-1960's sharing thoughts and perspectives on the evolution of Bedouin life.

ψ ψ ψ

To some, my changed situation, from growing up as a Bedouin to living in Riyadh, with a comfortable job, might seem a great achievement in a short time. To me, it seemed like I was taking slow steps forward. And for all that those steps required of me, in terms of effort and the sacrifice of my old way of life, it didn't seem as if I had gained much.

Even now, I occasionally feel very empty. It seems that my M.A. or even the Ph.D. I earned in economics will never give me a full feeling of accomplishment.

I believed that all that I had done so far was to promote the interest and selfish wants of Faisal alone. If you judged me alone, I would have agreed that I did a lot to transform myself from a nomadic person to an educated individual and a city-dweller.

But I don't want to judge myself from that angle. I believe that I should be judged according to how much I did for my family and my tribe. From that angle, my only contribution has been to show all my brothers, cousins, and other young children of the tribe that with hard work and determination one can transfer himself from a life of hardship to one that looks much better, that of an educated person, who is able to see beyond the close social environment in which he lives.

I am glad that so many are following me now and are working hard to upgrade their lives by schooling or specialized training that their fathers never had. Materially speaking, however, I have failed to truly help—and that is the source of my agony. At times, when I hear that the tribe is in bad shape, or that my family is fighting hard to meet basic needs, I feel frustrated. I feel that long fight for education contributed little to the welfare of that beloved tribe and family. No one can help that tribe, or any tribe, with outright gifts. What they need is stable help, which will come through a process of transformation like the one I went through.

I don't believe that every tribesman needs to be highly educated in order to leave that romantic, nomadic life. Rather, I think that a planned gradual transformation must be developed to settle any tribe in Arabia. And so, dear reader, excuse me while I theorize about the settlement of nomads in Saudi Arabia.

You must remember that this autobiography is not aimed to promote Faisal S. Bashir's case, but rather to help the world understand the problem of nomadic life through Faisal S. Bashir's struggle and transformation.

I am selfish, yes, and this theorizing may help me ease some of the frustrations I feel within me all the time.

ψ ψ ψ

The tribes, I know, were born free in the desert. Their freedom has been as absolute as the vast space they live in. That freedom looks as stable as the desert itself, but it could vanish as easily as the mirage in the big desert.

However, since tribes still believe that no matter how much governmental intervention they encounter, they will remain freer than city-dwellers, their disdain and disrespect for settlement persists. This is why I believe a system of settlement, one that offers cities as exciting as Brasilia to accommodate the Bedouins, would not succeed. The problem includes human and sociological factors. It is not strictly economic, as many analysts and planners believe.

In most of the world, and even in Saudi Arabia, many still look at the Bedouin exactly like a Hollywood director who decided that a good movie could be made out of nomadic life. We look at Bedouin life today from a romantic point of view and note its strangeness in comparison to modern and settled life. Most do not know how much nomadic life has changed since only 15 years ago. Because we begin by looking at the nomadic case with a narrow perspective, we prescribe solutions to its problem that have narrow validity. In fact, we attempt to impose the standards of modern, settled societal standards to a human being who does not, first of all, think that those standards are better than his own.

I believe a continuation of this course (no matter how great the expenditure involved) will hurt more than help the Bedouins. In Saudi Arabia, as well as in every country faced with nomadism, the most urgent need is to chart a government policy as clearly and simply as possible.

For example, the government of Saudi Arabia should ask itself whether it really wants the immediate settlement of the Bedouins, with the sacrifice of all their herds, which would in turn require increased imports of meat. Perhaps it should instead envisage a combination of increasing rural life and gradually decreasing nomadism, which would promote agriculture and preserve animal wealth at the same time. A clear understanding of the nature of nomadism is required before anyone proposes a solution.

Many experts have recommended to countries faced with nomadic problems the building of modern villages, to settle portions of the nomads, and to serve as an experiment to settle others. When they have tried this measure, which I call *forced settlement*, the results are not good. It is "forced" because it transfers a person suddenly from nomadic life to a settled life without giving that poor human being a chance to think.

One may argue that a Bedouin would be free to reject an offer of settlement. This may be—but the power of persuasion, and the promises that are made, rush the Bedouin into a position for which he is not prepared, and it leaves him feeling miserable in the end. Unfulfilled promises, coupled with impatience over the new idea of long waiting periods for concrete returns, in addition to the persuasion of non-settled kin, often convince the newly settled Bedouin to go back to his tribe.

Public expenditure in forced settlement projects have, in too many cases, eventually led to abandoned structures for historians to ponder about. When this happens, government officials usually place all blame for failure on the Bedouin and conclude that a Bedouin will remain a Bedouin forever, no matter how comfortable or profitable a life is offered to him. This kind of conclusion exists in the heads of high government officials in almost all the Arab Middle Eastern countries.

Forced settlement has so far brought about nothing more than worsening attitudes from those who could help nomadic people. On the part of the Bedouin, it has led to suspicion of anyone intervening in their lives. Those government officials in the Arab world who blame the Bedouin for so many failures are almost completely ignorant of Bedouin characteristics and, therefore, don't know how to approach them.

It is against any human being's nature to prefer restricted life to a free life. Forced settlement to a Bedouin is nothing more than a jail. When he realizes his condition, he attempts to break the door and escape.

Building modern villages to accommodate the Bedouin is a self-defeating approach to Bedouin transformation for all concerned. The reasons are many. The main ones are:

> 1. The cost of establishing villages is high. It is not economically feasible to build enough villages to accommodate the total nomadic population.
>
> 2. Since many of the young people have already left the tribes, looking for better opportunities in cities, there are mainly old people and very young children left in the tribes. I believe that this trend

will continue, and that nomadism in Saudi Arabia will vanish after the death of the old generation. As a consequence, model villages established now to settle Bedouin would end up as old-age centers, with welfare pay and government subsidies as the only major source of income.

3. Settled life requires feelings and customs, which don't exist in Bedouin life. Settled life requires organization and a sense of planning for tomorrow, the day after tomorrow, and the year after the present year. These qualities are not part of Bedouin traditions.

A nomadic person rarely thinks or plans beyond one season of the year. First, he will worry about rain in the fall. When one asks him how he will save his sheep and camels, if rain comes very late, his answer most likely will be, "I will worry about that problem when it comes." Through this unpreparedness, he always faces the possibility of losing most of his animals.

After rain comes, his first span of concern ends. During the end of winter season, when sheep usually give birth, the Bedouin does not have a definite plan for the use of then-available milk. He has the choice of selling it to a nearby station for cheese making, keeping it for processing himself, or using it to fatten the offspring. Only after the milk is actually available will he decide how to use it. In the spring, the Bedouin has to make a definite decision about the year's male lambs, whether to sell them immediately or to leave them until summer in expectation of higher prices. He faces each problem as it comes and as necessity demands an answer.

The Bedouin's cycle of projection ends with the summer season, when most tribes congregate around wells. A lack of long-term planning and projection costs the Bedouin a lot of capital and often leaves him at the mercy of city creditors. Time segregation, based on the four seasons of the year, leads the Bedouin to believe that the future will repeat this year's experience, with only occasional variations.

When you ask a Bedouin whether his life has changed over the past years, he will tell you flatly, "No." His father and grandfather lived in this tent as he does now, and so he expects his children will live there in the future. He does not visualize time as bringing change.

A Bedouin is an honest liar, when he says that Bedouin life has never changed; the Bedouin's pattern of short projection has accustomed him to expect immediate results in his life. Any time lags will not exceed three or four months. It will be a good year or a bad year, depending on whether the winter rain comes. There is no in-between.

Sudden settlement of that kind of person is a self-defeating process. A newly settled Bedouin will leave a village the moment he realizes it will take three or more years to pay for what he is getting. If this factor alone does not discourage him, he will leave when he realizes that he has to work hard all the year around to get returns, which may or may not be sufficient to meet his needs.

I believe that no kind of immediate forced settlement can be successful. The problem requires more human understanding.

You cannot convince a Bedouin suddenly that homogenized milk is safer or healthier than what is taken straight from a camel. He will tell you that his father and all his previous ancestors lived on unhomogenized camel milk and that nothing happened to them.

A Bedouin is a traditional fellow, whose way of life is as sacred as his religion. One would be as hard to abandon as the other.

Someday, nomadism will vanish from the Saudi Arabian social system as well as from the world as a whole. The end of nomadism will have its disadvantages as well as its advantages. Unless careful planning is done, one of the greatest disadvantages for Saudi Arabia will be the depletion of sheep and camel herds. The advantages are many, but the most important one I see is people's introduction to the twenty-first-century ideas of individualism, cooperation, and global understanding.

One cannot suggest a scheme of transformation that has no disadvantages or faults. But an agency or a government usually tries to choose the plan that will fulfill its targets at the least cost in regard to time, money, and human suffering.

Keeping these requirements in mind, I envisage transforming the Bedouin through a gradual process of learning, which I call gradual settlement, as opposed to sudden forced settlement. I pick the former method because:

> 1. It is more humane, in that it gives the poor Bedouin a chance to think alone with his tribe while he is walking on the road toward permanent settlement. Sudden change cannot be understood by an illiterate and simple person swathed in tradition, so it will not be acceptable to a Bedouin. He would be crushed and left as a lost person in a modern society with a fast pace of living.

> 2. It is the only feasible way to preserve the sheep, goat, and camel wealth of the country, as there is presently no substitute prepared for raising them in large numbers.

> 3. Gradual settlement, especially at the initial stages, which offer mainly help and advice, is the least expensive way of settlement, and one which permits the checking of results at each step.

In sudden forced settlement, there is a risk in attempting to visualize the results of building a village, to accommodate, say, 10,000 Bedouins, before the whole project is completed. This means that a waiting period of four or five years would be required before one could truly judge whether the project was a success or failure. Besides being more expensive, this kind of settlement has less probability of success because it does not take into account the human factor mentioned in number one.

In gradual settlement, there are some safety valves that can be opened the moment encouraging results appear, or shut (by reducing new expenditures) the moment there is discouragement. This means the gradual system of settlement permits frequent examination and adjustment to insure a successful project. Economically, this is better than the forced settlement plan where allotted funds (especially for fixed things) are used entirely before knowing the outcome of efforts.

Sheep and camel ownership have created two kinds of nomadic life in Saudi Arabia. Successful implementation and eventual success of any kind of settlement plan requires keeping this fact in mind. Sheep owners (mostly in the north) move less than camel owners (mostly in the south), and have, therefore, become closer to modern ways of living and thinking.

In a way, the two kinds of ownership lead to categorizing the Bedouin into:

a) the primitive group which represents, to a large degree, the classical life of nomadism as it existed in the past with camels being dominant, and

b) the less primitive group, which is composed of those who have abandoned camels and changed to sheep ownership.

The latter group is becoming more prosperous and more easily influenced by modern ways of living. The past example of the natural patterns of movement between these two groups can serve as a guide to future successful programs for Bedouin settlement. Any tribe or part of a tribe which has already settled has proved beyond doubt that a nomadic person who has made the transition from the most primitive to sheep ownership is the one likely to eventually settle.

Through a natural, gradual process, Saudi Arabia now has the highest portion of its nomadic people as sheep owners. These people who move no more than three or four times in a year, compared with thirty or forty times, in the case of camel owners, are the first ones to be encouraged to take the steps toward permanent settlement.

This does not mean that camel owners should be forgotten. The sheep-owning Bedouins who can settle successfully will serve as an example and convincing argument for the camel owners to consider change.

Starting with tribes or individuals who own sheep, I believe gradual settlement (which will lead to permanent settlement) could be achieved by implementation of the following steps:

> 1. Drilling wells in places tribes consider to be, from past experience, the best grazing areas. These wells must be spaced near enough to each other, say forty kilometers, so that sheep are always within a radius of easily accessible water sources. Sheep would never be beyond a distance where water could be carried to them by trucks, and so the wells would eventually become the nuclei for potential villages.

> 2. Establishing around every few wells (as needed) some kind of public services. These might be no more than a small hospital, veterinary clinic, dispensary, or police office.

> 3. Educating the children in schools around the wells. This is preferable to sending children into cities, where they would be far from their families.

Boarding schools, with all costs of living covered, would be the best arrangement, because a Bedouin would be reluctant to let his children go to school if it meant new expenses. The chances of convincing him to lose a laborer would be even less if he thought there would be new expenses on top of the loss. Furthermore, the child is more likely to remain in school if he is still near his family and tribe while he is introduced to a new environment. The school will affect the child immediately, by introducing him to a new environment and different ways of thinking.

In the longer run, when the child returns to his tent in summer, some of what he has learned in school will go with him. He will affect his family indirectly, by wanting clean clothes, a lamp to read by, etc. Parents' visits to their children through open-house programs will convince Bedouins that their children are well taken care of and will give them some new ideas about ways of living. Now, establishing any one or all of the above-mentioned steps will give Bedouins concrete evidence that the government is serious in trying to help them. They will see that, with cooperation, they and the government can do a lot of good things for their sheep, children, and life in general.

I don't believe that all three steps mentioned so far need to be established in every area where wells are provided, but that some of them should be provided at each of the wells without delay. At first, the Bedouins should not be asked to help financially in initiating any of the steps. They know that these services are presently provided by the government in most cities and would, therefore, be reluctant to cooperate.

There are some past examples to show that the gradual settlement approach will work. The establishment of pumping stations for the Trans-Arabian Pipeline Company, built to carry oil to Lebanon, created many small towns where twenty years ago the thought of such settlements would have been considered daydreaming. These stations convinced the government to provide dispensaries, police stations, water wells, schools, markets, etc., to meet local needs, mostly of Bedouins who chose to settle in their areas. Rafha, Qaisumah, Turaif, and Ar'ar are some of the now-prosperous small towns that started in this way. The pumping stations never employed more than a small minority of the Bedouins living in those towns, which supports the argument that providing the same facilities without necessarily having planned employment will lead to establishment of successful new villages.

With this background, we can continue to other points that should help in gradual settlement, such as:

> 4. Assigning drilled wells and their surrounding area to a specific tribe or tribes. This will give Bedouins a new sense of ownership of something beyond sheep and camels, and they will feel that every improvement or effort they make in the area will remain theirs. Each tribe, through its council, needs to be made aware that, if the need should arise, other tribes may use the well and the land but will not have the right to claim them as possessions. This kind of warning from the start will avoid some conflicts and orient the Bedouin to include a wider circle of people in his relationships. It will help individual tribesmen to realize that living a modern life requires more extensive cooperation, or at least peaceful coexistence with many different people as a major foundation for success.
>
> 5. Inducing camel owners to shift to sheep ownership. The latter ownership can be more profitable under present conditions, and it will make the owners easier to settle, for reasons previously explained.
>
> 6. Convincing the Bedouin of economic laws that will give them advantages in supplying their products to the market. Instead of selling their sheep, wool, ghee, and male lambs in one short period

(usually the end of spring), they can hold some of their products for later days and get better prices. The market will be saved from the sudden short periods of abundance of nomadic products and will have more stable prices for these goods. It will give the Bedouin much better deals than they are now accustomed to receiving.

7. Establishing credit agencies for Bedouins. To assure the success of step six, Bedouins must be saved from the outright cheating and theft they now face in getting loans from city-dwellers who demand exorbitant interest. These loans help them postpone sales to the market, but at the end of a yearly cycle, Bedouins are lucky if they break even. In a way, most Bedouins live in a kind of slavery that resembles that of feudal farmers of old. Credit agencies with fair rates are one way to begin breaking this vicious cycle. Besides giving loans, the agencies might help the Bedouin develop a sense of saving, which has not been part of his tradition up to this time.

8. Making the ownership of land and wells by tribes or individuals conditional upon a willingness to exert some self-help in using and improving the area. The people must realize that an outside agency can't do everything for them indefinitely, though it may willingly participate in providing equipment and giving advice. Also, tribes can be informed that any agricultural settlement that has been initiated through capital from the tribe can receive supplemental help and advice. Some tribes have already established such settlements on their own, and helping them succeed will encourage others to follow them.

9. Providing storage places for animal feed (hay, barley, etc.) in the vicinity of wells. This can be a combined effort of tribal and outside help.

10. Establishing small industries. With the passage of time, some products, acquiring sheep or camels as a source of raw materials (cheese, wool, tent weavings, etc.) could be processed near the wells.

11. Establishment of a central office, concerned with Bedouin affairs. This office would be known as a source of advice and guidance, and would serve as a place for working out Bedouin-government relationships. It would coordinate various Bedouin programs that might exist in other government or private agencies.

Steps that are taken along these lines will lead to the successful settlement of nomads in Saudi Arabia and other countries. With the progressive implementation of any of these steps, more and more families or parts of families will settle until the day when there are no longer any nomadic people. I believe there will be success, if various steps are executed, simultaneously, on a small scale at first, to eventually spread more uniformly over all grazing areas.

There is no short road to the successful settlement of the nomad. Such settlement is a social change, and as such requires time, patience, and understanding. Through my background and recent analysis of the Bedouin situation, I believe in the feasibility and potential success of each step I have described, despite the initial difficulties that are sure to be generated by the Bedouins' suspicion.

To researchers and government planners, who doubt the Bedouins can adapt and meet the requirements of each step, I make the following plea.

Leave your office analysis for a while and go out with the nomads, to see what changes they have accepted in the last 15 years alone. To city-dwellers, a Bedouin today is a Bedouin of thirty years ago, because he still lives in a tent. This is a naïve observation, without any depth, because the Bedouins' way of dressing, kinds of food, and manners of maintaining sheep have changed quite drastically. Some of these changes are not even obvious to the Bedouins themselves, because they have been so gradual.

Upon close examination, the poor, illiterate person has shown himself increasingly capable of adapting to changes, and in the future, he will become even more ready to accept new ways and ideas. Ask a Bedouin about his fashion in clothes, and he will not understand the word "fashion." He will tell you he wears a thobe (traditional men's dress, shaped something like a Western man's shirt reaching to the ground) exactly as his father and grandfathers did. This may be accepted as the truth and recorded as evidence of the Bedouins' unbreakable traditions. But if analysis went further, one would find that there definitely has been a change in dress in the last fifteen years. The thobe is worn shorter than it used to be. The full, loose sleeves have been replaced by tighter ones made with cuffs exactly like those worn in business offices, and often decorated with the latest styles in cufflinks.

If this change is pointed out, the Bedouin cannot reason out why it happened, but it is in fact part of the adaptation to a new way of life. As the Bedouin is riding in cars, and going into cities more often, the new thobe is a convenience as well as a reflection of new influences. Economically speaking, the new thobe consumes less fabric, and is cheaper than the old one.

Besides clothing, the diet of the Bedouin has changed. Before, camel or sheep milk with dates were his staple foods. Now he occasionally eats fresh fruits and vegetables. Canned foods have made headway in tents all over the country. Tea has become the most dominant beverage. In 1962, when I left my father's tent, I saw no canned food. Five years later, it was not only accepted but frequently used.

In caring for their sheep, many Bedouins now commonly use trucks to transport their animals to better grazing areas or to bring water to them. Even the Bedouin's way of thinking has changed. His knowledge has become more diversified, with the influx of radios. Bedouins now can talk about what is happening elsewhere in the world, though admittedly in a simple way. Radios in Saudi Arabia also help the Bedouins know where last night's clouds dropped their rain, according to information relayed to stations by governors of various provinces. Other changes could surely be found to supplement these few examples. However, these are enough to support the idea that the proposal for gradual change and settlement is logical and compatible with what has been going on in Bedouin life in the recent past.

To summarize the main reason why gradual settlement would succeed, it depends on the Bedouins' present way of living and doesn't introduce sudden schemes that require much adaptability. Since the basic Bedouin character is taken into consideration in gradual settlement, it will be acceptable to the Bedouins.

Nomadic people in Saudi Arabia are well aware that nomadism will vanish someday. It is the duty of people in positions of influence to recognize this belief and to create the best programs for the Bedouins' smooth transition to a new situation. They are willing to settle gradually, and with honest, sincere advice and sound programs their transformation can be economically feasible for themselves and their countries, as well as humane in nature.

Time is moving more quickly, all the time, so action must be taken while the Bedouin is still optimistic and unhurt by sudden, forced change or bad experiences. The song of a settled Bedouin girl reflects the willing and happy adjustment that can come with gradual settlement, which convinces the Bedouin he is doing the right thing and makes him feel he is gaining for himself at each step.

Oh! The tractor sound is reassuring, much better than the sounds the camels make. I see the teapot on the Brimus (kerosene stove).

And the glasses in the cupboard. I have no more tears to shed as a sign of regret over vanishing nomadic life.

My urgings for gradual settlement are a clear sign that I have accepted the inevitable, and that I now want to ensure that tribes are transformed in a humane way. I pray to God that I have contributed to the world's understanding of nomadic life, so that future solutions will be successful, largely because they include consideration for the human factor. If I contribute only that much, I believe that my struggle for education has been worthwhile.

Faisal S. Bashir Al-Mershed, you did it. But pray that other tribal children will have the same feeling of successful adjustment. You left nomadic life to become a member of the world's urban population that thinks its ways of life are the best, although you know generosity, freedom, and love are universal principles respected and pursued by Bedouins as well.

Farewell, nomadic life. Farewell, my beloved tribe, Al-Sba'a. And may God over us take care of every one of you, my beloved tribesmen.

Related Titles from Westphalia Press

The Limits of Moderation: Jimmy Carter and the Ironies of American Liberalism

The Limits of Moderation: Jimmy Carter and the Ironies of American Liberalism is not a finished product. And yet, even in this unfinished stage, this book is a close and careful history of a short yet transformative period in American political history, when big changes were afoot.

The Zelensky Method
by Grant Farred

Locating Russian's war within a global context, The Zelensky Method is unsparing in its critique of those nations, who have refused to condemn Russia's invasion and are doing everything they can to prevent economic sanctions from being imposed on the Kremlin.

Sinking into the Honey Trap: The Case of the Israeli-Palestinian Conflict
by Daniel Bar-Tal, Barbara Doron, Translator

Sinking into the Honey Trap by Daniel Bar-Tal discusses how politics led Israel to advancing the occupation, and of the deterioration of democracy and morality that accelerates the growth of an authoritarian regime with nationalism and religiosity.

Essay on The Mysteries and the True Object of The Brotherhood of Freemasons
by Jason Williams

The third edition of Essai sur les mystères discusses Freemasonry's role as a society of symbolic philosophers who cultivate their minds, practice virtues, and engage in charity, and underscores the importance of brotherhood, morality, and goodwill.

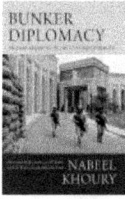

Bunker Diplomacy: An Arab-American in the U.S. Foreign Service
by Nabeel Khoury

After twenty-five years in the Foreign Service, Dr. Nabeel A. Khoury retired from the U.S. Department of State in 2013 with the rank of Minister Counselor. In his last overseas posting, Khoury served as deputy chief of mission at the U.S. embassy in Yemen (2004-2007).

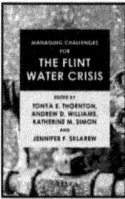

Managing Challenges for the Flint Water Crisis
Edited by Toyna E. Thornton, Andrew D. Williams, Katherine M. Simon, Jennifer F. Sklarew

This edited volume examines several public management and intergovernmental failures, with particular attention on social, political, and financial impacts. Understanding disaster meaning, even causality, is essential to the problem-solving process.

User-Centric Design
by Dr. Diane Stottlemyer

User-centric strategy can improve by using tools to manage performance using specific techniques. User-centric design is based on and centered around the users. They are an essential part of the design process and should have a say in what they want and need from the application based on behavior and performance.

Masonic Myths and Legends
by Pierre Mollier

Freemasonry is one of the few organizations whose teaching method is still based on symbols. It presents these symbols by inserting them into legends that are told to its members in initiation ceremonies. But its history itself has also given rise to a whole mythology.

Abortion and Informed Common Sense
by Max J. Skidmore

The controversy over a woman's "right to choose," as opposed to the numerous "rights" that abortion opponents decide should be assumed to exist for "unborn children," has always struck me as incomplete. Two missing elements of the argument seems obvious, yet they remain almost completely overlooked.

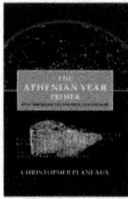

The Athenian Year Primer: Attic Time-Reckoning and the Julian Calendar
by Christopher Planeaux

The ability to translate ancient Athenian calendar references into precise Julian-Gregorian dates will not only assist Ancient Historians and Classicists to date numerous historical events with much greater accuracy but also aid epigraphists in the restorations of numerous Attic inscriptions.

Siddhartha: Life of the Buddha
by David L. Phillips,
contributions by Venerable Sitagu Sayadaw

Siddhartha: Life of the Buddha is an illustrated story for adults and children about the Buddha's birth, enlightenment and work for social justice. It includes illustrations from Pagan, Burma which are provided by Rev. Sitagu Sayadaw.

Growing Inequality: Bridging Complex Systems, Population Health, and Health Disparities
Editors: George A. Kaplan, Ana V. Diez Roux, Carl P. Simon, and Sandro Galea

Why is America's health is poorer than the health of other wealthy countries and why health inequities persist despite our efforts? In this book, researchers report on groundbreaking insights to simulate how these determinants come together to produce levels of population health and disparities and test new solutions.

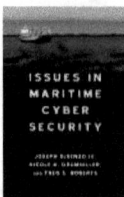

Issues in Maritime Cyber Security
Edited by Dr. Joe DiRenzo III, Dr. Nicole K. Drumhiller, and Dr. Fred S. Roberts

The complexity of making MTS safe from cyber attack is daunting and the need for all stakeholders in both government (at all levels) and private industry to be involved in cyber security is more significant than ever as the use of the MTS continues to grow.

Female Emancipation and Masonic Membership: An Essential Collection
By Guillermo De Los Reyes Heredia

Female Emancipation and Masonic Membership: An Essential Combination is a collection of essays on Freemasonry and gender that promotes a transatlantic discussion of the study of the history of women and Freemasonry and their contribution in different countries.

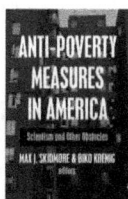

Anti-Poverty Measures in America: Scientism and Other Obstacles
Editors, Max J. Skidmore and Biko Koenig

Anti-Poverty Measures in America brings together a remarkable collection of essays dealing with the inhibiting effects of scientism, an over-dependence on scientific methodology that is prevalent in the social sciences, and other obstacles to anti-poverty legislation.

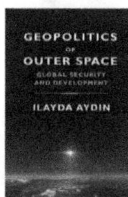

Geopolitics of Outer Space: Global Security and Development
by Ilayda Aydin

A desire for increased security and rapid development is driving nation-states to engage in an intensifying competition for the unique assets of space. This book analyses the Chinese-American space discourse from the lenses of international relations theory, history and political psychology to explore these questions.

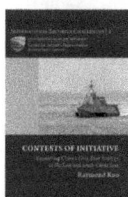

Contests of Initiative: Countering China's Gray Zone Strategy in the East and South China Seas
by Dr. Raymond Kuo

China is engaged in a widespread assertion of sovereignty in the South and East China Seas. It employs a "gray zone" strategy: using coercive but sub-conventional military power to drive off challengers and prevent escalation, while simultaneously seizing territory and asserting maritime control.

Discourse of the Inquisitive
Editors: Jaclyn Maria Fowler and Bjorn Mercer

Good communication skills are necessary for articulating learning, especially in online classrooms. It is often through writing that learners demonstrate their ability to analyze and synthesize the new concepts presented in the classroom.

westphaliapress.org

Policy Studies Organization

The Policy Studies Organization (PSO) is a publisher of academic journals and book series, sponsor of conferences, and producer of programs.

Policy Studies Organization publishes dozens of journals on a range of topics, such as European Policy Analysis, Journal of Elder Studies, Indian Politics & Polity, Journal of Critical Infrastructure Policy, and Popular Culture Review.

Additionally, Policy Studies Organization hosts numerous conferences. These conferences include the Middle East Dialogue, Space Education and Strategic Applications Conference, International Criminology Conference, Dupont Summit on Science, Technology and Environmental Policy, World Conference on Fraternalism, Freemasonry and History, and the Internet Policy & Politics Conference.

For more information on these projects, access videos of past events, and upcoming events, please visit us at:

www.ipsonet.org